# GOD'S WARRIORS

KNIGHTS TEMPLAR, SARACENS AND THE BATTLE FOR JERUSALEM

OSPREY
PUBLISHING

# The Authors

**Dr Helen Nicholson** is Reader in History at Cardiff University. She has written extensively on the history of the military orders, the crusades in general and the Templars in particular. Her best-known publications include *The Knights Templar: A New History* (Sutton Publishing, 2001) and *Templars, Hospitallers and Teutonic Knights: Images of the Military Orders 1128–1291* (Leicester University Press, 1993).

**Dr David Nicolle** worked in the BBC Arabic service for a number of years, before taking an MA at the School of Oriental and African Studies, London, and a doctorate at Edinburgh University. He later taught world and Islamic art and architectural history at Yarmuk University, Jordan. David has written many books and articles on medieval and Islamic warfare, and has been a prolific author of Osprey titles for many years. He lives and works in Leicestershire, UK.

# GOD'S WARRIORS

KNIGHTS TEMPLAR, SARACENS AND THE BATTLE FOR JERUSALEM

DR HELEN NICHOLSON & DR DAVID NICOLLE

First published in 2005 by Osprey Publishing
Midland House, West Way, Botley, Oxford OX2 0PH, UK
443 Park Avenue South, New York, NY 10016, USA
E-mail: info@ospreypublishing.com

Previously published as Campaign 19: *Hattin 1187*; Warrior 10: *Saracen Faris AD 1050–1250*; and Warrior 91: *Knight Templar 1120–1312*.
This paperback edition first published in 2006.

Every attempt has been made by the publisher to secure the appropriate permissions for materials reproduced in this book. If there has been any oversight we will be happy to rectify the situation and written submission should be made to the Publishers.

A CIP catalogue record for this book is available from the British Library

ISBN-10: 1-84603-143-5
ISBN-13: 978-1-84603-143-4

Helen Nicholson has asserted her right under the Copyright, Designs and Patents Act, 1988, to be identified as the Author of 'Knight Templar'.

Design: Ken Vail Graphic Design, Cambridge, UK

Index by Alan Thatcher

Maps by The Map Studio Ltd

Originated by The Electronic Page Company in Cwmbran, UK and PPS Grasmere Ltd in Leeds, UK

Printed in China through World Print Ltd

06 07 08 09 10   10 9 8 7 6 5 4 3 2 1

FOR A CATALOGUE OF ALL BOOKS PUBLISHED BY OSPREY PLEASE CONTACT:

NORTH AMERICA
Osprey Direct c/o Random House Distribution Center, 400 Hahn Road, Westminster, MD 21157, USA
E-mail: info@ospreydirect.com

ALL OTHER REGIONS
Osprey Direct UK, P.O. Box 140, Wellingborough, Northants, NN8 2FA, UK
E-mail: info@ospreydirect.co.uk

www.ospreypublishing.com

Front cover image:
'Battle of Stamford Bridge', in L'Estoire de Seint Aedward le Rei, by Matthew Paris (Cambridge University Library, Ms. Ee. 111.59, f.32v). Reprinted by permission of the Syndics of Cambridge University Library.

Image on spine:
© David Nicolle

# CONTENTS

# PART ONE

# HATTIN 1187

## INTRODUCTION

The Crusades seemed to erupt into the late 11th-century Middle East without warning. Yet in reality they were the culmination of a century during which Catholic Western Europe had been changing at an increasing rate, not least in its attitudes towards war and religion. The 11th century had also seen considerable economic and population growth and, although there were ups and downs, it would be wrong to see the First Crusade as a product of poverty, despair and religious hysteria. Hysteria there may have been, but this did not create the Crusades.

In early Christian times warfare had been seen as, at best, an unfortunate necessity. Now, however, the concept of Holy War spread, along with such phenomena as the Holy Banner given by the Church to a military leader, and of the *Militia Christi* or Warrior of Christ, and the growing cult of warrior saints. It was also increasingly accepted that men who fell fighting for the Church now died as martyrs. Whether these ideas owed anything to the Islamic concept of 'lesser' *jihad* – widely mistranslated as Holy War – is hotly debated, as is the influence of early Byzantine concepts of religiously justified warfare upon the idea of military *jihad* in the first place. What is clear is that, in Christian Western Europe, co-existence with Islam was increasingly denied. Christ's supposed enemies must be defeated and destroyed – 'truth' was to be proved by the sword.

During the 12th century, four so-called Crusader States were established in the Middle East, in and around the Holy Land of Christianity but also in the heartland of Islamic civilization. Furthermore 'Frankish' or Western European Latin or Catholic Christians now occupied Jerusalem, a city that was sacred to all three monotheistic religions, Judaism, Christianity and Islam. In fact, the First Crusaders had expelled the Muslim and Jewish inhabitants of the Holy City with great slaughter. The First Crusade had indeed been a resounding, and even today astonishing, success from the Westerners' point of view.

By the 1180s the realms carved out following the First Crusade were no longer real 'Crusader States', because the descendants of the First Crusaders were no longer striving to expand. Instead they were struggling to survive and to protect the Holy

The ivory cover of Queen Melisende's Psalter, made in Jerusalem AD 1131–43. It symbolizes the King of Jerusalem's claim to rule as King David's successor. The warriors reflect Byzantine or Islamic arms and armour, particularly 'Fortitude' who slays 'Avarice' below and to the right of 'David and Goliath'. (British Museum, London)

The ancient Roman city of Ba'albak in Lebanon was the centre of a strategic frontier governorate in Saladin's empire. Many ancient buildings were incorporated into its fortifications and new defences such as the Southern Tower on the right of this picture were added. (David Nicolle)

Places of Christianity from Muslim reconquest. Leadership was also passing to men who were working towards co-existence with the surrounding Muslim peoples.

The Kingdom of Jerusalem remained the most important of the Latin States in Syria and Palestine. Of the others the County of Edessa (Urfa) had already been reconquered by the Muslims, the Principality of Antioch had fallen under Byzantine influence and even the small County of Tripoli now resisted Jerusalem's suzerainty. In the early 1180s the Kingdom of Jerusalem had 400,000 to 500,0000 inhabitants, no more than 120,000 of whom were Latins (Christians of Western European origin). The rest consisted of indigenous 'Oriental' Christians, Muslims, Jews and Samaritans. The balance of power between feudal lords and ruler in late 12th-century Jerusalem is not entirely clear, but in general it seems that the king and lesser aristocracy were losing out while the leading barons grabbed ever more control. Meanwhile the Military Orders (Templars and Hospitallers) were growing in power, being given more castles which only they seemed able to garrison effectively.

The defence of the Kingdom of Jerusalem was theoretically the responsibility of all Western European Christians, yet in reality the Latin States had to rely on themselves after the fiasco of the Second Crusade in 1148. What its leaders now wanted were professional soldiers and financial support – not hordes of belligerent Crusaders who stirred up trouble then went home. Meanwhile the catastrophic Byzantine defeat by the Saljuq Turks at Myriokephalon in 1176, and a massacre of Latins in Constantinople eight years later, meant that help from the Byzantine Empire was an illusion. The Kingdom of Jerusalem also faced problems within its borders. Few Armenians settled in Palestine and the warlike Maronite Christians of the mountains lived away from the main centres of power while the majority of Syriac-Jacobite Christians remained deeply suspicious of the Latins. The Latins' adoption of some eastern habits of dress and cleanliness was superficial and the cultural gulf between Latins and locals remained unbridged until the end. Relations between the Latin States and neighbouring Muslim states remained rooted in war, lasting peace probably being impossible as each side clung to ideologies that could not accept the other's existence. Attitudes based on the easy victories of the First Crusade meant that the military elite of the Latin States was still hugely overconfident. This did wonders for their morale but would soon lead to military disaster. Yet elements of doubt were already creeping in, and the second half of the 12th century saw the building of many defensive castles.

The eastern frontier of the Kingdom of Jerusalem actually consisted of distinct sectors. In the north (the Litani valley) were some impressive castles. The central sector from Mount Hermon (Jabal al Shaykh) along the Golan Heights to the Yarmuk valley was supposedly shared with the rulers of Damascus. The Muslims thought this zone should have extended as far as the Balqa hills around Amman but in fact the Latins dominated a fertile plateau between the River Yarmuk and the Ajlun hills. Southward again lay the Latin territory of Oultrejordain, lying between the River Jordan, Dead Sea and Wadi Araba in the west, and the strategic road from Amman to Aqabah. From Oultrejordain the Latins had levied tolls on Muslim traffic between Syria and Egypt, even on Muslim *Haj* or pilgrim caravans travelling south to Mecca and Medina. Then, in the early 1170s, Saladin's reconquest of territory south of Montreal (Shawbak) had a profound psychological impact, 'liberating the Haj Road' so that pilgrims, at least from Egypt, no longer paid humiliating tolls to the infidel.

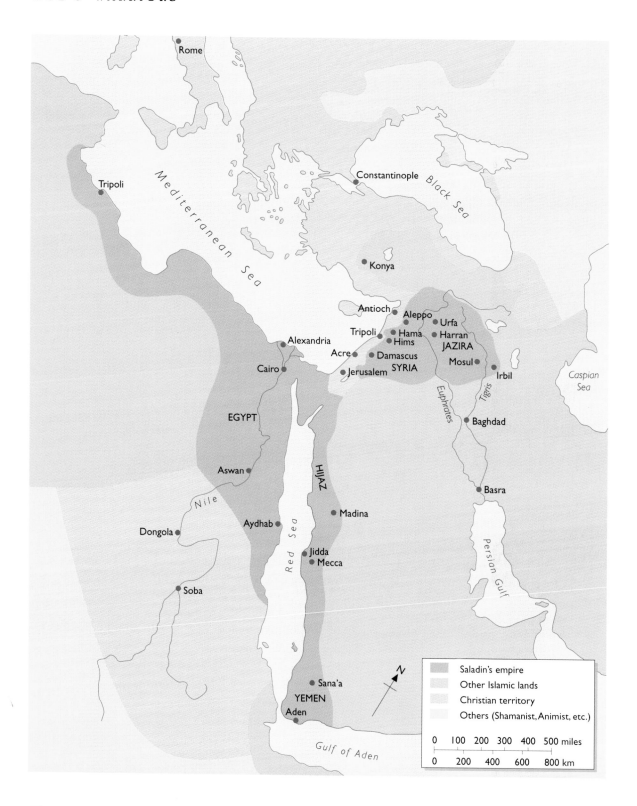

Rome

Mediterranean Sea

Tripoli

Constantinople

Black Sea

Konya

Antioch

Aleppo

Urfa

Tripoli

Hama

Harran

Hims

JAZIRA

Acre

Damascus

Alexandria

Mosul

Jerusalem

SYRIA

Irbil

Caspian Sea

Cairo

Euphrates

Tigris

EGYPT

Baghdad

Aswan

HIJAZ

Nile

Basra

Dongola

Aydhab

Red Sea

Madina

Persian Gulf

Jidda

Mecca

Soba

Sana'a

YEMEN

Aden

Gulf of Aden

N

Saladin's empire

Other Islamic lands

Christian territory

Others (Shamanist, Animist, etc.)

| 0 | 100 | 200 | 300 | 400 | 500 miles |
|---|-----|-----|-----|-----|-----------|
| 0 | 200 | 400 | 600 | 800 km | |

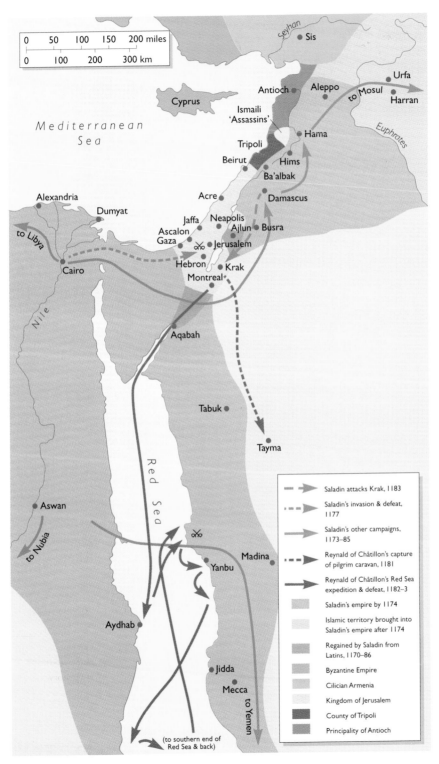

Saladin attacks Krak, 1183

Saladin's invasion & defeat, 1177

Saladin's other campaigns, 1173–85

Reynald of Châtillon's capture of pilgrim caravan, 1181

Reynald of Châtillon's Red Sea expedition & defeat, 1182–3

Saladin's empire by 1174

Islamic territory brought into Saladin's empire after 1174

Regained by Saladin from Latins, 1170–86

Byzantine Empire

Cilician Armenia

Kingdom of Jerusalem

County of Tripoli

Principality of Antioch

(to southern end of Red Sea & back)

Qala'at al Rabadh
outside Ajlun was built
for Saladin in 1184–85.
This picture, taken
by a German aircraft
on 9 April 1918, shows
a small castle of
rectangular plan. The
four main towers date
from Saladin's reign;
some outer defences
were added in the 13th
century. (Royal Jordanian
Geographical Centre)

The most striking development on the Muslim side of the frontier had been Saladin's unification of Islamic territory neighbouring the Latin States. Only in the far north did the Latins now have any neighbour other than Saladin, and that was the fellow Christian state of Cilician Armenia. Yet there had been other equally important changes in the Muslim Middle East. The concept of *jihad* as war against the infidel, long dormant, was revived by 12th-century Sunni Muslim scholars. *Jihads* became organized campaigns to recover the Holy Land, just as Crusades had been to conquer it. They were not, however, intended to convert the enemy by the sword since Islam has always frowned on forcible conversion. Nevertheless the 12th century did see a hardening of religious attitudes, greater intolerance and increased pressure on indigenous Oriental Christians. This Sunni Muslim revival was also directed against the Shi'a Muslim minority.

The loss of Jerusalem to the Crusaders had actually increased the city's importance to Muslims, being followed by an outpouring of *fada'il* or 'praise literature' about the Holy City. The responsibilities of rulers were also described in a number of books known as 'Mirrors for Princes', and one of the most interesting was written by an anonymous Syrian living near the Crusader frontier a year or so after Saladin's death. It went into great detail about *jihad* and although the best *jihad* was still against evil in one's own heart, fighting the unbeliever came a good second. In fact the inhabitants of Syria's cities, particularly Aleppo in the north, had long traditions of scientific siege warfare and the 12th century saw the building of many new fortifications in Muslim Syria, just as it did in the Latin States. Meanwhile the Arab bedouin of the desert fringes remained strong but, having lost political dominance to the invading Turks, now generally preferred to be left alone. The people of Egypt, on the other hand, largely left warfare to their rulers, yet even here fundamental changes were taking place. The Arabization of the country really started under the Fatimids who had ruled Egypt from AD 969, and the Arab bedouin of Egypt continued to prosper after Saladin seized control in 1171.

Islam's relations with Europe, rather than just the Latin States in Syria, were also changing. By the 12th century Islamic naval power in the Mediterranean was in steep decline while Italian merchant republics such as Pisa, Genoa and Venice controlled the sea lanes. Saladin would, in fact, be the last ruler of medieval Egypt to attempt a serious revival of Egyptian naval power – an attempt that ultimately failed. In the Red Sea, however, Egypt remained dominant, defeating Latin Crusader raids and piracy with relative ease.

Saladin's unification of so much of the Middle East took decades of war and diplomacy. From his power base in Egypt he and his family, the Ayyubids, won control of Yemen (1173), Damascus (1174) and Aleppo (1183). By 1186 Saladin also imposed his suzerainty over the Jazira (eastern Syria, south-eastern Turkey and northern Iraq), a rich region which provided a reservoir of military manpower. Overconfident the leaders of the Latin States may have been, but they watched the growth of Saladin's power with alarm and sent embassies to various parts of Europe seeking support. King Henry II of England had long been sympathetic, though his help took the form of cash rather than troops. A special tax in aid of Jerusalem had already been levied and in 1172, as part of his penance for the murder of Becket, Henry promised to support 200 knights for one year in Jerusalem. Five years later he sent a chest of money to Jerusalem and in 1185 promised yet more. In fact these donations may have totalled 30,000 marks, a huge sum for those days and one that would play a crucial role in the forthcoming Hattin campaign.

Within the Latin States a census was conducted to discover their real military potential, while taxes were raised and castles strengthened. The strategic importance of Oultrejordain also increased now that Saladin controlled both Egypt and Syria. Here Reynald of Châtillon, who ran an effective intelligence service among the bedouin, planned to smash the Muslim ring surrounding the Latin States and perhaps even break into the Indian Ocean with its fabulous wealth of trade. In 1181–82 Reynald raided the Hijaz and the support he got from some local tribes clearly worried Saladin. Reynald's spectacular but disastrous naval expedition into the Red Sea the following year sent shock waves throughout the Islamic world and dented Saladin's status as Protector of the Muslim Holy Places in Mecca and Madina. The Sultan struck back immediately, and then again in 1183. In response the Christians fielded the largest army so far raised by the Latin States, but adopted a defensive stance by refusing to meet Saladin in a set-piece battle. This strategy was effective and the Muslims withdrew. Yet the invasion caused great damage and many people blamed Count Raymond, on whose advice the passive strategy had been adopted, for missing a chance to destroy Saladin.

Painted fragment from a mid-12th-century Egyptian manuscript showing Muslim warriors wearing full mail hauberks and turbans, supported by unarmoured infantry with large kite-shaped shields, emerging from a fortress to fight Crusaders. The Muslims are probably Fatimid troops and the fortress may represent Ascalon. (Dept of Oriental Antiquities, British Museum, London)

Iron mines were almost as important as water sources and the Jabal Ajlun to the north of Oultrejordain had such mines. These hills had come under Saladin's control by 1184 and the Sultan sent Izz al Din Usamah, previously governor of the iron-rich mountains near Beirut, to build a new castle overlooking Ajlun itself. But although the Muslims were nibbling away at the Kingdom of Jerusalem, Saladin faced problems away in the east. A severe drought also struck Palestine in 1185 and so it was with some relief that both sides agreed to a four-year truce. This did not mean peace on all fronts, of course. In 1186 the Principality of Antioch raided its Christian neighbours in Cilicia while in south-eastern Anatolia a bloody struggle broke out between Kurds and Turcomans (nomadic Turks), both of whom were vital sources of military manpower for Saladin's armies. The Byzantine Empire was also wracked by dissention. Two leading noblemen, Isaac and Alexius Angelus, had sought refuge at Saladin's court but in 1185 Isaac Angelus returned to Constantinople and overthrew the Emperor Andronicus to become Byzantine Emperor himself. The following year his brother Alexius was imprisoned in the Latin States as he made his way home. There were similar tensions on Saladin's eastern border. In 1180 the new caliph Al Nasir had succeeded to the throne of Baghdad and under his energetic rule the once mighty Abbasid dynasty saw a final burst of glory. Yet Al Nasir's ambitions clashed with Saladin's plans in northern Iraq and relations between the two Muslim leaders were cool.

In Jerusalem the leper king, Baldwin IV, died in 1185 and in August 1186 his child successor Baldwin V also died, throwing the Kingdom into a major crisis. The regent, Count Raymond of Tripoli, was ousted in a coup by a belligerent 'Court

Party' who wanted a tougher policy towards the Muslims. They had Sibylla, sister of Baldwin IV, crowned queen and thus her husband, a French nobleman named Guy de Lusignan, became king. For months many Jerusalem nobles refused to recognize the coup – though in the end only Count Raymond continued to deny homage to King Guy. Instead Raymond retired to Tiberius, capital of the seigneurie of Galilee, which he held through his wife Eschiva of Galilee. Naturally Saladin watched this crisis with interest. He released some of Raymond's knights who had been prisoners of war and sent his own troops to support Raymond in Tiberius and for a while it looked as if King Guy would attack Raymond. Beyond Jerusalem Prince Raymond III of Antioch also refused to recognize Guy, though he would do so after war broke out with Saladin.

# THE OPPOSING LEADERS

## THE MUSLIM COMMANDERS

Saladin has traditionally been seen in Europe as a paragon of virtue and a hero. Recently, however, a critical view has portrayed him as an ambitious, ruthless and devious politician, and less brilliant as a commander than once thought. As usual the truth probably lies between these extremes, though all agree that Sultan Saladin was the greatest man in the history of the 12th-century Middle East. Saladin's family, the Ayyubids, was of Kurdish origin and had served Nur al Din, the Turkish ruler of Syria and northern Iraq. Saladin himself was educated and given military training in the cultivated surroundings of a Turkish court in Arabian Syria, though it was in Egypt that he rose to power. As a ruler he listened to advice, particularly on political matters, and made use of existing military structures as well as new ideas. Contemporary Muslim biographers tend to idealize his character, emphasizing his humanity, his forgiving nature, piety, love of justice, generosity, courage. They may have exaggerated but there is no doubt that Saladin made a profound impact on those around him. Even his Christian foes trusted Saladin's honour.

Contrary to some romantic views, the Sultan was no military 'innocent' thrust into warfare against his will. He had had considerable experience as a staff officer under Nur al Din and fought in several battles before taking over as vizier (chief minister) of Egypt in 1169. Saladin did not become official ruler of that country until 1171, and even then Egypt theoretically remained part of Nur al Din's realm until the latter's death in 1173. As a commander Saladin was willing to take considerable risks and he had a clear understanding of broad strategy. On the other hand he made mistakes, for example allowing Latin resistance to crystalize at Tyre (Sur) after his overwhelming victory at Hattin.

Nevertheless Saladin remained the noble and tragic – though 'pagan' – hero of various European tales. His greatness was such that the Latins seemed unable to

This early 13th-century carving over the Bab al Tillism gate of Baghdad was destroyed by an explosion in 1917. It showed a 'hero-ruler' in Turkish costume – long plaits and rich tunic plus an elaborate turban – seizing two dragons. (Photograph via the Staatliche Museen zu Berlin)

accept that he was a 'mere Saracen'. So legends grew up claiming that Saladin was the grandson of a beautiful French princess forced to marry a valiant Turk named Malakin. He, it was said:

> ...lived long and tenderly with his wife. Neither were they childless, for of this lady, who was called the Fair Captive, was born the mother of that courteous Turk, the Sultan Saladin, an honourable, a wise and a conquering lord.

Saladin had great respect for his nephew Taqi al Din who, like so many Islamic leaders of this period, was described by contemporary Muslim writers as deeply religious and very generous. This may have been true, but what comes across most clearly was his physical courage and preference for leading troops in person. Taqi al Din had demonstrated his initiative long before Hattin, his prompt action saving the day at the battle of Hama (against the troops of Muslim Aleppo and Mosul) in 1175. Now Saladin gave him the toughest military tasks, often placing him in command of the right wing which, in the traditional tactics of the Middle East, usually took an offensive role while the left wing acted defensively.

In addition to being an outstanding commander, Taqi al Din was impetuous and obstinate. His political ambitions aimed at a power base larger than the central Syrian province of Hama which he had governed since 1178. Saladin was fully aware of the tempestuous Taqi al Din's desire for independence – perhaps seeing him as a kindred spirit – but the Sultan still made him governor of Egypt while he himself was away. Taqi al Din next dreamed of carving out a state in North Africa, but Saladin feared that he would take away too many valuable troops. Dismissed as governor of Egypt, he almost rebelled against Saladin and quarrelled openly with Saladin's son Al Afdal. Yet Saladin was soon reconciled with his warlike nephew, adding the mountainous frontier region around Mayyafariqin in Anatolia to Taqi al Din's existing Syrian fief of Hama. Here the young warrior had a chance to expand his territory without clashing with other members of the family. Even so Taqi al Din virtually deserted Saladin during the crisis of the Third Crusade, only to die suddenly a bare 17 months before the great Sultan himself.

Muzaffar al Din Gökböri was one of Saladin's leading *amirs* or military commanders. Like all such *amirs* he governed large provinces from which he drew revenues to pay his troops. Gökböri, which means 'Blue Wolf' in Turkish, was a son of the governor of Irbil. His father had been a loyal follower of the great Zangi whose conquest of Edessa in 1144 was the first step in rolling back the Crusades. Gökböri himself served Zangi's son Nur al Din and became governor of Harran in what had been the Latin County of Edessa. In 1175 he led the right wing of a combined Aleppo-Mosul army against Saladin at the Horns of Hama, but after Nur al Din's death Zangi's dynasty was falling apart and a new Muslim hero arose – Saladin. Gökböri's defection to Saladin was a major factor in the Sultan's success. Yet it was also a dangerous move because if Saladin failed, Gökböri would lose everything. In the event Saladin defeated the remaining Zangids and added the cities of Edessa (Urfa) and Samsat to Gökböri's governorate. He also gave one of his sisters, Al Sitt Rabia Khatun, to the 'Blue Wolf' in marriage.

Gökböri's military skills were widely recognized, Saladin's secretary, the chronicler Al Isfahani, describing him as '...the audacious, the hero of well thought out projects, the lion who heads straight for the target, the most reliable and firmest chief'. He remained a leading *amir* after the Hattin campaign and though he had to give his original fiefs to Taqi al Din, he was compensated with his father's old governorate around Irbil. This he ruled until dying at the age of 81. In Syria Gökböri was remembered as a great warrior, but in Irbil in what is now Iraqi Kurdistan the old Turk was remembered as a patron of scholars such as the historian Ibn Khallikan. He built colleges, hospitals, almshouses and hostels for pilgrims and merchants. Gökböri was also the first ruler to patronize the previously unofficial Mawlid al Nabi (Birthday of the Prophet Mohammed) festival, perhaps in imitation of a large Christian community which then lived in Irbil. Only five years after his death the Mongols arrived, destroying Gökböri's cultural works, and all that seems to remain is the beautifully decorated brick minaret of Irbil's Old Mosque.

Little is known about the Hajib Husam al Din Lu'lu's background. He was almost certainly a *mamluk* as the name Lu'lu, meaning 'Pearl', was usually given to slaves. He may also have been of Armenian origin. Even his title of Hajib (chamberlain) does not say much. Under the previous Fatimid rulers of Egypt, when Lu'lu may already have been a courtier, the Hajib was an important court official though not a military one. Under the Saljuqs of Iran the Hajib was a court official who could also lead armies.

Early 13th-century ceramic bowl from Persia showing a Muslim ruler holding a *gurz* (mace). He is seated between two military leaders who wear full mail *dir'* (hauberks) beneath sleeveless surcoats. (Toledo Museum of Art, Ohio, Edward Drummond Libbey Gift)

According to one chronicler, Husam al Din Lu'lu was a *shaykh* or man of religion. But it was as commander of Saladin's fleet that he earned fame, defeating Reynald of Châtillon's audacious raid into the Red Sea in 1183 and personally leading marines in a naval battle which led to the capture of Gibelet (Jubayl) four years later. After taking a relief fleet to Acre in 1189 Lu'lu seems to disappear from the records. Was he among 2,700 men of Acre's garrison slaughtered on Richard the Lionheart's orders in 1191? A senior officer named Husam al Din was still in Al Adil's service in 1194, but there is no certainty that he was the same man.

Whether or not Lu'lu died at Acre, retired after the destruction of the Egyptian Mediterranean fleet at Acre, or went on to serve Al Adil, he had already won enough fame to be included alongside Saladin in a panegyric by the poet Ibn al Dharawil. Saladin's secretary Al Isfahani was also full of praise for Lu'lu,

...whose courage was well known to the infidels, whose violence against the enemy was extolled. He was without equal when it came to raids with which none but he were associated... happy in all he undertook, agreeable in character.

Ibn al Athir, a less flowery chronicler, simply described Husam al Din Lu'lu as '...an emir known for his bravery, prudence and good humour' and as '... a brave and energetic man, a naval and military expert full of useful initiative'.

## THE CHRISTIAN COMMANDERS

Most of the original sources are unsympathetic to Guy, King of Jerusalem (1186–92), as the ruler who lost Jerusalem to the Muslims. Guy and his French knights were also disliked by the local Latin aristocracy. He was clearly handsome and won the heart of Queen Sibylla of Jerusalem, but whether he was as weak and frivolous as most chroniclers suggest is less certain. He emerges as a far more decisive character after Hattin than before it. Traditional historians still describe Guy as an ineffective *bailli* (regent) during the crisis of 1183 and as being tight with money even before he became king. The late R.C. Smail, however, gives Guy some credit for forcing Saladin's withdrawal in 1183. On the other hand he does appear to have been easily influenced by friends who offered conflicting and not always sound advice. As a result King Guy tended to change his mind at crucial moments.

A war-galley in a Byzantine manuscript of the 12th century. A number of illustrations of Byzantine warships exist, and several give the vessels red-painted prows and sterns. Perhaps this was a form of identification that could be seen from a great distance. Otherwise the written sources suggest that it could be very difficult to identify friend from foe in Mediterranean naval warfare. (*Sermons of St Gregory Nazianzus*, Monastery of Panteleimon, Mount Athos, Greece)

Of course the basis of Guy's authority was weak, as the laws of the Kingdom of Jerusalem reflected a European ideal of 'constitutional' feudal monarchy rather than the reality of conditions in the Latin States. Even Guy's command of the army was rather theoretical and he constantly had to consult his barons and other men before issuing an order. Confusion, resentment, jealousy and insubordination were rife throughout the Kingdom and Guy could rarely impose effective discipline. On the other hand his final decisions and the tactics he adopted, even at Hattin, were fully in line with the accepted strategy of the time – a strategy which had served the Latin States well in the past.

In many ways Count Raymond III of Tripoli was the most tragic figure in the whole Hattin saga. Perhaps the most intelligent of Latin leaders, he often tried to achieve peaceful co-existence with neighbouring Muslim rulers. He also emerged as the best tactician among the Kingdom of Jerusalem's military leaders. Yet in the end Raymond was branded a traitor, as the man responsible for Christian defeat by Saladin, and he retired to die a broken man within a few months of that catastrophe.

Raymond became count of Tripoli at the age of only 12, after his father was killed by Isma'ili 'Assassins'. By 1175 his ability and experience had made him leader of the local barons and he was later the natural choice to be regent, ruling the Kingdom of Jerusalem in the name of the dying leper King Baldwin IV. In this role Raymond showed himself patient, careful and ingenious in dealing with various factions in the Kingdom and with its neighbours. The calculating Count Raymond was also capable of adapting to a changing situation, an adaptability rare among his hidebound contemporaries in Jerusalem. Eight years as a prisoner in Aleppo had made him fluent in Arabic and given him considerable knowledge of Islam, plus a certain admiration rather than hatred for his captors. Unlike newly arrived Crusaders, Raymond no longer saw the Muslims merely as foes but as neighbours – though rivals – with a shared interest in the harvest, the uncertain rainfall and in trade. For their part the Muslims regarded Raymond III of Tripoli as the bravest as well as the shrewdest of Latin leaders. But when the final crisis came he fought as hard as any to save the Kingdom and if Guy had followed Raymond's advice the battle of Hattin might have been avoided or even won.

Of all the leading characters in the story of the loss of Jerusalem, none is more colourful than Reynald. The traditional view portrays him as a recklessly brave, handsome but undisciplined adventurer who came to the Latin States in 1153 without wealth or followers yet won the hand of the young Princess Constance of Antioch. Unscrupulous and brutal he may have been, but Reynald had an astonishing grasp of geopolitical strategy. Unfortunately for the Kingdom of Jerusalem, his vision far outstripped the military or economic capabilities of the Latin States. Unlike Raymond of Tripoli, who had also spent years as a prisoner among the Muslims, Reynald's captivity in Aleppo (1161–75) had left him with a burning hatred for Islam – though also a great knowledge of its geography. He

Late 12th- to early 13th-century stucco relief from Persia showing horsemen fighting with spears held in both hands. They wear lamellar *jawshan* (cuirasses), which on the right has flaps to protect the upper arms. (Museum of Art, Seattle)

emerged as a fanatical Crusader. The Muslims in turn well knew that 'Arnat', as they called him, was their most dedicated foe.

By the time of Reynald's release, his wife Constance had died and so, without delay, Reynald married the heiress to Krak (Karak) and thus became master of the great seigneurie of Oultrejordain. Here he gradually built up a state-within-a-state, perhaps one day hoping to make it an independent lordship like the County of Tripoli or the Principality of Antioch.

Balian, the Lord of Rama (Ramlah), came from the most famous feudal family in the Latin Kingdom of Jerusalem. Yet this d'Ibelin family had humble origins, being part of a 'new aristocracy' which rose from the rank-and-file of knights who carved out the Kingdom in the early 12th century. By the 1180s Balian d'Ibelin had become one of the most respected local barons and enjoyed semi-autonomous authority in the south of Palestine. Trusted by all sides, he had acted as an intermediary in negotiations between King Guy and Count Raymond of Tripoli. Balian was also well known as a negotiator among the Muslims and was counted a personal friend by Saladin himself.

Nevertheless Balian remained a convinced Christian and a dedicated defender of the Kingdom. Released by Saladin after Hattin, he swore never again to take arms against the Sultan. Yet Balian d'Ibelin allowed himself to be absolved from this oath by the Patriarch of Jerusalem and took command of the Holy City's defences where he showed enormous courage and determination. It says a great deal for the respect between Balian and Saladin, qualities that bridged the religious divide, that the Sultan could understand Balian's oath-breaking and forgive him when Jerusalem finally fell on 2 October 1187.

# THE OPPOSING ARMIES

### SALADIN'S FORCES

Medieval Muslim armies were highly organized compared to their Crusader enemies and some aspects of their structure, tactics and traditions went back to the ancient Romano-Byzantine or Persian empires. Warfare was largely left to professional soldiers although religious volunteers did play a role against the invading Crusaders. Possession of a horse also gave status in medieval Islamic society, as it did in Europe. On the other hand the elite of the Muslim countries had lived in towns since at least the 9th century, rather than in scattered castles like the feudal aristocracy of the West. Regular soldiers also dwelt within the city walls, though irregulars camped outside. The Turks and Kurds who formed the bulk of such professionals were rough compared to the cultured Arab *amir*s of the old Fatimid regime, while the sophisticated urban populations regarded them as a barbarous but necessary addition to their streets. Such men often came from long-standing military families in which young warriors acquired experience of leadership and tactics fighting alongside their relatives. Unlike the fully professional *mamluks* of slave origin, such free-born warriors often had other activities including trades to keep them busy in time of peace. Among those who rose high in Muslim armies were men of humble birth, but in Saladin's day most leaders were drawn from free-born soldiers rather than the slave-recruited *mamluks*.

'Gulshah arrives to remove her veil', in a superbly illustrated copy of the *Warqa wa Gulshah*, a Persian epic poem. Made in western Iran, Azerbayjan or eastern Turkey, probably in the 13th century, it shows the arms, armour and costume of the Turkish military elite. (Topkapi Library, Ms. Haz. 841, p. 131, Istanbul)

Painted panels from Capella Palatina, Palermo. Near top, an Arab cavalryman with a spear and long kite-shaped shield. Another horseman below is indulging in the universal aristocratic pastime of hawking. (David Nicolle)

The proportion of various ethnic groups within 12th-century Islamic armies is not easy to judge, as the origins of leaders did not necessarily reflect the men they led. Saladin's armies grew out of those of his Zangid predecessors and, like all the states which emerged from the fragmentation of the Great Saljuq empire in the early 12th century, the Zangids were highly militarized and looked east for cultural, political and military inspiration. The force which Nur al Din sent to Egypt in 1169, in which Saladin served as a staff officer, consisted of 6,000 Turcomans, 2,000 Kurds and a tiny elite of 500 *mamluks*. It was around this force that Saladin built his own army when he took over Egypt a few years later. At first he also used some of the old Fatimid regiments but most of these were disbanded within a short while.

Two warriors on a mid-13th-century tile from Kashan in Persia. The man in front carries a small round shield, the man behind is wielding a spear with both hands. (Museum of Oriental Art, Rome, inv. 1056; photograph – David Nicolle)

In Syria and the Jazira region Saladin made a policy of trying to recruit the troops of defeated Muslim rivals. The loyalty of those who did join him was strengthened by flattering their sense of 'asabiyah (family pride) and Saladin's armies soon proved that they had greater experience as well as better discipline than Muslim forces from eastern Anatolia or Persia. As Saladin's authority spread, so regional armies grew up under various provincial governors. Their recruitment often differed from that of the Sultan's own forces. Aleppo relied primarily on Turcoman tribes such as the Yürük, Damascus recruiting Arab tribesmen from central Syria, and Kurds playing a prominent role around Mosul. Nevertheless, the core of most such forces remained slave-recruited *mamluks*. Fiercely loyal to the man who had bought, educated and then freed them, such warriors had formed the bodyguards of Abbasid caliphs for centuries. Now Saladin combined the old Abbasid and newer Fatimid practices, mostly buying slaves of pagan Turkish origin from Asia. This elite joined the Sultan's guard which also looked after the main arsenals, garrisoned important fortifications and were stationed in the centre of Saladin's army in battle.

The largest ethnic group in the army was that of the Turks who had been the dominant military element in Syria since the early 12th century. Some tribes had migrated into northern Syria in the 1120s but the majority of Turkish troops were still recruited from Turcoman tribes in the Diyarbakr region. Second in numerical importance were the Kurds who fought as cavalry and archers, though apparently they were not using the horse-archery tactics of their Turkish rivals. Saladin recruited them either as individuals or as whole units from various tribes, such tribal units generally fighting as one block in battle. A third important ethnic element was the Arabs. There had been a resurgence of nomadism in northern Syria following a

Byzantine military revival of the 11th century. But although these Arab nomads were rich in horses they had few archers, fighting instead with spear or sword. Nevertheless the bedouin continued to supply vital auxiliary cavalry to the rulers of 12th-century Syria – though they were deeply mistrusted by the settled Arab peasantry and city dwellers. Such bedouin featured in Saladin's army as *qufl*, infantry raiders who specialized in harassing an enemy's communications, and as *lisus*, cavalry infiltrators whose role was to interrupt enemy supplies.

The *mutatawi'ah* or religious volunteers often served for very short periods, but they could be quite effective, particularly when harassing enemy stragglers. Unlike the *ahdath* (urban militias), the true religious volunteers were difficult for a government to control. Meanwhile the *ahdath* tended to be recruited from the poorer sections of city populations. By the 12th century its main duty was to police a city or town, though it could also fight alongside the regular army in an emergency. Under Fatimid rule the *ahdath* of Palestinian towns may have included Jews as well as Muslims, but whether this was true of Saladin's *ahdath* is not known. Other local troops included the often despised *rajjalah* infantry. Specialist infantry would have been professionals, even if part-time, and the wealthy city of Aleppo was famous for warriors who also seem to have had a well-developed sense of humour. Back in 1071, when the Saljuq Turks were attacking Aleppo, the defenders wrapped a bale of silk around their strongest tower and sent a message to the enemy saying that the Turks' stone-throwing machines had given it a headache! Aleppo was still famous for its miners and siege engineers in Saladin's day, while the garrison of Aleppo's

Arab bedouin warrior stopping a fight between two travellers. This example of the *Maqamat* of Al Hariri was made in Mosul in 1256 and shows the very long spear characteristic of Arab horsemen. (British Library, Ms. Or. 1200, London)

citadel were also looked after by a professional government-paid doctor. Engineers from far-away Khurasan may have served Saladin, and the Sultan was certainly delighted to get a squad of specialist fire-troops from the Abbasid caliph of Baghdad. Meanwhile North Africa played its part by supplying naval crews, of which Saladin was always short, the Maghribis (North Africans) being regarded as the best sailors in the Muslim world.

### Organization of Saladin's Forces

Saladin's army was subdivided into units of various sizes, though the terms used often overlapped. The smallest were the *jarida* (70 men) and the *tulb* (70–200 men) with their own flag and trumpeter. The *jama'a* was probably a tactical formation consisting of three *jarida*s. The *sariya* was an ad hoc band of about 20 cavalry, often used in ambushes, while the *saqa* was a small advance guard or reconnaissance party. Unlike their Latin foes the Muslims also had specific *amir* (officer) ranks, ranging from an *isfahsalar* (army leader) down through the *ustadh al dar* and *hajib* (chamberlain) senior commanders, to the *amir hajib*, *amir jandar*, *khazindar* (governor of an important citadel), *amir kabir* (great officer) and ordinary *amir*. A

A scene on a damaged early 13th-century candlestick-base from Persia showing a horseman from the rear. (Victoria & Albert Museum, inv. 1593–1888; photograph David Nicolle)

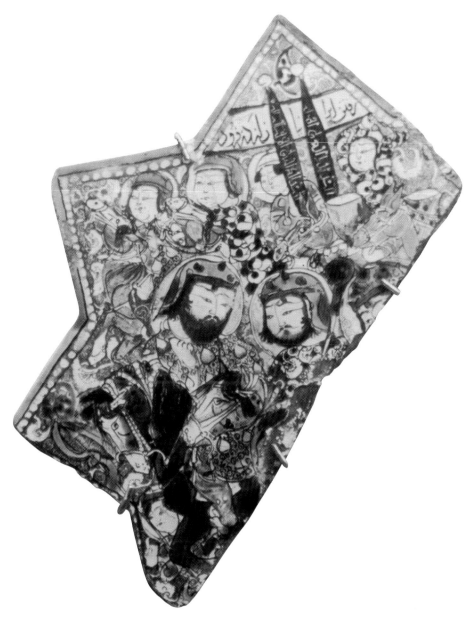

'Iranian army leaving the castle of Furud', scene from the *Shahnamah* on a broken early 13th-century tile from Persia. Four warriors have helmets with extended neck protections. The leading horseman wears a mail hauberk, the second carries a massive *gurz* (mace). In the rear-right one man carries two furled banners while another beats upon drums carried by a mule. (Museum of Fine Arts, Boston; photograph David Nicolle)

*ra'is* headed the *ahdath* militia while the *shihna* was chief of police. Regular soldiers were paid regular *jamakiyah* (salaries) or held *iqta'* (land-grants), which had features in common with European feudal fiefs. The pay structure was controlled by a *Diwan al Jaysh* (Army Ministry). This *Diwan al Jaysh* also listed the troops' names and where they were stationed, and held reviews to check training and equipment. Registered soldiers received weapons from government arsenals free, but if they lost this equipment the cost was deducted from their pay. Any changes of rank, status or unit were also noted on the registers.

The *iqta'* or fief was vital to this military system. It was really a system of tax-farming in which the holder took a proportion of revenues in return for ensuring that taxes were collected. One vital characteristic that distinguished an *iqta'* from a European feudal fief was that the land could be taken back at any time. In return for an *iqta'* the *muqta* (land-holder) also maintained and equipped a specified number of troops. Some *iqta's* were huge estates given to members of the ruling family. Others were governorships of towns, castles and strategic districts bestowed on senior officers. Then there were villages and smaller estates given to lesser *amir*s. Salaries or pensions drawn from government properties could also be *iqta's*. The value of land-grants varied considerably, even within a single region. Only a generation after Saladin's death a survey showed *iqta's* ranging from one maintaining 250 horsemen, to another that included the towns of Nablus and Jinin supporting 120 horseman, to a small *iqta'* maintaining 70 horsemen. Inferior land went as *iqta's* to *ajnad* militia or bedouin auxiliaries. Yet the *muqta*s only lived on these estates if they had fallen from political favour.

Among various categories of troops the slave-recruited *mamluks* generally formed a ruler's elite *'askar* bodyguard. Fiercely disciplined and proud of its status, an *'askar* also looked after siege engines, arsenals and other vital facilities. The *halqa* seems to have been a larger formation, perhaps comparable to a household regiment. The *tawashiya* included, by Saladin's day, both *mamluks* and freely recruited cavalrymen, each with his own horse, page or *mamluk* follower, about ten animals to carry baggage, and a salary to purchase equipment. Organized into first-rate regiments which remained close to the ruler on campaign, each *tawashi* was expected to serve in the army for a certain number of months every year. Men of the *ajnad* or territorial army had lower status but were still properly equipped cavalry, though few seem to have been trained horse-archers. The infantry had even lower status, despite their essential role in siege warfare. Most were archers, crossbowmen, or fought with spear and shield. The *janib* may have operated as mobile mounted infantry, sometimes riding mules, but the only real elite among foot soldiers were the *nafatin* (fire-troops). All professional foot soldiers were paid salaries, at least while on campaign. The same was probably true of siege engineers such as the *naqqabun* (miners or engineers), *hajjarun* (masons) and *najjarun* (carpenters).

It was the support services, however, that really set this army apart from its Latin enemies. Considerable emphasis was put on good communications: a government *barid* (postal service) used carrier pigeons and couriers, while beacons could carry warnings from the frontiers at extraordinary speed. Equally important was the distribution of weapons. Most cities had arms bazaars and many, like Aleppo, Damascus, Cairo and Mosul, had their own weapons-manufacturing quarters. Arms were issued to the troops from the *zardkhanah* (arsenal) at the start of a campaign. On the march, however, armour and most weaponry would remain in the *thuql* (baggage train). This made the troops light and fast moving but could be disastrous if intelligence failed and there was a surprise attack. Consequently the *thuql*

A late 12th- to early 13th-century lustre plate from Persia showing a soldier carrying a tall shield, the base of which is flattened. Such *januwiyah*, or mantlets, were specifically for infantry use. The man's turban and the hilt of his straight sword represent styles known in the Islamic Middle East long before the coming of the Saljuq Turks. (Keir College, London, inv. 151)

was commanded by an experienced and reliable *amir*. The *thuql* also incorporated fire-troops, blacksmiths to repair weapons, siege equipment with engineers and surveyors. Non-combatants in the *thuql* included servants, horse handlers, mule and donkey drivers, cameleers, scribes, religious functionaries, doctors and surgeons. The sophisticated medical services formed, in fact, a mobile hospital. The division of booty had always been carefully regulated in Muslim armies, one-fifth going to the government and the rest being distributed among the troops. Much would then be sold to the merchants of the *suq al-'askar* (soldiers' bazaar) which formed part of the baggage train. This *suq al-'askar* also supplied additional weaponry and other military supplies when needed.

Physical appearance, costume and a rudimentary form of heraldry distinguished individuals and groups within Saladin's military. While the Ayyubid family and the Turks wore their hair long, the Arabs with the possible exception of the bedouin shaved their heads. Almost all Muslim men had beards or moustaches, Saladin's sailors having to shave in order to pass themselves off as Crusaders when slipping through a Latin blockade. A tall yellow cap called a *kalawta* was used by the Ayyubids while Central Asian Turkish forms of wrap-around tunic also became popular in the ruling class. A *hiyasa* (belt) made of linked metal plates actually distinguished the elite while officers wore the *sharbush*, a stiff fur-trimmed cap with a raised front. A band of richly embroidered *tiraz* fabric bearing an inscription had long been given by rulers to their followers as a mark of allegiance. Inscriptions also appeared on shields in the 11th century and would become more common later. Other devices and colours indicated Iranian influence, perhaps via the widely popular *Shahnamah* (epic poem), but there would be no real system of Islamic heraldry until the Mamluk dynasty of the mid-13th century onwards. Devices remained personal, not hereditary, and there was never a governing body to regularize 'heraldry' as in Europe.

Taqi al Din's personal flag was described by a Crusader witness as looking like a pair of trousers, but what the ignorant European probably saw was either a doubled 'windsock' banner such as had been used by Turks and Persians for hundreds of years, or a flag bearing the double-bladed 'Sword of Ali' or a Turkish tribal *tamga* device. Taqi al Din's troops certainly marched beneath a yellow banner, yellow being the Ayyubids' favoured colour. It was not, however, one of the normal colours of Islamic symbolism (green, white, black, red), having been regarded with some disfavour in earlier years. While Arabs and Kurds used various types of flag, the Turks also held *tuq* or horsetail standards aloft.

### Tactics of the Muslim Forces

Saladin continued to use the age-old *razzia* raiding tactics of the Arab Middle East though there had been a change in the way these were carried out. The old mixed infantry and cavalry armies now gave way to smaller elites of *mamluk* horse-archers supported by auxiliary cavalry using Turkish tactics of rapid manoeuvre, dispersal and harassment. Military manuals from the Islamic Middle Ages may reflect theory rather than reality, but the organizing of a battle array, an encampment, line of march, siege or counter-siege were very similar in works from the Fatimid, Ayyubid or even Mamluk periods. Saladin's siege tactics were almost entirely the same as those of his Fatimid predecessors, while his cavalry tactics were far more flexible than those of the Crusaders. Saladin's horsemen would even, if the situation were suitable, stand against a full-scale charge by the enemy's knights. Considerable skills were, in fact, demanded of a late 12th-century cavalryman. Literary sources give primacy to the spear, which could be wielded with one or both hands and thrust at the foe's arms or legs as well as his body. Once lances were broken horsemen drew their swords. Only in specifically Turkish sources are bows given much prominence.

Cavalry manuals dating from a generation or so later deal with the initiating and maintaining of an attack, feigning retreat, wheeling around in battle, evading the enemy and renewing an attack. Horse-archers are instructed how to control their mounts and how to shoot. The advantages of various forms of bow and arrow, as well as the use of thumb-rings for long-distance shooting, are all discussed. So is the use of the javelin from horseback. The training of foot soldiers received less attention, but manuals did give advice for infantry archers, describing the skills they needed to fight in the open. A little later military experts were suggesting that infantry must be able to march long distances, recognize dangerous enemy formations that indicated an impending attack, know how to take cover, check and chase cavalry, and how to scatter or scare an enemy's horses.

Once in enemy territory any force should always keep its escape route open. This was particularly true of lightly equipped raiding parties whose function was to sow confusion and fear among the enemy. Arab bedouin auxiliaries excelled in setting ambushes, particularly if they were natives of the area. If a raid were to be made at night, cloudy, windy and rainy weather was best. If the enemy were strong, it was

Carved 11th- to 12th-century relief from the window of a mosque in Kubachi, Daghestan. Only in such isolated Turkish areas could one find representational sculpture on an Islamic religious building. This portrays a horse-archer with a typically Turkish Central Asian form of box-like quiver on his right hip. (Metropolitan Museum of Art, New York; photograph David Nicolle)

'Defending a castle' in a Mozarabic manuscript from Catalonia written in about 1100. It provides one of the clearest representations of a *lu'ab*, the smallest form of man-powered stone-throwing mangonel, widely used in both Muslim and Christian Spain and in the Middle East. (Biblioteca Nazionale, Turin, inv. J. II. 1, ff.189v-190r)

advisable to attack him just before dawn while he was still confused and sleepy. Set-piece battles were generally avoided but when they did take place it is difficult to tell how far the tactics of Saladin's day really followed the theories.

The *jandariyah* guard remained with the ruler and though Saladin normally placed his best *halqa* regiments in the centre, *halqa* troops also operated as independent formations. Heavy cavalry were certainly used in the charge, operating much like Latin knights, and, like knights, were divided into small *tulb* squadrons. Yet horse-archery remained the cavalry's most effective tactic. At long distance it could disrupt enemy formations by wounding horses and infantry. At close range the Muslims' composite bow could penetrate most 12th-century armour. Islamic infantry may have declined in importance after the 11th century but they still appeared in major set-piece battles as well as siege warfare. Although infantry were dismissed by many Muslim chroniclers as *harafisha* (rabble), Saladin's tactics often relied on separating an enemy's infantry from his cavalry even when fighting fellow Muslims. Terrain would be used to full advantage. Shirkuh lured Latin cavalry into an impossible charge up a slope of soft sand in 1167 and Saladin used a *tal* (artificial hill of debris from long habitation, typical of the Middle East) to hide his reserves. But such sophisticated battlefield tactics demanded reliable battlefield communications and here the Muslims were well served by musical instruments, flags and *jawush* or *munadi* (criers).

Siege warfare was the main purpose of large expeditions. Lightly armed troops would be the first to reach and invest an enemy castle. The attackers would then protect their position with palisades before digging entrenchments. Siege towers might be built and miners would start undermining the enemy's walls. Mining operations, which demanded skilled personnel and careful direction, were in fact used by the Muslims more than by the Crusaders. In addition to battering rams the Muslims had a variety of stone-throwing engines, some of which were large enough to damage a wall or at least the battlements which gave cover to the defenders. The numerous smaller engines were essentially anti-personnel weapons designed to clear defenders from their positions prior to a general assault. One of the attackers' most important tasks was to protect their wooden siege engines and mines from defenders who might make a sortie. Once a breach had been made or a wall undermined, the garrison would be given an opportunity to surrender. If this were refused assault parties would be organized under the best available officers. When these managed to seize the breach they might again stop while the enemy was offered a final chance to surrender. Sieges could go on for months and in such cases the besiegers' camp could turn into a temporary town. Outside Acre in 1190 Saladin's position had 7,000 shops including 140 farriers, all controlled by a police force. Several markets included those for clothing and weaponry old or new, plus an estimated 1,000 small bath-houses mostly managed by North Africans. The contrast with the stinking disease-ridden camps of the Crusaders could hardly be more striking.

Muslim armies were just as sophisticated in defence of fortifications, most of which were based on long-established designs going back to the pre-Islamic period. The *burj* or tower was basic to Islamic military architecture. Covered galleries along the top of a wall were also widespread while city walls tended to be high rather than thick. Major architectural changes appeared early in the 13th century as a result of the invention of the counterweight *mangonel*, but these had not appeared by Saladin's time. Garrisons included masons, sappers, crossbow-men, javelin-throwers, fire-troops and operators of stone-throwing machines. If an attack were imminent troops should pollute all the neighbouring water sources, and even attempt to spread disease downstream with the aid of carcasses. If possible the attackers should themselves be attacked by the garrison before they could establish their camp. Once the siege had begun the defenders must make night sorties to burn the enemy's machines, but if a sortie were attempted in daylight it could be in a strictly disciplined square formation.

Many of these ideas were used in naval warfare. Nevertheless the main role of Saladin's fleet was to transport troops rapidly from Egypt to Syria, and to hamper traffic between the Latin States and Europe. Marines would sail aboard larger merchant ships as well as fighting galleys and could include archers, fire-troops and operators of stone-throwing machines as well as boarders. When faced with an enemy fleet Muslim galleys made use of crescent-shaped or compacted formations, feigned retreat and used coastal features for cover. Although Muslim naval power had been in decline for more than a century, a naval manual of the 13th century could still claim that the Muslims were superior to Byzantines in naval warfare – but made no comparison with the now dominant Italian fleets. Saladin's ships were essentially the same as those of his enemies. A *shini* was the standard fighting galley, but many cargo vessels were also powered by oars. Others, of course, relied on sails and it is now known that three-masted ships were built by Muslim Mediterranean shipwrights more than a century before they reappeared in Christian fleets. As early as AD 955 one great ship was 95 metres long and almost 40 metres broad. The warships built in sections in Egypt and then transported across Sinai on camel-back to the Gulf of Aqabah in 1170 must, however, have been small. Other Indian Ocean vessels could be astonishingly large. Here there was less use of oars, partly because of reliable monsoon winds but more importantly because water sources were scarce and so smaller crews were an advantage. The hinged stern rudder, a Chinese invention, was also known to eastern Arabian sailors by at least the early 12th century.

### Muslim Weapons

Saladin rose to power in the central regions of the Muslim world which were acutely short of iron and of fuel for working metals. The nearest important source of iron ore was eastern Anatolia, but otherwise Saladin's empire had to rely on imported ingots plus small mines in the mountains near Beirut and around Ajlun – both of which virtually straddled the frontier with the Latin States. Not surprisingly long-distance trade in pig-iron and refined steel, much of it from India, was vital for Saladin's armies. Despite such difficulties Egypt already had three state arsenals under the Fatimids, one employing 3,000 craftsmen, which Saladin inherited. In addition to sword making in Damascus, Mosul had an arms market as did neighbouring Baghdad.

Saladin was criticized for seizing horses and weaponry from Nur al Din's arsenals when the latter died, yet it was clearly important for an ambitious ruler to get his hands on as much scarce military *matériel* as possible. The value of such equipment made the capture of enemy stores worth recording and when a Latin garrison surrendered, it invariably had to leave its arms behind. The Muslims could also demand tribute in weapons even including horse armours from the Latin States, while in January 1188 a Byzantine embassy, as a mark of friendship, gave Saladin 400 mail hauberks, 4,000 lances and 5,000 swords captured from an Italo-Norman army.

Swords were also imported commercially from both Byzantium and Europe – the latter in direct contravention of a papal ban. But an extended campaign could pose huge problems of supply.

The weapons used in Saladin's armies included spears, swords, maces, axes, javelins, composite bows, crossbows and occasionally lassos, the main protection being shields, lamellar cuirasses, mail hauberks including the padded cloth-covered *kazaghand*, and helmets. The popular image of lightly armed Saracens wielding

A soldier with a turban and a straight sword, probably hung from a baldric rather than a belt. He appears in a medical manuscript written in Iraq in AD 1224. (Freer Gallery of Art, Washington, inv. 575121; photograph David Nicolle)

equally light sabres is far from reality. Many if not most Islamic swords were still straight though the curved sabre, long known in Turkish Central Asia, had appeared in Persia by the 9th or 10th centuries. The composite bow had long been the main missile weapon of the Middle East but one notable change during the Crusading era was from the angled, so-called 'Hun' bow to the smoothly recurved 'Turkish' type (see page 132). Sources indicating the ineffectiveness of Islamic archery against Crusader armour are widely misunderstood, referring as they do to long-range harassment intended to injure unprotected horses rather than to kill men. Tests have, in fact, shown that mail offered little resistance to arrows. On the other hand the shock-absorbing lamellar armours of the Turks would almost certainly have given greater protection.

### The Size of Saladin's Army

Even today it is widely assumed that Islamic armies were huge and that the valiant Crusaders were overwhelmed by numbers. This is not borne out by the facts. Of course the manpower potential of the Muslim states was far greater than that of the Latin States in Syria and Palestine, but, as in Europe, only a small proportion normally took part in warfare. Nevertheless large auxiliary forces could be mustered – for a short while – around a ruler's professional 'askar. Egypt could afford quite large armies, though even under the Fatimids these were nowhere near as big as sometimes believed, reaching a maximum of 25,000 at best. In his early days as Nur al Din's governor in Egypt, Saladin inherited some Fatimid regiments and records show that in 1169 he had 8,640 regulars, excluding naval troops, of whom the most reliable were his own family's 500-strong following plus 3,000 Turcomans. At another review held on 11 September 1171 Saladin mustered 174 *tulb* cavalry squadrons (about 14,000 cavalry) while a further 20 squadrons were on duty elsewhere, plus some 7,000 Arab bedouin auxiliaries. A pro-Fatimid coup attempt in 1174 led to most of the old Fatimid units being disbanded and bedouin auxiliaries were reduced to about 1,300. A further *ard* (review) held in 1181 listed Saladin's forces at 6,976 *tawashi* cavalry plus 1,553 *qaraghulam mamluks*. To this could be added the forces maintained by the governors of Syrian cities, though not all would be committed to one campaign at one time. Damascus is estimated to have had a garrison of about 1,000, Hims 500, Hama and its dependent towns 1,000 and Aleppo 1,000. The Jazira region could field a further 2,000 to 4,000 men including Mosul's own garrison which numbered 1,500 in the early 12th century.

**LEFT AND OPPOSITE**
'Fight between Roland
and Faragut': relief
carvings of c. AD 1138
on the façade of the
Church of San Zeno in
Verona. The ideal of
knightly combat began
with the 'breaking of
lances' and concluded
with swords, as it did in
the Islamic heroic tales
of the Arab Middle East.
(David Nicolle)

## THE CRUSADER FORCES

Most leading families of the Latin States rose from relatively humble origins, having made their fortunes early in the 12th century. Even so there were never enough trained warriors to defend the new territories and qualifications for knighthood were lowered so that pilgrims would settle. Even indigenous Christians were sometimes knighted in 12th-century Jerusalem. This, and the many marriages between Crusader warriors and local Christian women, led to a certain 'orientalization' of the Latin aristocracy. Yet this was very superficial and many of the supposed 'eastern fashions' were Byzantine rather than Middle Eastern. An influx of bourgeois Italian merchants was meanwhile seen as a social threat by the new aristocracy of Jerusalem. Knights claiming French origin also looked down on knights of Italian blood, and all were despised as half-breeds by men newly come from Europe.

The *maréchal* of each Latin State was in charge of recruitment, but his powers were limited by customary law. Knights, for example, were excused service on foot or where their horses could not carry them. Nevertheless men from knightly families would be involved in warfare from the age of 15 and remained liable for military summons until 60. On the other hand service was not due if a knight lost his fief to the enemy. The frequent mention of *sodees* ('soldiers') did not always refer to paid mercenaries as in Europe. Instead many Latin *sodees* had fiefs of money or rent rather than land. Troops would also be drawn from other organizations owing feudal obligations such as the Church, towns, indigenous Christian landholders and the military orders. These would supply knights and mounted sergeants, plus large numbers of infantry. In emergencies an *arrière ban* would be declared in which,

A carved capital in the cloisters of Monreale Cathedral, Sicily, made in the late 12th century. The many carvings at Monreale show a greater variety of arms and armour than do the carvings of northern Europe and may reflect both climate and a specifically Mediterranean military tradition shared with Byzantium, the Arab countries and the Latin States of the Middle East. (David Nicolle)

again theoretically, all free men had to muster. Infantry could also be recruited from visiting pilgrims, of whom there were many in the Kingdom of Jerusalem. As such sources still remained inadequate the Latin States increasingly relied on mercenaries and the majority of mounted sergeants were probably hired outside the Middle East. Western mercenaries often stayed in almost permanent service though their contracts may have been renewed monthly. Penalties for deserting before a contract expired were, however, severe: a knight forfeiting his armour and other equipment, a common soldier having his hands pierced with a hot iron.

The military orders of Templars and Hospitallers tended to reflect the aggressive attitudes of the newcomers, rather than the more cautious Latin settlers, and their motivation had much in common with the *mutatawi'ah* religious volunteers of the Muslim side. Among indigenous and non-feudal troops, the *turcopoles* were by far the most important. The concept and the name were copied from the Byzantines but also had something in common with the Muslim system of slave-recruited *mamluks*, most being converted Muslim prisoners of war. No Muslim soldiers could be found in Latin service, though the Latin States did employ Muslim clerks. Nor were Jews enlisted as they were regarded as sympathetic to the Muslim side. Siege engineers were recruited from various indigenous Christian communities and here Armenians took a leading role. In fact Armenians proved to be the most sympathetic of eastern Christian sects, but were mostly found in the north, in the Principality of Antioch where they provided the bulk of the infantry. Maronites from what is now Lebanon furnished the Kingdom of Jerusalem with infantry archers but were not fully integrated into the new feudal structure. Except for the largely pro-Muslim Nestorians, most of whom lived beyond Latin territory in what is now Iraq and Iran, Syrian Orthodox or Jacobite Christians were regarded as the least reliable, yet even they were needed as guides.

## Organization of the Crusader Forces

As in feudal France, which the Latins of Syria took as their model, the King of Jerusalem commanded the army. His authority might be expected to have been great because the Latin States were highly militarized and the army of Jerusalem was a permanent structure due to the almost constant state of war. Failure to expand much beyond the coastal strip and failure to conquer any of the inland cities except Jerusalem meant that the Kingdom had to maintain an abnormally large defensive army but it also meant that it lacked land to support such an army by normal feudal means. Theoretically the king could demand that his knights serve a full year, much longer than was seen in the West, but in reality the period was negotiated at the *Haute Cour* (High Court) as each campaign was planned. Even when war broke out the king was only first among equals, and divided authority

'Devils and Sinners' carved on the façade of the church of Ste-Foy, Conques, AD 1120–30. On the left a fully mailed knight, probably representing the sins of war or pride, is tipped on to his head. On the right devils are armed with 'demonic' weapons including a pick, a ball-and-chain and a crossbow. (David Nicolle)

led to difficulties when facing a disciplined foe. The Kingdom of Jerusalem was also financially weak, which caused great problems for an army relying so strongly on mercenaries.

By the late 12th century most Latin knights, even those who had land fiefs, lived in the towns like their *iqta'*-holding Muslim counterparts. Money fiefs had been known since at least the 1130s, their holders receiving rents from ports, markets, tolls, commercial or industrial properties. In return they, like any feudal fief-holder, had specified military obligations such as maintaining a certain number of fully equipped knights or sergeants. In addition to knightly fiefs there were also sergeantry fiefs, some of which supported *Turcopoles*.

The command structure of the army of Jerusalem stuck closer to the established European system. The three great military officers of state were the *senéchal*, the *connétable* and the *maréchal*. The *senéchal* was responsible for all fortifications, except the king's own palace, garrisons and provisions. On campaign the *senéchal* usually led the king's own *bataille* or division under the king's direct command. The *connétable* commanded the army except when the king was present. He also organized the muster, sorted out various *bataille* divisions in battle or on the march, gave them their duties and checked the readiness of knights, sergeants and squires.

Infantry are shown in this small mid-12th-century relief carving of 'The Betrayal' in the crypt of Pistoia Cathedral. The men lack body armour but have helmets, spears and long shields which can cover them from chin to feet. (David Nicolle)

The knights were in fact the *connétable*'s particular responsibility. The *maréchal*, of whom there might be more than one, was second in command to the *connétable*. He was directly in charge of recruitment, particularly of mercenaries, controlling their pay and equipment as well as organizing other military *matériel*, horses and baggage animals for the army. The *grand turcopolier* commanded the King's *turcopoles* and was under the immediate command of the *maréchal*, the only other *turcopoles* being those of the military orders.

This pair of confronted archers on an 11th- to 12th-century carved altar in the church of Santa Maria in Valle Porclaneta, southern Italy, both have the old form of angled composite bow. (David Nicolle)

A knight often led four or five mounted sergeants, but in general sergeants seem to have formed a military reserve, not normally summoned to the first muster. The numbers of fighting troops expected from different fiefs varied considerably, great baronies like that of Jaffa or Galilee supporting 100 knights while a small fief like that of 'the wife of Gobert Vernier' supported only one. The numbers of sergeants also varied, 500 being maintained by the Patriarch of Jerusalem and 25 by the fief of Le Herin (Yarin), as did the numbers of mercenaries, ranging from 500 from the Patriarch of Jerusalem to 25 from Le Herin.

Heraldry may have been more advanced in the Latin States than in many parts of Europe. The Kingdom of Jerusalem certainly had its own great banner in the late 12th century, the Arab chronicler Baha al Din describing it as being '...on a staff as tall as a minaret and set up on a cart drawn by mules. It had a white background with red spots. The top of the staff was surmounted by a cross.' In other words it was a *carroccio* like those used as rallying points by the armies of medieval Italian cities. There is, however, no evidence for any form of permanent navy in the Kingdom of Jerusalem during the 12th century, though the coastal cities did have their own local shipping.

### Crusader Tactics

There clearly was a 'Science of War' in 12th-century Europe, spanning broad strategic thinking to the employment of specialized troops. Large-scale set-piece battles were, however, rare, simply because they were unpredictable and very risky. So, in addition to sieges, Western warfare revolved around raids and skirmishing in which there was plenty of scope for tactical skill. When a large battle did take place it hardly ever depended on cavalry alone, despite the dominant position of the knight. These traditions of warfare were transplanted to the Latin States in Syria and Palestine where there were few changes during the 12th century. The role of infantry in support of cavalry remained the same while the latter may even have lagged behind their European cousins when it came to adopting new tactics such as the couched lance.

How far the armies of the Latin States were influenced by their neighbours remains unclear. Even the knights were essentially part-time warriors and this may have limited their ability to learn from professional Byzantine soldiers, while cultural factors made it difficult for the Latins to copy their Muslim foes. Many Latin knights had experience of fighting within – as well as against – Muslim armies because it was common for men of the Latin States to serve as mercenaries under the Saljuq sultans of Anatolia. Events prove that the Latins did evolve effective tactics against the Muslims. These, however, were essentially defensive and were designed to ensure the survival of the Latin States, not the total destruction of their foes. Major battles were avoided in the knowledge that if the field army were seriously weakened the towns and castles of the Kingdom would be vulnerable, particularly as the mustering of a large army meant reducing garrisons to a bare minimum. Obtaining enough remounts was another perennial problem for the

Combat between galleys and a two-masted merchant ship on a late 13th-century painted beam from Catalonia. Both galleys have their beaks or rams supported by rope or chain, exactly as shown in a 5th-century late Roman manuscript. (Art Museum of Barcelona)

Latin armies. In the Western tradition of knightly warfare it was considered bad form, as well as financially stupid, to kill or injure an enemy's horse. The Muslim armies, however, made a point of attacking the Crusaders' horses with spears and arrows.

Weather had a major impact on warfare in the Middle East. As a result summonses to muster were usually issued in early spring. Troops, pack animals and any additional livestock would be assembled. The army would then remain in camp to watch an invading enemy or be arranged into an order of march known by the originally Arabic name of *caravan*. According to the Old French Rule of the Templars, knights would assemble ahead of their squires, but the squires would be sent ahead with the knights' lances, shields and warhorses (which were only to be ridden in battle) during the actual march. The need to maintain cohesion on the march was fully understood, as was the vital role of infantry in protecting the knights' horses from enemy harassment. In open country such armies marched in a box-like formation with infantry surrounding the cavalry. In broken or mountainous terrain an army generally marched in columns.

Raiding and reconnaissance operations were given the French name of *chevauchées*. Here knights carried their own armour behind their saddles. Infantry would sometimes also be carried on the horses' cruppers. *Turcopoles* played a leading role on such expeditions and reconnaissance was the only time when the *turcopolier* could command knights.

If the Latin army did commit itself to a set-piece battle, infantry were drawn up in front of the cavalry, the latter charging through gaps in the foot soldiers' ranks. The role of the infantry was to protect the cavalry's horses, rather than the riders, yet the infantry remained essential if a knightly charge was to be effective. On the

Late 12th-century carved capital in the cloisters of Monreale Cathedral, Sicily. The two men fighting on foot lack body armour. (David Nicolle)

other hand the Latins' reliance on infantry made their armies slow and unmanoeuvrable compared to those of their Muslim foes. The structure and size of cavalry *eschielles* or squadrons varied but in general it seems that, in the Middle East, horsemen were split into smaller units than in Europe in an attempt to deal with fast and tactically flexible foes. Such small groups, however, were always in danger of being surrounded and engaged to exhaustion even if protected from mortal wounds by their heavy armour.

Although the knightly charge remained the Latin armies' only real offensive tactic it was effective if used properly, but, because it was a response to the enemy's actions, a charge could rarely be planned beforehand and it also left the initiative with the enemy. As the Muslims developed counter-measures so the effectiveness of the Latin charge declined. Lighter Muslim horsemen were in any case generally able to get out of the way by opening and closing their own ranks or wheeling aside.

When such manoeuvres were not possible the Muslims could feign flight, whereupon the knights often lost their cohesion if they attempted to pursue. Even Muslim infantry, once they had learned the bitter lessons of the early 12th century, generally seem to have been able to escape such charges.

In contrast with this information about the cavalry, almost nothing is known of the organization of infantry in open battle, though more is known about siege warfare. Most Crusader castles were not sited on the frontiers, but, occupying the same sites as previous Byzantine and Islamic fortifications, were scattered about. These castles, often built at great speed, had varied designs depending on their situation. Throughout the 12th century most were simple and even primitive,

'Pharaoh's Army in the Red Sea', on a late 12th-century carved font in the church of San Frediano, Lucca. Both horsemen wear mail hauberks while the leading rider also has mail *chausses* covering his legs. (David Nicolle)

45

the great Crusader castles which now dot the region either dating from the 13th century or having been extensively rebuilt by Muslim architects after their recapture. Not until the 13th century, when the Latins finally accepted that they had been forced on to the defensive, were fortifications provisioned to withstand a long siege. Each would have been commanded by a *châtelain*. Town garrisons would include knights and sergeants who manned both walls and gates, while the untrained burgesses were only entrusted with defending the walls, using crossbows and javelins.

## Weaponry of the Crusader Forces

The Latin States were never famous centres of weaponry manufacture though some burgesses of Jerusalem were listed as shield-makers. By far the bulk of their military equipment was imported from Europe and probably came from Italy or via Italian merchants. Captured Islamic weapons were also reused and the Order of Templars had special rules concerning these. Otherwise the equipment used in the Latin States were the same as those of Western Europe. Radulfus Niger, writing allegorically in the very year of Hattin on how the Kingdom of Jerusalem should be supported, listed these as spurs, *chausses* (iron leggings), hauberks, *cuirie* (leather cuirass), helmets with face protection, swords, horses, shields, lances, horse-harness, horse-armour, infantry weapons, flags and banners, and a variety of siege machines. How far the mid-13th-century Rule of the Temple reflected the 12th-century situation is unclear, but it stated that a brother knight should have mail hauberk and *chausses*, a light brimmed *chapel de fer* helmet, mail *coif*, possibly an arming cap, an *espaliere* shoulder-piece (perhaps of mail or padded), a quilted jupon or *gambeson*, a sword, lance, *masse turque* (Turkish form of mace), shield and *couteau d'arme* (large dagger plus two smaller knifes for non-military uses). His horse would have a *caparison* (covering cloth) and the knight should also keep a leather sack for his mail hauberk. Sergeants, again in the Rule of the Templars, had a smaller mail *haubergeon* which lacked mittens for the hands, and their mail *chausses* should lack feet to that they could walk in comfort.

Specific information about infantry equipment is rare but the *chansons de geste* poems of the period constantly refer to the foot soldiers' mail hauberks, long-hafted *gisarme* axes, 'Danish' axes which probably had heavy bearded blades, maces, *faussars* which may have been early forms of single-edged *falchions*, pikes, javelins, bows and crossbows. The European knight's prejudice against archery has perhaps been exaggerated. None the less the adoption of the crossbow as a weapon of war instead of merely a hunting weapon was seen as a social and a military threat. In 1139 the Pope's Lateran Council attempted to ban the use of the crossbow, and perhaps also the ordinary bow, in war except when used against 'infidels'. Early crossbows often seem to have been made of laburnum wood and they had a very long draw compared to later medieval versions. Bows of composite construction, giving much greater power-for-weight, were incorporated into crossbows late in the 12th century, but when this idea reached the Latin States is uncertain. A lack of

OPPOSITE
Demons on a carved
capital from the Church
of the Annunciation,
Nazareth, late 12th
century. They reflect
the Latin image of their
Muslim foes – leather
shields, no body armour
and with an emphasis
on archery. (Plaster cast
in Victoria & Albert
Museum, London:
photograph – David
Nicolle)

direct influence from the Middle Eastern composite hand-held bow upon the European composite crossbow is suggested by the fact that the two weapons are constructed in totally different ways.

Horse harness was a major concern for the knightly elite. In addition to a leather-covered, wood-framed saddle with its *afeutremens* (felt padding) and *arcons* (raised cantle), the knight's horse would have had a saddle-cloth, single or doubled girths, breeching and breast straps. The latter or *poitral* had to be very strong to take the shock of impact when a rider struck with his couched lance.

The siege machinery available to the Latin States was basically the same as that used by the Muslims. *Fondifles* were slings, probably of the staff-sling variety, while the main stone-throwing devices were *mangonels* and *perières* or *petraria*.

The fully developed counterweight *trebuchet* was an astonishing machine. Recent experiments with a trebuchet having a 200-kilogram counterweight threw a 15-kilogram ball 180 metres and a 47-kilogram ball 100 metres, all within a target six metres square. The term *perière* or *petraria* was used more loosely but often included torsion engines like the ancient Roman stone-throwing devices. The *petraria turquesa* (Turkish stone-machine) of about AD 1202 was clearly a torsion-powered device, probably similar to the twin-armed crossbow-like machine known in Islam as the *qaws ziyar*.

## The size of the Crusader Army

Contrary to yet another widespread myth, the military elite or knightly class of the late 12th-century Kingdom of Jerusalem was neither enfeebled nor degenerate. The settlers had not gone soft, as their uncultured European contemporaries claimed, but had learned to take a realistic approach to warfare with their Muslim neighbours. Even the town-based knights of the Latin States clung to the ideas and aspirations of knightly chivalry, following the latest fashions from France and Italy.

Until the massive losses of territory which followed Hattin, the Kingdom of Jerusalem could field a substantial army. According to a register based on records from the reign of Baldwin IV, the total military establishment of the Kingdom numbered 675 knights and 5,025 sergeants plus *turcopoles* and mercenaries. At best Jerusalem could muster up to 1,000 knights including contingents sent from the 200 knights maintained by the County of Tripoli and the 700 of the Principality of Antioch. At most times there would also be knights among visiting pilgrims from Europe.

Meanwhile the Templars maintained a highly disciplined regiment of up to 300 knights in the Latin States, plus several hundred sergeants and *turcopoles*. In 1168 the Hospitallers had promised 500 knights and 500 *turcopoles* for an invasion of Egypt, though whether they could really muster such a force remains unclear as there never seem to have been more than 300 brother knights in the Middle East at any one time. Local indigenous troops would also push up the size of the army.

# THE OPPOSING PLANS

'The Betrayal' in a Coptic Gospel manuscript made in AD 1179/80. The soldiers reflect a local Egyptian militia rather than the elite troops of the Islamic Middle East. They have typically Arab straight, broad swords with down-turned *quillons*. Some men also carry the tall, flat-bottomed shields used by Middle Eastern infantry rather than cavalry. (Bib. Nat., Ms. Copte 13, f.79r, Paris)

The Sultan had to make a major effort against the Latin States to maintain his prestige among fellow Muslims. Saladin's recovery from a serious illness may also have made him realize that death was not far off and that it was now or never. The first part of the year was taken up with raiding to test the enemy's strength and to weaken him. But once Saladin's main force was committed across the frontier there was no further raiding. All efforts were directed to enticing the Latin field army into a major battle. This also had to be done quickly for it was difficult for Saladin's army to remain in the field for a long time. The Sultan may also have taken into account the losses inflicted on the military orders at the Springs of Cresson earlier that year, since they were the most effective troops in the Latin army.

Skirmishing failed to lure the Latins out of their strong defensive position so Saladin committed his forces to a full-scale assault on Tiberius. In so doing he put himself in a very dangerous position with the possibility of being caught between two enemy forces, but the gamble worked and the Christians marched to relieve Tiberius. Everything depended on not allowing the Latins to reach adequate water supplies once they left Sephorie (Saffuriyah) and Saladin then staked

The interior of Saffuriyah (Sephorie) castle in Galilee. The basic structure dates from the Crusader period. (David Nicolle)

'Chedorlaomer defeated by Abraham', mid-13th-century painted ceiling in the Baptistry, Parma. Such scenes portray the ideal of European cavalry combat with lances, though here only the first knight on the left is using his lance in the approved couched manner.

everything on a major battle before the Latin field army came off the dry plateau to reach water at Lake Tiberius. The likely area of battle had, of course, already been reconnoitred by Saladin's scouts. His plan for the following day was simple. The enemy must still not reach water, his infantry must be separated from his cavalry and none must escape. In the event things turned out almost exactly as Saladin hoped, although more Latin troops did escape from the battle than is generally realized.

Events after Saladin's victory at Hattin were simply a case of taking full advantage of the destruction of the Latin field army by capturing as many fortified places as possible before another European Crusade arrived. Saladin's preoccupation with the threat from the West is shown by his seizure of the coastal towns first, before going on to take the greatest prize of all – the Holy City of Jerusalem.

Having assembled the largest army he could at the traditional mustering point of Sephorie, King Guy at first stuck to traditional policy when faced with an invasion from the direction of Damascus. The army stayed put in its strong situation and by threatening Saladin's more exposed positions, hoped that the Muslims would eventually retreat. It was a predictable reaction to a predictable attack. The fact that Guy then decided to relieve Tiberius and meet Saladin in battle has been described as unusual, yet such a reaction had been attempted before – successfully. Guy may have feared blame for the damage being caused by Saladin's troops, but he may also have hoped to catch and destroy the Muslim army west of Lake Tiberius, where its escape would be difficult.

Once Saladin had outmanoeuvred the Latins, however, the latter faced a battle seriously low on water but still within striking distance of the springs at Hattin village. Guy therefore marched in that direction, with his infantry, as usual, protecting his cavalry. The only other course would have been an all-out attack on Saladin's main force. This suggestion was rejected, though the sources do not say why. Perhaps the Christian army's poor morale and raging thirst made a move away from water impossible.

Following the disaster at Hattin all that the remaining Latin garrisons could do was make the best terms they could or hang on until relief arrived. The latter was very long in coming but for the coastal cities there was always hope of help arriving by sea. This was why some garrisons fought so hard and why the efforts of Tyre (Sur) were eventually rewarded.

# THE CAMPAIGN

Despite a truce between Saladin and the Kingdom of Jerusalem, the situation east of the River Jordan was volatile by the start of 1187, while farther south Reynald of Châtillon was still demanding tolls from Muslim caravans travelling between Egypt and Syria. Suddenly, that winter, Reynald attacked a large caravan, capturing the travellers and their escort. Perhaps he felt that such a large escort breached the truce, or that Saladin's support for Count Raymond in his quarrel with King Guy (see above) had already done so, or perhaps he was simply 'piratical' as some Muslim chroniclers believed. The story that one of Saladin's sisters and her son were with this caravan is untrue, but Reynald's actions, plus King Guy's inability to get the prisoners released, gave Saladin a perfect excuse to renew the war.

At the start of the Muslim year of 583 AH (13 March 1187) the Sultan led the troops in Damascus to the well-watered area of Ras al Mai' and sent letters to neighbouring countries asking for volunteers for a forthcoming *jihad*. A week later his brother Al Adil, the governor of Egypt, led his forces out of Cairo towards Syria. Meanwhile Husam al Din Lu'lu took 15 galleys down the Nile to Alexandria. Far to the north Taqi al Din and his troops reached Aleppo, from where they watched the

## CAMPAIGNS OF 1187 – CHRONOLOGY

| | |
|---|---|
| Winter | Reynald of Châtillon captures Muslim caravan. |
| 13 March | Saladin sets up camp at Ras al Mai' and summons troops to *jihad*. |
| 20 March | Al Adil leads Egyptian forces towards Aqabah. The Hajib Lu'lu takes warships to Alexandria. |
| 29 March | Taqi al Din reaches Aleppo to guard the northern frontiers. |
| Early April | Saladin leads contingent south of Busra to protect pilgrims. |
| 26 April | Saladin attacks Krak. |
| 29 April | Delegation leaves Jerusalem to seek reconciliation with Count Raymond. |
| 30 April | Envoy from Al Afdal asks Count Raymond's permission for reconnaissance party to cross the count's lands. |
| 1 May | Muslim reconnaissance force attacked by Christian forces near Springs of Cresson defeats the Christians and returns same day. |
| 27 May | Saladin instructs Ayyubid forces to muster at Tal 'Ashtarah. King Guy instructs his army to gather at Sephorie. |
| 26 June | After reviewing his army Saladin marches off, making camp at Khisfin. King Guy holds a council of barons at Acre. |
| 27 June | Saladin's army camps at Al Qahwani, reconnaissance parties sent into Christian territory. |
| 28–29 June | Christian army completes muster outside Sephorie. |
| 30 June | Saladin makes camp near Cafarsset. (Some scholars believe that Saladin did not personally cross the Jordan until 2 July.) |
| 1 July | Saladin approaches Christian army at Sephorie then makes reconnaissance of Lubia area. |
| 2 July | Part of Muslim army attacks Tiberius, which falls except for Citadel. |
| Night of 2/3 July | King Guy decides to relieve Tiberius. |
| 3 July | Christian army marches towards Tiberius. Saladin leaves a small force to watch Tiberius. Christian army forced to stop at Manescalcia. |
| Night of 3/4 July | Saladin organizes troops and supplies. |
| 4 July | Christian army defeated at **Horns of Hattin**. |
| 5 July | Countess Eschiva surrenders Tiberius citadel. |
| 8 July | Muslim army arrive outside Acre. |
| 10 July | Acre surrenders to Saladin. |
| 14 July | Tyre breaks off surrender negotiations with Saladin. |
| 26 July | Toron surrenders to Saladin. |
| 29 July | Sidon surrenders to Saladin. |
| 4 August | Gibelet surrenders to Saladin. |
| 6 August | Beirut surrenders to Saladin. |
| 25 August | Saladin and Al Adil start siege of Ascalon. |
| 5 September | Ascalon surrenders to Saladin. |
| 20 September | Muslim army reaches Jerusalem. |
| 25 September | Muslim army stops attacking western wall of Jerusalem. |

| 26 September | Muslim army starts attacking northern wall of Jerusalem. |
| 29 September | Breach made in wall. |
| 2 October | Jerusalem surrenders to Saladin. |
| 1 November | Saladin sends army to besiege Tyre. |
| 30 December | Combined land and naval attack on Tyre beaten off. |
| 1 January 1188 | Saladin disbands half his army, raises siege of Tyre. |

frontier with Antioch. It was now the Muslim month of Muharram when huge numbers of pilgrims would be travelling home from Mecca. So Saladin left the troops who were assembling at Ras al Mai' under the command of his son Al Afdal and, perhaps fearing another raid by Reynald of Châtillon, took his own guards south of Busra to keep watch on the pilgrim road. On 20 April Taqi al Din moved forward to the fortress of Harenc (Harim), right on the frontier of Antioch and, at about the same time, Saladin's small force raided south into Oultrejordain. On 26 April, the day that Al Adil's Egyptian army was expected to reach Aqabah, Saladin attacked Krak itself, confining the garrison so that Muslim irregulars could ravage the entire province. Saladin also ordered Al Afdal to raid neighbouring Latin territory but then countermanded these orders, telling Al Afdal to await further developments.

Meanwhile the leading barons of the Kingdom of Jerusalem assembled to persuade King Guy to seek a reconciliation with Count Raymond who was still holed up in his wife's town of Tiberius. A delegation was sent, including Balian d'Ibelin, the Master of the Hospitallers, the archbishop of Tyre, Reynald of Sidon and Gerard de Ridefort, Master of the Temple. It left on 29 April, making its leisurely way towards Tiberius. But next day an envoy from Al Afdal arrived at Tiberius with a message from Saladin. This politely asked his 'friend' Count Raymond to allow a Muslim reconnaissance party across his land the following day. They wished, the letter said, no harm to Raymond's lordship of Galilee, but wanted to reach King Guy's Royal Domain around Acre. Not knowing of the approaching delegation Raymond agreed on condition that the Muslims returned the same day and inflicted no damage.

On the morning of 1 May the Muslim party passed beneath Tiberius' walls and turned west. It was commanded by Muzaffar al Din Gökböri with his troops from the Jazira, and other Turkish amirs including Qaymaz al Najmi with a squadron from Damascus and Dildirim al Yaruqi with men from Aleppo. Al Afdal himself seems to have remained with a larger force at Al Qahwani south-east of Lake Tiberius. Count Raymond now learned of King Guy's approaching delegation from Jerusalem and sent them a warning. By that time the delegation no longer included Reynald of Sidon or Balian d'Ibelin who had agreed to catch the others up at La Feve (Al Fulah). The main part of the delegation had also heard about the planned Muslim reconnaissance the previous night, through Raymond's warnings to his own troops in Galilee. Gerard de Ridefort summoned all Templar troops in the area and at nightfall on 30 April the Marshal of the Temple brought 90 knights from the castle at Caco (Al Qaqun). Next morning Gerard led these and his own followers to Nazareth where they were joined

**RIGHT**
The campaigns of 1187

**OPPOSITE**
Jabal Tabur (Mount
Tabor) rising above the
other hills of Galilee,
seen from the Arab
village of Ayn Mahil,
close to the Springs of
Cresson where Gökböri
and his men utterly
defeated Gerard de
Ridefort's Templars who
attacked them on 1 May
1187. (David Nicolle)

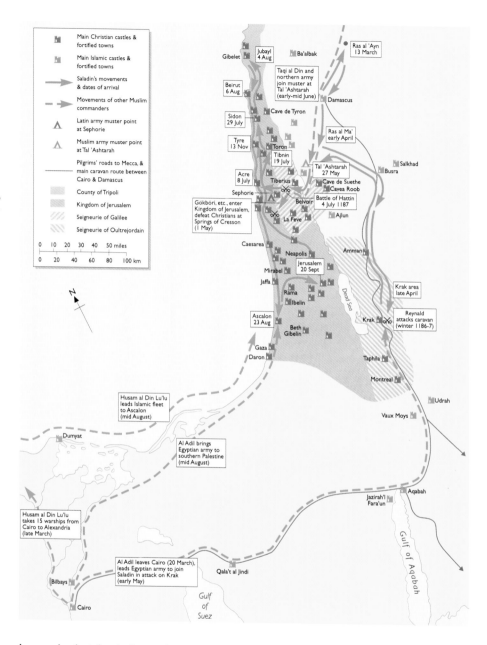

by secular knights before riding east towards the Springs of Cresson (Ayn Juzah) near
the present village of Ayn Mahil. By this time Gerard had a force of about 130 knights,
an unknown number of *turcopoles* and up to 400 infantry. Gökböri's force was said
to consist of 7,000 men though this is a huge exaggeration, 700 seeming more likely.

The course of the battle which followed is clear, even if the numbers are not.
Against the advice of the Master of the Hospital and the Marshal of the Temple,
Gerard insisted on a sudden charge against the Muslims. This has been presented as

a case of suicidal overconfidence, yet the Muslim chroniclers indicate that the brief struggle was a close-run thing fought out in a forest. The Templars, Hospitallers and other cavalry caught their enemy unawares, though in so doing they left their infantry behind. Dildirim al Yaruqi's troops from Aleppo received the brunt of the charge and were praised for standing firm. It seems that Gökböri and Qaymaz al Najmi then led a counter-charge with spear and sword, the Latin cavalry being surrounded and overwhelmed. Only Gerard de Ridefort and a handful of knights escaped death or capture, the Muslims then scattering the Christian infantry before pillaging the surrounding area. The fact that Gökböri's force then returned across Raymond's lands without doing further damage says a lot for their discipline.

This rout at the Springs of Cresson on 1 May 1187 had a greater impact than might be realized. Although it encouraged King Guy and Count Raymond to patch up their quarrel, the Hospitallers had lost their chief and the Templars had suffered severe losses. Latin morale may not have been affected but that of the Muslims certainly increased. At about the same time a fleet from the Byzantine Emperor Isaac raided Cyprus which was being held by a rival claimant to the imperial throne. Unfortunately this rebel was an ally of the Latin Principality of Antioch and as a result Isaac Angelus was accused of siding with Saladin. Relations between Latin and Greek Orthodox Christians thus sunk to a new low on the eve of Saladin's final assault.

## THE ARMIES MUSTER

To the south Al Adil's army had joined Saladin's own small force to ravage Oultrejordain and encourage local peasantry to migrate into Muslim-ruled areas. By late May all that Reynald was holding were the castles of Krak and Montreal. Nevertheless Gökböri's victory at the Springs of Cresson may have undermined Saladin's strategy as it was now clear that the enemy was moving to meet a threat from Damascus rather than coming to rescue Oultrejordain. So Saladin returned north with some of the Egyptian troops while Al Adil returned to Cairo. He also told Al Afdal to check the condition of pasture and water-supplies for he needed a mustering point for a large army. In the end Nur al Din's camping ground at Tal 'Ashtarah was selected. There Saladin and Al Afdal joined forces on 27 May. Urgent messages were sent throughout Syria and the Jazira for troops to join them. So far Taqi al Din's role had been to inhibit military action by the Principality of Antioch or the Armenians of Cilicia, but at the beginning of June he made a truce with Antioch and led the bulk of his troops south to join Saladin. Soon there were troops from all over Syria, Mardin, Nisibin, Diyarbakr and neighbouring regions of what is now south-eastern Turkey, plus Mosul and Irbil in northern Iraq, encamped around Tal 'Ashtarah. On 24 June a great *ard* or review was held at Tasil a few miles away, and the army was found to number some 12,000 professional cavalry plus a large number of less effective troops, a total of about 45,000.

Events were also moving in the Kingdom of Jerusalem. After the disaster at the Springs of Cresson Count Raymond sent home the troops Saladin had sent to strengthen Tiberius, then publicly did homage to Guy as king. Yet great bitterness

remained beneath the surface, particularly between Raymond and Gerard de Ridefort, Master of the Templars. Latin losses at Cresson may have included 130 knights while Saladin's ravaging of Oultrejordain also weakened its potential. Faced with such a serious situation King Guy sent out the *arrière ban* at the end of May, summoning all able-bodied free Christian men. Meanwhile Gerard de Ridefort handed over money given by King Henry II and with this the king recruited mercenaries, mostly mounted sergeants, who now displayed the arms of the king of England. His army mustered at springs just south of the castle of Sephorie (Saffuriyah). By the end of June it totalled some 1,200 knights, up to 4,000 lighter cavalry sergeants and *turcopoles*. Its 15,000 to 18,000 infantry would have been of mixed value, ranging from professional crossbowmen to inexperienced locals. This gave Saladin a numerical advantage of three to two though the Muslims were inferior in armoured cavalry. Christian leaders included the Masters of the Temple and the Hospital, the Count of Tripoli, Reynald de Châtillon, Balian d'Ibelin, Reginald of Sidon, and Walter Garnier, the Lord of Caesarea.

During Saladin's review of his army the basic array had been agreed. Taqi al Din commanded the right, Gökböri the left, Saladin the centre, which may also have included van and rearguards. On 26 June they set out on the first stage of their march and made camp at Khisfin on the Golan Heights. The following day the army

The springs at Muzayrib in early spring. The fertile plain north of the Yarmuk valley has many such springs which served as muster points for Muslim armies before campaigns against the Crusaders. Here there would be not only water for men and animals but also grass for the horses. (David Nicolle)

The small Crusader castle at Saffuriyah (Sephorie) with its elaborately carved doorway. The upper part of the building was reconstructed by the local Arab leader Tahar al Umar in 1745. In June 1187 the Latin army mustered at the nearby springs. (David Nicolle)

wound down the southern tip of the Heights to encamp at Al Qahwani, a marshy area between Lake Tiberius and the Rivers Jordan and Yarmouk. Small parties were now sent across the Jordan to ravage a wide area between Nazareth, Tiberius and Mount Tabor – the invasion had begun.

King Guy was holding a council of leaders in Acre but moved up to Sephorie on hearing the news. Precisely when Saladin's main force crossed the Jordan is not clear, but it is likely to have been on 30 June. Tiberius was blockaded while scouts went towards Sephorie and the bulk of the army camped at Cafarsset (Kafr Sabt). Here there were several springs midway between Tiberius and the enemy's main position. On 1 July Saladin himself approached Sephorie, perhaps hoping to lure King Guy out. That same day the Sultan made a reconnaissance of Lubia (Lubiyah) which lay on an alternative route between Sephorie and Tiberius.

On 2 July Saladin attacked Tiberius with part of his army, including the siege engineers and their cumbersome equipment, thus placing them between the Tiberius garrison and the main Christian army if the latter moved from Sephorie. With the lake on one side and steep hillsides on the other, escape would have been difficult in case of defeat and to guard against this Saladin remained at Cafarsset with most of the cavalry. Fortunately the Tiberius garrison had been reduced to an absolute minimum and the town fell by nightfall. The defenders and Count Raymond's gallant wife Countess Eschiva retreated to the citadel from where they continued to defy the Sultan's army.

Meanwhile King Guy held another council at Sephorie. Count Raymond argued against marching to raise the siege of Tiberius because this was clearly what Saladin wanted. If they stayed put, however, Saladin would either have to retreat or attack the Christian army in a strong position. If the army marched east in high summer it would suffer acute thirst on a road that lacked adequate water sources and crossed a 'desert', by which Raymond probably meant that they would find no fodder for their horses. Many of the men at the council still suspected Raymond of being a traitor because of his previous alliance with Saladin, and Gerard de Ridefort also accused him of cowardice. Yet for now Count Raymond's reasoning won the day

The falls at Al Hamah near the western end of the Yarmuk gorge. Such abundant water sources are rare in this part of the Middle East and both sides sought to control them. These falls lay within the Terre de Suethe, which formed an eastern extension of the Latin seigneurie of Galilee. (David Nicolle)

and the army stayed put. During the night of 2/3 July, however, Gerard de Ridefort continued to badger King Guy with political as well as military arguments. Perhaps he also pointed out that King Henry of England's money had been spent without consulting Henry – and that it should not now be wasted.

The Christian army awoke before sunrise on 3 July to hear that they were marching towards Tiberius after all. A variety of routes were available. They could swing south via Casal Robert (Kafr Kana) then north-east to join the main road to Tiberius near Touraan (Tur'an) which had a small spring, or they could head directly for Touraan by marching north and then east. A few kilometres east of Touraan the road divided, the main branch continuing via Saladin's main position at Cafarsset while another, also leading to Tiberius, ran in a northerly sweep via Lubia and the Horns of Hattin. About two kilometres from Tiberius both roads plunged down steep slopes to the lake. The northern road between Touraan and Tiberius itself divided about two kilometres west of Lubia. From here a track went in an even more northerly sweep around the other side of the Horns of Hattin, down a steep slope to Hattin with its abundant spring and the even more spectacular Wadi Hammam gorge to the lake at Magdala (Al Majdal).

King Guy chose to go via Casal Robert. The army probably broke camp at about sunrise, then marched in three divisions with Count Raymond commanding the vanguard. King Guy led the centre where Christendom's greatest relic, the Holy Cross on which Christ was believed to have been crucified, was guarded by the bishops of Acre and Lidde (Lydda). Balian d'Ibelin commanded the rearguard where the Templars were also stationed. Each division would have consisted of cavalry protected on all sides by infantry. Portents and signs were already eroding the army's morale, which was perhaps never high as any local soldier knew that they were in for a long, hot, dusty and very thirsty march even if the enemy left them alone. As the march began, a half-crazed Muslim woman was thought to have laid a curse upon the army. A fire in which the nervous soldiers tried to burn the unfortunate lady supposedly left her unscathed and so a soldier split her head with an axe. The horses were said to have refused to drink before setting out – a very serious matter given the lack of water on the way.

When Saladin, outside Tiberius, heard that the enemy was on the march he immediately led his guards back to the main camp at Cafarsset, leaving a small force to watch Tiberius. Detachments were then sent to harass the Christian army but Saladin's main force does not appear to have made contact until King Guy reached Touraan at about 10 o'clock in the morning. Some Christians on the left flank may have drunk at Touraan's spring but the bulk of the army pressed on. Being denied a drink further eroded their morale. Harassment intensified as the Christians moved across Saladin's front, closer to his base at Cafarsset, with heat, thirst, dust, throbbing Muslim drums and now a steady wastage of horses struck down by arrows. At noon repeated attacks slowed the Christians' pace to a crawl and soon Count Raymond in the vanguard, which had reached the road junction near Manescalcia (Miskinah), was told that the rearguard had been forced to halt. At this point there was a major change of plan. Believing that the army could no longer fight its way across Saladin's front, Count Raymond convinced King Guy that they should swing left down a track to the springs at Hattin only six kilometres away. From there they could reach Lake Tiberius the next day.

The army was now probably spread over at least two kilometres on a relatively level plain, with Jabal Tur'an stretching along its left flank in a series of wooded slopes ending in a small hill topped by the village of Nimrin. On its right flank, the villages of Sejera (Shajarah) and Lubia stood on other wooded hills. Ahead rose the Horns of Hattin with the waters of Lake Tiberius just visible to their right. The cool waters might have seemed close to desperately thirsty men, but actually lay 12 kilometres away. The Christian army now attempted to change direction and promptly fell into confusion. Saladin, who almost certainly had a clear view from hills to the south, realized what they were trying to do and sent Taqi al Din's division to block the way to Hattin. If Taqi al Din were still in command of Saladin's right wing his men would have been skirmishing with Count Raymond's troops since the Muslim main force committed itself to battle. Raymond, knowing that the Muslims would attempt to stop him seizing the spring at Hattin, urged speed but this proved impossible. Just how Taqi al Din got ahead and to the left of the Christians' vanguard is unclear. Perhaps his troops had been on the small hillock north-east of Lubia, blocking the main road to Tiberius. Being faster than their foes they could have moved sharply right, perhaps now anchoring their right flank on a larger hill by the village of Nimrin. This would have blocked the track from Manescalcia to the edge of the plateau and thence to Hattin spring. But this could have opened up the main road due east once again, so Saladin may also have moved the Muslim centre farther to the right. The Sultan certainly set up his headquarters on the hill of Lubia village the following night.

Gökböri, with Saladin's left wing, would have been on hills around Sejera and it was probably his troops whose determined attacks on the Latin rearguard forced King Guy to order another halt. The Templars charged in the hope of driving their tormentors away but failed. It was then that Count Raymond announced, 'Alas! Alas! Lord God, the war is over. We are betrayed to death and the land is lost.' He also advised Guy to have the exhausted army make camp around Manescalcia, though others urged an attack on Saladin's own position as the only remaining chance of victory. This time the king took Raymond's advice, perhaps hoping his army would be able to strike out for Hattin spring in proper formation the following morning. Meanwhile Saladin's troops harassed them until nightfall.

The hills around the spot where the Christian army made camp were then quite wooded. Taqi al Din's division held the open plateau between Nimrin and the Horns of Hattin while Saladin's held the hills around Lubia. Nothing is known of Gökböri's division but this is likely to have closed the valley up which the Christians had just marched. During the night both sides are said to have been so close that their pickets could talk to one another. Thirsty and demoralized, the Latin army listened to the drums, prayers and singing of their enemies, while conditions in the Muslim camp

GOD'S WARRIORS

were very different. That night Saladin brought up the rest of his troops from Cafarsset, presumably including the infantry. Four hundred loads of arrows were distributed, the troops having used up most of their immediate supplies. Seventy camels loaded with more bundles of arrows as a reserve were made ready to be sent where needed on the morrow. While the Christians gasped with thirst, the Muslim army had a caravan of camels carrying goat-skins of water up from Lake Tiberius. These were emptied into make-shift reservoirs dug in the camps of each Muslim division. Morale was, of course, high. Saladin's men also collected brushwood from the surrounding hills which would have been full of bone-dry thistles at that time of year. These they piled on the windward side of the Christian camp to be lit the following morning. It also seems that brushwood was placed along the Christians' expected line of march.

The march to Hattin

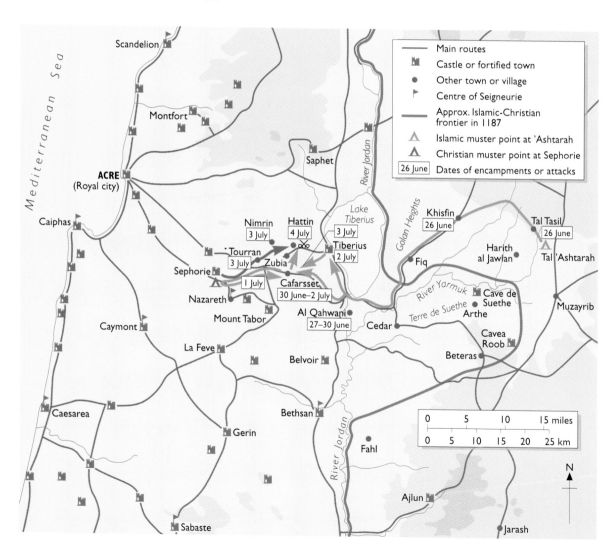

## THE BATTLE OF HATTIN

Before dawn on the morning of 4 July 1187 the Christian army awoke and formed up ready to move. Count Raymond again commanded the vanguard, accompanied by Raymond of Antioch with his contingent. The Latin army was already in a bad way but Saladin did not disrupt its preparations, perhaps unsure whether it would make a dash for Hattin village or a desperate attack on his own position. Quite when the Muslims set fire to their stacks of brushwood is also unclear. Some say they did so before the enemy set off, others as they marched, or as the crumbling Christian force retreated to the Horns of Hattin. Given Saladin's careful preparations, these fires may have been lit in sequence as the enemy marched. The final fires were ignited by volunteers; the shifting of the prepared stacks of kindling was a task suited to Saladin's numerous but untrained *mutatawi'ah*. The Muslims also taunted the Christians by pouring water on the ground, this coming from the temporary cisterns dug the night before. It may have been now that one or more knights with experience of serving in Islamic armies urged King Guy to make a sudden attack on Saladin's own position. But they were overruled and the army began its march to the Hattin spring which lay only five kilometres away.

View from the northern Horn of Hattin looking south-west towards the modern kibbutz Lavi beyond which lay the abandoned village of Lubiyah. King Guy probably attempted to make a defensive camp here at the foot of the Horns. (David Nicolle)

So bad was the Christians' thirst and morale that six knights and some sergeants chose this moment to desert to Saladin, telling him that their comrades were as good as beaten. They included Baldwin de Fotina, Raulfus Bructus and Laudoicus de Tabaria. Saladin now seems to have sent his centre, and perhaps his left flank under Gökböri, into the attack. The Templars counter-charged while Count Raymond's vanguard also made a charge, presumably against Taqi al Din and the Muslim right wing who blocked the way forward. The only chronicler to hint at how near the Christians came to breaking through is Ibn Khallikan in his biographies of Gökböri and Taqi al Din. He wrote:

> They both held their ground although the whole army was routed and driven back. The soldiers then heard that these two chiefs still resisted the enemy, whereupon they returned to the charge and victory was decided in favour of the Muslims.

Saladin also lost one of his most trusted young *amirs* named Manguras, early in the battle. He was probably fighting in the right wing, having previously served as Taqi al Din's deputy governor in Hama. Manguras charged forward alone and one source says that he challenged a Christian champion to fight him man-to-man but was thrown from his horse, dragged into the enemy lines and beheaded. Another states that he was simply overwhelmed by numbers.

Aerial view of the battlefield of Hattin seen in the late afternoon. The abandoned village of Nimrin lay in the rugged hills on the left, the abandoned village of Hattin at the foot of the shadowed gorge in the centre. The Horns of Hattin appear in the lower right corner and here the walls of an ancient, perhaps Bronze Age, settlement are clearly visible. (Israel Exploration Society)

The Christian army had set out in its standard formation with ranks of infantry, including archers and crossbowmen, protecting the cavalry while the latter stood ready to drive back the Muslims with controlled charges. The cavalry did drive back Saladin's first attacks but also lost many horses. More importantly, however, the morale of the Christian infantry now cracked and numbers started to drift eastwards. Muslim sources assume that the thirsty foot soldiers were heading towards Lake Tiberius, though this was much farther away than the spring at Hattin. Christian chroniclers state that the infantry sought refuge on the Horns of Hattin. What both original sources and most modern historians fail to explain is how they got through the middle of what should have been Saladin's army! Joshua Prawer, the greatest expert on the battle, assumed that Saladin had turned his entire army round the previous night, making Taqi al Din's division the left wing and Gökböri's the right, and placing his own central division somewhere to the west of the Latin forces. But Saladin's main position during the night had been at Lubia to the south, and his primary objective was still to stop the enemy reaching water – either at Hattin village to the north-east or Lake Tiberius to the east.

A possible explanation is that Taqi al Din blocked the path to Hattin by holding a position from the foot of the Horns to Nimrin hill, that the centre of the Muslim army was arrayed between the foot of the Horns and Lubia hill blocking the main road to Tiberius, and that Gökböri's division stood between Lubia and the massif of Jabal Tur'an blocking any retreat west to the spring at Touraan village. Anchoring one's flanks on hills was a common tactic in Turco-Muslim cavalry armies, whereas placing a hill at the centre was more characteristic of infantry forces. Clearly Saladin feared that the Christians might break out towards Lake Tiberius and he gave strict orders that they be stopped. This suggests that Count Raymond's first charge had weakened the link between Taqi al Din's division and Saladin's. If this were the case, the Christian infantry who drifted eastward may have hoped to reach the lake which could still have been visible to the right of the Horns. If Saladin now extended the right of his own division he would have shepherded any enemy drifting east on to the Horns of Hattin. In an effort to provide a barrier against further attacks by Muslim cavalry, King Guy ordered his army to halt and put up tents, but in the confusion that followed only three were erected 'near a mountain' – almost certainly a short distance west or south-west of the Horns. Smoke from the burning brushwood certainly now played its part, stinging the eyes of the Christians and adding to their appalling thirst. The wind was, as usual at this time of year, from the west which suggests that the *mutatawi'ah* were acting almost independently in the wooded hills between Jabal Tur'an and Nimrin. Any Muslim troops still around the Horns of Hattin would also have suffered from this smoke unless a clear gap had now opened between Saladin and Taqi al Din's positions.

At about this time Count Raymond of Tripoli made his notorious charge northwards and consequently escaped the debacle. This was not, however, an act of treachery but an attempt to force a break in the Muslim ring and enable the army to reach water at Hattin village. The charge was probably ordered by King Guy. One

View from the northern Horn of Hattin looking west. The closest hill may be where the Muslim dead of the battle were buried. Beyond it is the deep cleft down which Count Raymond and his men rode out of the battle after Taqi al Din's division swung aside to let them pass. Beyond that is another cleft and the wooded hills around the abandoned village of Nimrin. (David Nicolle)

thing is certain: instead of trying to stop Raymond, Taqi al Din had his more nimble soldiers swing aside and let the Christians continue down the gorge. Some writers, still imagining 12th-century European knights to be juggernauts weighed down by armour, assume that the momentum of Raymond's cavalry hurtled them down the path to Hattin village, but this is fanciful. Taqi al Din's men promptly returned to their positions at the top of the path, making it virtually impossible for Raymond to turn and charge back up the steep and narrow track. In fact Raymond had no alternative other than to continue across the fields beyond Hattin and down Wadi Hammam to Lake Tiberius. From there he chose not to join his wife in the trap of Tiberius but rode north to Tyre.

On the plateau, confusion in the Christian ranks was getting worse and most of the infantry were now streaming towards the Horns of Hattin where they took up a position on the northern Horn. This might be significant, for if Taqi al Din had pulled his men up to Nimrin hill to let Raymond past he would have enlarged or

finally opened up a gap between himself and Saladin's troops south of the Horns. Perhaps the Christian infantry had been moving north-eastward in support of Raymond's charge or had simply tried to follow Raymond in hope of escaping. Once the path to Hattin had been closed again it would be natural for them to drift left towards the smaller but closer northern Horn. Morale now collapsed with the infantry on this northern Horn refusing to come down and rejoin the cavalry who were still fighting around three tents at the foot of the Horns. King Guy ordered and the bishops begged. They must defend the Holy Cross, they said, but the foot soldiers replied, 'We are not coming down because we are dying of thirst, and we will not fight.' Meanwhile the unprotected horses of the knights were struck down by enemy arrows until most knights were also fighting on foot.

There was now nothing for Guy to do but order his army on to the Horns of Hattin where the knights took position on the larger flat-topped southern Horn. The royal tent, bright red and visible from a great distance, was probably set up on the southern Horn. Quite when the Holy Cross was captured remains unknown, though it was clearly seized by Taqi al Din's division. Some sources suggest that Taqi al Din made a fierce charge after allowing Count Raymond to escape and that the bishop of Acre, who carried the Cross, was killed, the holy relic then being taken by the bishop of Lidde before falling into Taqi al Din's hands. Others suggest that the bishop of Lidde took the Holy Cross up on to the southern Horn where it was finally captured during one of the last charges by Taqi al Din's troops. Whenever it happened, the loss of this relic must have had a devastating effect on morale.

A Western depiction of the battle of Hattin from Matthew Paris's *Chronica majora*. Saladin rides in from the left and seizes the relic of the Holy Cross from King Guy of Jerusalem, who struggles to hold it. (Cambridge, Corpus Christi College MS. 26, page 279 [140]: © the Master and Fellows of Corpus Christi College, Cambridge)

The Muslims now attacked the Horns of Hattin from all sides. The northern and eastern slopes are too precipitous for cavalry although a steep path does climb the northern side of the northern Horn. Muslim infantry now took on the Christian foot soldiers early in the afternoon and after a bitter struggle those Christians who were not killed or thrown down the slopes surrendered. Saladin also ordered Taqi al Din to charge the Latin knights as they made their last stand on the southern Horn. It would have been impracticable, though not impossible, for horsemen to attack up the southern slopes, and Saladin himself would have been covering this sector. So it seems likely that, while the Muslim infantry fought on the northern Horn, Taqi al Din rode up the gentle western slope that led between the Horns. For their part those Latin knights who still had horses regrouped, probably in this flat space, and made two vigorous counter-charges. One came close to Saladin himself who urged his men on, crying out, 'Away with the Devil's lie!' It may be that the Latins still hoped to slay the Sultan and snatch victory at the very moment of defeat. That they came close enough to endanger Saladin suggests that the centre of the Muslim army had now come right up to the south-western foot of the Horns. Twice the Muslim cavalry charged up the slope, finally winning control of the saddle between the Horns. Young Al Afdal was at his father's side and cried out, 'We have conquered them!', but Saladin turned and said, 'Be quiet! We shall not have beaten them until that tent falls.' Even as he spoke the Muslim horsemen fought their way on to the southern Horn; someone cut the guy-ropes and the royal tent fell.

That, as Saladin had predicted, marked the end of the battle. The exhausted Christians threw themselves to the ground and were captured without further struggle. Remarkably few of the well-armoured knights had been killed or even wounded, though the losses of horses and infantry was far higher. Nothing is recorded of Gökböri and the Muslim left wing during these last stages. His division may have found itself almost out of the battle as the Latin army was swallowed up between Saladin and Taqi al Din. On the other hand a number of knights from the Latin rearguard, including its leader, Balian d'Ibelin, escaped near the end of the battle. Reginald of Sidon may also have got away at this time. Perhaps this indicates some carelessness on the part of the normally reliable Gökböri and maybe the Muslim chroniclers did not want to cast a shadow on a great victory.

Among those taken captive were King Guy, his brother Geoffrey de Lusignan, the *Connétable* Amalric de Lusignan, Marquis William de Montferrat, Reynald of Châtillon, Humphrey de Toron, the Master of the Templars, the Master of the Hospitallers, the bishop of Lidde and many other leading barons. Virtually the entire leadership of the Kingdom except for Count Raymond, Balian d'Ibelin and Joscelyn de Courtnay had fallen into Saladin's hands. Obviously feeling generous after his staggering victory, the Sultan offered a cup of cooled sweetened water to King Guy, but after he drank Guy passed the cup to Reynald of Châtillon whom Saladin had sworn to kill. According to Arab custom a man who had taken food or drink from his captor was thereafter safe from harm. 'This criminal was given water without my consent,' observed the Sultan, 'and as such my safe-conduct does not extend to him.'

**OPPOSITE TOP**

A track winds around and up the southern Horn of Hattin to the saddle between the Horns. Here Taqi al Din's right flank division and Saladin's central division made several charges before the Latin army finally surrendered. (David Nicolle)

**OPPOSITE BOTTOM**

The summit of the Horns of Hattin looking from the southern Horns where King Guy and his knights made their final stand, to the northern Horn where the Christian infantry fled earlier in the battle. (David Nicolle)

Reynald knew that his doom was sealed and answered Saladin's questions with arrogant courage until at last the Sultan's patience snapped. Whether he himself killed Reynald de Châtillon or ordered his men to strike off the Lord of Oultrejordain's head depends on which chronicler one believes. Saladin then placed a finger in his enemy's blood and rubbed it into his own face as a sign that he had taken vengeance. Not surprisingly the other captives were terrified but now the symbolic act was over the Sultan assured them that they were safe. Victors and vanquished remained on the battlefield that night but the following day, 5 July, Saladin rode down to Tiberius where Countess Eschiva surrendered her citadel.

All captured *turcopoles* would, as renegades from the Muslim faith, probably have been killed on the battlefield. The rest of the prisoners reached Damascus on 6 July and there Saladin made a decision which has been seen as a blot on his humane record. All captured Templars and Hospitallers were given the choice of converting to Islam or execution. Conversion under threat of death is contrary to Muslim law but on this occasion Saladin seems to have considered that the military orders, as dedicated fanatics with a bloody record of their own, were too dangerous to spare – 230 were slaughtered. A few converted and one Templar of Spanish origin later commanded the Damascus garrison in 1229, though if he were a survivor of Hattin he would have been a very old man. Other knights and leaders were ransomed but many of the infantry went into slavery.

Perhaps as many as 3,000 men from the Latin army escaped from the battle of Hattin and fled to nearby castles and fortified towns. Some time later Saladin had a small monument, the Qubbat al Nasr or Dome of Victory, built on the southern Horn. Nothing now remains, although its foundations were recently discovered. Muslim dead would have been buried with honour though it is not known where. A possible location could be the ruined Muslim shrine of Shaykh al Lika ('Old Man of the Encounter') just to the north-west of the Horns overlooking the spring of Hattin.

## CONQUEST OF THE KINGDOM

Events now unfolded at astonishing speed. On 7 July Saladin sent Taqi al Din to seize Acre which, contrary to expectations, resisted. Saladin himself arrived outside the walls on the 8th, but as the Muslims prepared their assault envoys came out to discuss terms. These were soon agreed, though there was rioting among the citizens when they heard the news. Saladin actually invited the Western merchants and feudal elite to remain under his rule but few if any of the inhabitants accepted. The fall of Acre also released the Byzantine emperor's brother who had been held by the Latins. Saladin promptly sent him home and thus strengthened his already good relations with Byzantium. Meanwhile Al Adil was ordered to invade southern Palestine with the Egyptian army which advanced rapidly and captured the powerful castle of Mirabel (Majdalyabah). The conquest of Acre also altered the naval situation by providing the Egyptian fleet with a base on the Palestinian coast for the first time since 1153, and a squadron of ten galleys was immediately sent from Alexandria. Saladin now split his forces into several sections, since there was no

The southernmost inner walls of Ascalon curving round to enclose the site of the medieval city, with the sea in the distance. The city would also have enclosed fields or gardens and, being on a flat sandy coastal plain, had doubled walls. (David Nicolle)

enemy field army to fear, and sent them to mop up the various provinces of what had been the Latin Kingdom of Jerusalem. In many areas the local Muslim peasants and Jews rose in revolt, confining their Latin overlords and settlers in scattered castles until Saladin's troops arrived. The quantity of plunder and the number of prisoners taken was staggering, not to mention the 4,000 Muslim slaves who were released from Acre alone. By the end of the campaign more than 20,000 Muslims had been released while in return Saladin's men took more than 100,000 Latins captive.

Yet there were already problems. Taqi al Din had tried and failed to seize Tyre (Sur). Reginald of Sidon, having escaped from Hattin, got there first and took command as hordes of Latin refugees flocked in from all over the northern part of the Kingdom. He learned that his great castle of Belfort (Al Shaqif Arnun) still held out. Even so Reginald seems to have opened negotiations for a peaceful hand-over while Taqi al Din went inland to besiege the exceptionally strong castle of Toron (Tibnin). Then Conrad of Montferrat supposedly took command of Tyre. The story of his arrival from Constantinople and seizure of command on 14 July has been seen as a turning-point, but it now seems that instead of sailing into Tyre in the midst of surrender negotiations Conrad really arrived one month later. Even if it were Reginald of Sidon who kept the Christian banners flying over Tyre in those desperate first months, Conrad's arrival clearly had a major impact on morale and the city went on to become the rallying point from which a truncated Latin Kingdom would later be reconquered.

Having left Acre on 17 July, Saladin led a lightning campaign up the coast of what is now Lebanon before returning to Tyre which was put under a loose blockade while Reginald retired to Belfort. From there he again negotiated with Saladin, offering Belfort in exchange for a position and pension in Damascus while in reality strengthening the castle's defences. Many of Saladin's troops now wanted to go home. The harvest was in and *iqta'* holders needed to check that their revenues had been collected. Neglecting their wives for more than four months could also give the women grounds for divorce under Muslim *ila* laws. Saladin clearly feared that his great army might drift away before he could take the greatest prize – Jerusalem. But before Saladin could attack Jerusalem he had to clear the enemy from the coastal ports through which help might flow from the west. Al Adil's Egyptian army was already operating in this area, having taken Jaffa, Jerusalem's main outlet, in July. By the time the Sultan joined Al Adil on 23 August the Kingdom of Jerusalem had been reduced to Gaza and a few other isolated castles in the south, Ascalon, Tyre, Safed and perhaps still Belfort in the north, the castles of Oultrejordain almost forgotten in the east, and of course Jerusalem. But the key to southern Palestine remained Ascalon (Asqalan) until the arrival of the Egyptian fleet under Husam al Din Lu'lu to blockade the city sealed its fate.

The siege of Ascalon began on 25 August and by the following day the Muslims had taken the outworks. The siege was far from easy, however, and cost Saladin the lives of two of his best *amir*s including the chief of the Banu Mihran bedouin tribe. Negotiations eventually started and on 5 September Ascalon accepted the same generous terms as Acre, the garrison being allowed to leave with their families. They were then escorted to Egypt where they were given decent housing until repatriation to Europe. On that same day a delegation from Jerusalem arrived in the victor's camp – but they did not come with an offer of surrender. The remaining Latin castles and towns of southern Palestine then fell in quick succession before or during Saladin's final march on Jerusalem, which he reached on 20 September.

Not surprisingly the morale of Saladin's army was high as it marched to Jerusalem. Discipline only wavered once when the fortified abbey of Bethany (Al Azariyah) was sacked, perhaps in reaction to a successful sortie by Jerusalem's garrison which killed an *amir* who, according to Ibn al Athir, had been advancing without proper caution. Despite the disasters suffered by the Kingdom of Jerusalem, the Christian garrison still had plenty of fight left and scoured the region for supplies before Saladin arrived. The Patriarch Heraclius was in charge but he was no soldier. An eclipse of the sun had also increased the sense of impending doom. Then Balian

'David's Tower', the citadel of Jerusalem, seen from within the city. The lower part is of Crusader work but the upper part probably dates from the Ottoman restoration of Jerusalem's defences in the 16th century. (David Nicolle)

d'Ibelin arrived. He had been in Tyre when Saladin gave him safe conduct to fetch his family from Jerusalem. On reaching the Holy City, however, Balian was surrounded by people urging him to take command of their defences. Heraclius even absolved him from his promise to Saladin. Torn between honour and his religious duty, Balian wrote a letter to the Sultan explaining that he had no choice but to take command and bid defiance to the man who had given him safe conduct. Saladin in turn seems to have accepted this from a man he regarded as a friend – though still an enemy. Balian d'Ibelin now reorganized the city's defences with typical efficiency and churches were stripped of their treasures to pay fighting men. Jerusalem was also full of refugees eager to fight. Nevertheless trained soldiers were few.

Having arrived before Jerusalem on 20 September, Saladin and his engineers studied the walls while the army made camp. At dawn the following day Saladin's troops attacked the north-western corner of the city between the Bab Yafa (David Gate) and the Bab Dimashq (St Stephen Gate). Both sides yelled their battle cries and arrows poured down on the defenders. All surgeons in the city were employed plucking them from the bodies of the wounded. The anonymous author of *De Expugnationae Terrae Sanctae* records that he himself was struck on the bridge of

75

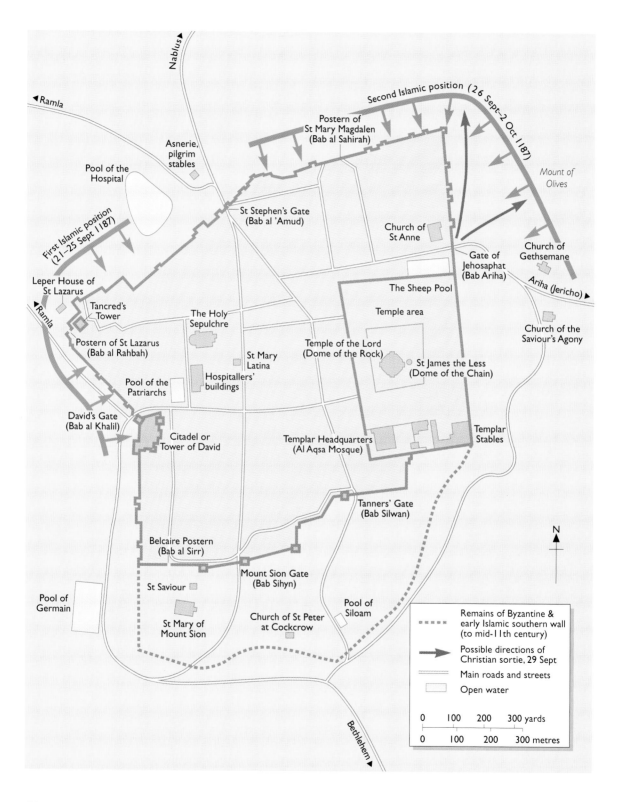

Nablus ▲

◄ Ramla

Second Islamic position (26 Sept–2 Oct 1187)

Postern of
St Mary Magdalen
(Bab al Sahirah)

Asnerie,
pilgrim
stables

Pool of the
Hospital

Mount of
Olives

First Islamic position
(21–25 Sept 1187)

St Stephen's Gate
(Bab al 'Amud)

Church of
St Anne

Church of
Gethsemane

Gate of
Jehosaphat
(Bab Ariha)

Leper House of
St Lazarus

◄ Ramla

Tancred's
Tower

The Holy
Sepulchre

The Sheep Pool

Temple area

Ariha (Jericho) ▶

Church of the
Saviour's Agony

Postern of St Lazarus
(Bab al Rahbah)

St Mary
Latina

Temple of the Lord
(Dome of the Rock)

St James the Less
(Dome of the Chain)

Pool of the
Patriarchs

Hospitallers'
buildings

David's Gate
(Bab al Khalil)

Citadel or
Tower of David

Templar Headquarters
(Al Aqsa Mosque)

Templar
Stables

Tanners' Gate
(Bab Silwan)

Belcaire Postern
(Bab al Sirr)

Mount Sion Gate
(Bab Sihyn)

Pool of
Germain

St Saviour

Pool of
Siloam

St Mary of
Mount Sion

Church of St Peter
at Cockcrow

Bethlehem ▼

N

Remains of Byzantine &
early Islamic southern wall
(to mid-11th century)

Possible directions of
Christian sortie, 29 Sept

Main roads and streets

Open water

| 0 | 100 | 200 | 300 yards |
| 0 | 100 | 200 | 300 metres |

his nose and that 'the metal tip has remained there to this day'. *Mangonels* of various kinds bombarded the walls, towers and gates while the Christians' own engines on the Towers of David and Tancred kept up a counter-barrage. The defenders fought with fanatical fury and made several effective sorties, damaging Saladin's siege engines and driving his troops back to their protected camps. Parts of the defences were damaged by powerful stone-throwing engines but not enough to force a breach. For five days both sides kept this up. The morning sun would be in the attackers' eyes, giving an advantage to the defence, while in the afternoon the opposite was the case. Muslim engineers even loaded their *mangonels* with dust which, driven by the prevailing wind, blew into the eyes of the defenders while assault parties tried to win the walls. Muslim losses were heavy and included senior men such as the *amir* Izz al Din Isa, whose father held the beautiful castle of Jabar overlooking the Euphrates in northern Syria.

By 25 September Saladin realized that his men were making no headway against the western walls so the attack was called off. The *mangonels* were dismantled, the tents pulled down and the troops marched out of sight behind the hills. For a while the defenders thought that the siege was over, but the following day, 26 September, the Muslims reappeared to the north of Jerusalem. Even by the Christians' own admission this caught the defence off guard and the Muslims quickly erected *zaribas* cut from olive trees to protect themselves as they established a new siege position. From there they attacked the northern walls as well as the northern sector of the eastern wall. Their main effort was focused east of the Bab Dimashq, a notoriously weak sector of the defences, but a part of which had a doubled wall which seems to have extended east beyond the small Bab al Sahirah (Postern of St Mary Magdalen). There was also a small postern in the north-eastern stretch of the walls through which a sortie could be made, but it was difficult to use because of the doubled wall.

Up to 40 *mangonels* were said to have been erected and these hurled rocks and *naft* (Greek fire). At least one was probably a new and powerful counterweight *trebuchet* and according to Balian d'Ibelin's squire, Ernoul, it struck the wall of the city three times on the very day that the Muslims renewed their siege. Next day Saladin sent forward three selected battalions of armoured engineers who advanced beneath large shields while archers gave covering fire. Having reached the ditch they began demolishing the base of the outer wall. Elaborate devices were erected, some covered with sturdy wooden roofs, beneath which Muslim miners cut away at the foundations. One tunnel, dug in two days, ran for 30 metres and was supported by wooden props which, when burned away, brought down a wide swathe of the wall on 29 September. To guard against sorties from the Bab Dimashq Saladin kept a large force of armoured cavalry on standby. The defenders also found the covering fire so intense that they were unable to shoot at the sappers while the rain of rocks from Saladin's siege machines hindered their countermining efforts. It is worth noting that the so-called Solomon's Quarry lies beneath the northern wall between Bab Dimashq and Bab al Sahirah. If the Muslim miners could have reached these tunnels extending beneath the city they could have worked with virtual impunity.

OPPOSITE

The Siege of Jerusalem

A desperate sortie by every man in Jerusalem who had horse and weapons was made through the Bab Ariha (Jehosaphat Gate) but why they chose this gate is unclear for it led directly down a steep slope into the Kidron valley. Perhaps they hoped to cross the valley and attack Saladin's headquarters on the Mount of Olives opposite. Perhaps they tried to follow a narrow path beneath the city wall and come around the Laqlaq Tower to catch the Muslims in their flank. The attempt was, however, crushed by Saladin's cavalry.

With about 60,000 people inside the walls, refugees as well as the Latin, Syriac-Jacobite and Orthodox Christian inhabitants, opinions varied on what should now be done. The Patriarch Heraclius and other barons promised to pay 5,000 'bezants' – an enormous sum – and distribute weapons to any 50 sergeants who would guard the newly made breach for a single night. They were not found for it was clear that Saladin's final assault was due. On the other hand other leading citizens proposed a suicidal night sortie, seeking death in battle rather than slaughter within the walls. Heraclius, however, dissuaded them by pointing out that they might win Paradise but they would leave women and children to lose their souls by abandoning Christianity.

On 30 September Balian d'Ibelin, as a personal friend of the Sultan, was sent to the Muslim camp where Saladin was already in contact with the non-Latin Christian communities within Jerusalem. Relations between the Latins and the Syriac-Jacobites had always been bad but now relations with the Orthodox were also at a low ebb. Joseph Batit, one of Saladin's closest aides and an Orthodox Christian born in Jerusalem, was actually negotiating with his co-religionists to open a gate in the north-eastern quarter of Jerusalem where most of them lived. Balian's negotiations were hard but not long. Twice he was refused an audience while an attempt by Saladin's troops to seize the breach was driven back. Next day Balian returned to Saladin's camp to learn that the Sultan had been discussing the matter with his *amir*s and religious advisers. Should the Holy City be taken by storm and the defenders slaughtered as they had slaughtered the Muslim and Jewish inhabitants in 1099? Saladin reminded Balian how the offer of honourable surrender made to Jerusalem's delegation outside Ascalon had been scornfully rejected. He also pointed out that he had sworn to take Jerusalem by storm and was known as a man of his word.

Perhaps believing that any sign of weakness would make matters worse, Balian threatened that if necessary the garrison would kill its own families, its own animals and the 5,000 Muslim prisoners still in its hands, destroy its own treasures, demolish the Dome of the Rock and the Aqsa Mosque – among the holiest buildings in Islam – then march out to meet Saladin's troops, '...thus we shall die gloriously or conquer like gentlemen'. Whether this threat showed that the fanaticism of the First Crusaders was still alive in Jerusalem, or whether it was a last desperate gamble, no one knows. But neither Saladin nor his officers seemed prepared to risk a holocaust worse than that of 1099. Instead a peaceful surrender was agreed for 2 October, on which day Saladin's banners were raised over Jerusalem and trusted *amir*s posted at each gate.

The non-Latin Christians could remain but the invading Crusaders must go. Every man was to pay ten dinars, with five for every woman, one for each child. A lump sum of 30,000 bezants would pay for 7,000 poor people who could not afford their own ransoms. Saladin allowed 40 days for the money to be paid. Now it was time for haggling over ransoms, though most of the quarrelling was within the Christian ranks. The Military Orders seemed unhappy about using their accumulated treasure to help those poor who could not pay ransoms and there is doubt about how

**OPPOSITE**

The Laqlaq Tower at the eastern end of the northern walls of Jerusalem. The First Crusade in 1099 and Saladin's army on 29 September 1187 both broke through the Holy City's defences a short distance to the right. (David Nicolle)

hard Heraclius tried to help those unable to pay. The Latins could take any property they could move, but much was sold in the *suq al-'askar* which always followed Saladin's army. When the 40 days was up there were still many poor trapped without means of paying for their freedom. So while the Christian rich struggled down the road to the coast laden with what valuables they could carry, Saladin himself paid the ransoms of many poor people. So disgusted were Saladin's *amir*s at the lack of Christian charity that they urged their Sultan to confiscate the wealth flowing out of the Bab Yafa (Jaffa Gate). Saladin refused to break his agreement, but even so there were up to 15,000 still in Jerusalem when the deadline came.

Some of the leading ladies of the Kingdom were also found in the city. King Guy's wife Sibylla was taken to see her husband now imprisoned in the citadel of Neapolis (Nablus) and the Lady Stephanie, widow of Reynald de Châtillon, was given her son, captured at Hattin, in return for ordering the garrisons of Krak and Montreal to surrender. When they refused, the Lady sent her son back to Saladin who was so struck by this honourable gesture that he soon let the young man go again. Even before the last ransoms were paid, the Muslims re-entered the Holy City to reclaim it for Islam. Their first task was to cleanse various buildings, making them fit for worship once more. On 9 October 1187 Saladin and many senior religious figures entered Jerusalem to make their *salat* (prayers) in the restored Al Aqsa Mosque. New buildings were commissioned while a palace once used by Patriarch Heraclius was given to *sufis* (Muslim mystics) as a convent. The headquarters of the Hospitallers became a religious college while most of the Latin churches were handed over to other Christian sects.

The fall of Jerusalem did not mean the end of the struggle. An unrecorded campaign was still being fought east of the Jordan where the remaining Latin possessions around the Yarmuk valley fell. Far to the south in Oultrejordain the castles of Montreal and Krak did not fall until 1188 and 1189 respectively. Meanwhile the defenders of Tyre recovered their confidence and sat tight behind the walls of a city built on a rocky peninsula that could only be approached across a narrow, sandy isthmus. They were also supported by numerous ships. Saladin was determined to renew the siege of Tyre and returned to the area with a small force on 12 November, the rest of his army coming up to assault the city 13 days later. It was a hard fight, the attackers being supported by as many siege engines as could be trained on the enemy. The isthmus was narrow and Christian ships filled with archers, crossbowmen and stone-throwing engines were moored on each side to shoot at the Muslims' flanks. The attacks failed and the siege dragged on with occasional attacks by the Muslims and frequent sorties by the defenders, among whom a Spanish knight, dressed in green and with a pair of stag's horns in his helmet, earned praise even from Saladin himself.

It was now clear that only by winning command of the sea could Tyre be taken, so a squadron of ten galleys and an unknown number of support vessels came up from Acre under the command of Abd al Salam al Maghribi, an experienced North African sailor. This was highly risky in the squalls of winter – the Mediterranean sailing season normally running from early April to late October – but the Muslim

**OPPOSITE**

Unlike Asqalan and some other coastal cities, Jerusalem was crammed with narrow streets and houses. In September 1187 it would also have been full of refugees. Once the city had surrendered to Saladin on 2 October, the Muslims returned to reclaim the sacred buildings occupied by Latin Christians for almost a century. The most important would have been the Aqsa Mosque hidden to the right of this picture and the Dome of the Rock, here seen down Bab al Qattanayn Street. (David Nicolle) fleet did force the Christian galleys into harbour. Meanwhile winter arrived, the besiegers' camp becoming a sea of mud and slushy snow as sickness broke out.

Then came disaster at sea. A Muslim squadron of five galleys, having kept watch through the night of 29/30 December, lowered their guard with the coming of dawn, but as they slept they were surprised by a fleet of 17 Christian galleys with ten smaller boats which darted out of Tyre and captured them. The five remaining Muslim galleys and other ships were then ordered to retire to Beirut because they were now too few to be effective. As they left they were pursued by galleys from Tyre which soon overhauled the exhausted Muslim crews. Most were beached, their crews escaping ashore and the vessels being destroyed on Saladin's orders, though one large sailing ship, described as being 'like a small mountain' and manned by experienced sailors, was able to escape. Following this setback the troops made a final unsuccessful attack on the defences of Tyre after which Saladin summoned a conference of his *amir*s. Some wanted to fight on but most said that the army was exhausted and their men wanted to go home. So next day, New Year's Day 1188, Saladin dismissed his army except for his own personal regiments whom he led back to Acre.

# AFTERMATH AND RECKONING

The events of 1187 shook Western Europe, the loss of Jerusalem being seen as casting shame on all Christians. On 20 October Pope Urban III died, of grief it was said. Nine days later his successor, Pope Gregory VIII, sent out letters urging Christendom to

save what was left of the Crusader Kingdom, letters which eventually led to the Third Crusade. On 19 December Pope Gregory also died. Meanwhile the survival of Tyre was a military disaster for Saladin, providing a perfect base from which the Third Crusade would start reconquering a rump Kingdom of Jerusalem in 1191. Yet this revived Crusader Kingdom was never what it had been. Hattin had demolished its feudal structure and undermined the basis of royal power. Western European interference in its government also increased rapidly.

On the Muslim side the liberation of Jerusalem had an enormous impact on Saladin's prestige. Barely noticed amid the excitement, a merchant caravan had set out from Damascus on 23 September, even before Jerusalem fell, heading for Cairo by the coastal route. It was the first for more than 87 years to travel this route without paying tolls.

## PERFORMANCE OF THE MUSLIM ARMY

The battle of Hattin was a typical encounter of its kind in which Saladin relied on varied but long-established tactics. Muslim morale may have been superior as a result of the Latin leaders' decision to lead their men on an exhausting, thirsty march, but although the Christians blundered, Saladin showed obvious tactical superiority. In the end the battle was won by the superior military capabilities of the Muslim troops in the situation in which the two armies fought. With better logistical support, superior speed of manoeuvre, greater ability to change position while retaining cohesion and probably better battlefield communications, one might think that the Muslims were bound to win – but in many other clashes they had not. Muslim capabilities in close combat have often been denigrated on the grounds that they wore lighter armour, wielded lighter weapons and rode smaller horses. The former two points are over-simplifications while the third is probably just wrong. In the end Hattin was won because Saladin got his enemies to fight where he wanted, when he wanted and how he wanted.

## PERFORMANCE OF THE CHRISTIAN ARMY

Christian morale and potential may have been damaged by a previous defeat at the Springs of Cresson, while the events surrounding that smaller battle had clearly undermined the prestige of the Latin army's ablest commander, Count Raymond of Tripoli. Sir Charles Oman's suggestion that the Latin army could have reached water at the Wadi al Hammam, many kilometres north of Hattin, was almost certainly wrong. In fact the only major mistake that King Guy made was marching east from Sephorie in the first place. Having made that decision, however, he and his advisers seem to have done whatever they could, and probably whatever they should, to trap Saladin in a disadvantageous position. Once battle was joined, the Christian army stuck to the tactics which had served it well in the past. The fact that these now failed was partly because of improvements in the opposing Muslim forces, but mostly because of the exhaustion of the infantry. They in turn let their cavalry down by failing in their primary task of protecting the knights' horses. Horse-armour may have been used in the Latin army but would have been extremely rare in 1187. It would also have made the knights even more unwieldy than they were. The supposed military-technological superiority of the European armoured knight is still accepted by many historians who should know better. Given the circumstances in which he had to fight in the Middle East, we should leave the last word with Saladin's friend and biographer, Baha al Din:

> A Latin knight, as long as his horse was in good condition, could not be knocked down. Covered by a mail hauberk from head to foot... the most violent blows had no effect on him. But once his horse was killed, the knight was thrown and taken prisoner.

# PART TWO
# RIVAL MILITARY ELITES

## INTRODUCTION

The Middle Ages saw an increasing imbalance in the manpower resources of a relatively over-populated Christendom and a generally under-populated Islamic world. This naturally resulted in different forms of military organization and recruitment. It also led to different methods of facing military challenges, and the results were particularly fascinating when the two civilizations met on the battlefield.

Military recruitment in the Islamic world during the Crusading era reflected established traditions until the coming of the Mongols in the 13th century. For example most eastern Islamic states recruited multi-ethnic armies which included indigenous elites and local volunteers as well as large numbers of soldiers of slave origin called *mamluks* or *ghulams*. Even the Saljuq Turks had turned to such traditional methods as their authority spread across most of the Middle East. Non-Turks, including people who would today be called Arabs, continued to play an important role in the armies of several successor states in 11th- and 12th-century Syria and Iraq. At the time, however, the name Arab was generally reserved for the bedouin tribes rather than the settled peoples of the Fertile Crescent and Egypt.

The most significant military development in the heartlands of Islamic civilization was a continuing professionalization of most armies because the skills demanded of a soldier were now so high that the old militias and tribal forces could not compete. This was despite the fact that, after the fragmentation of Great Saljuq Sultanate, many of the states involved were remarkably small and could only maintain small armies. Most rulers could only afford a small *'askar* bodyguard of slave-recruited *mamluks* which formed the core of a larger force of provincial soldiers, mostly Turks, Kurds and Arabic speakers. *Ahdath* urban militias played a minor role in some cities while further south bedouin Arab tribes continued to dominate the semi-desert and desert regions.

Saladin and his Ayyubid successors built a large and powerful military system in Egypt, Syria and northern Iraq, making use of existing Zangid-Turkish and Fatimid-Egyptian structures. Though Saladin was himself of Kurdish origin, the role of Kurds

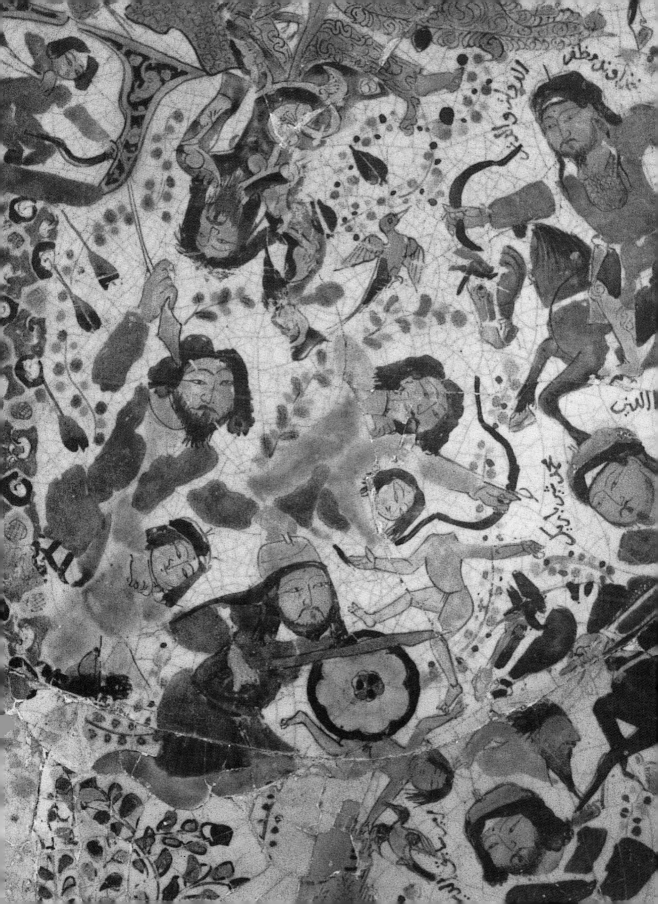

in Ayyubid armies has been greatly exaggerated and the *halqa* or elite of Saladin's army were largely slave-recruited Turks. Thereafter *mamluks* continued to form the elites of subsequent Ayyubid forces, though it was not until later that they came near to dominating in a numerical sense.

Among the more exotic troops in Saladin's army were ex-Fatimid infantry of black African slave origin, but these proved unreliable and were soon disbanded. The same applied to most of the ex-Fatimid Armenian soldiers. Many North Africans were recruited by the Ayyubid navy while large numbers of renegade European or Crusader warriors served Saladin and his successors after Saladin's reconquest of most of the Crusader States.

In almost complete contrast to the origins of most troops in the Islamic armies, Crusader forces initially consisted almost entirely of religiously motivated volunteers. Despite the astonishing but unrepeated success of the First Crusade, the inadequacy of such a system of military recruitment and organization very soon became apparent. The forces which had first marched east were unlike normal Western European armies in their composition, though not in their organization. The participants grouped themselves around the most senior lords present, though virtually all those involved were men of relative prosperity. Crusading was very expensive and poorer knights apparently had to pool their resources since, contrary to a widespread myth, Crusading was not a means of escape for a poor knight seeking his fortune overseas. Similarly the bulk of foot soldiers on all the early Crusades appear to have been

A contemporary depiction of the battle at La Forbie, 1244, between the Franks of the Kingdom of Jerusalem and the Khwarezmians, showing the Templar standard-bearer fleeing the field to the right. In fact the Templar standard-bearer did not flee, and virtually all the brothers of the military religious orders in the Frankish army died on the battlefield. From Matthew Paris's *Chronica majora*. (Cambridge, Corpus Christi College 16, fol. 170v; © the Master and Fellows of Corpus Christi College, Cambridge)

prosperous peasants and townsmen, plus professional sergeants. Women sometimes accompanied their husbands on Crusade and proved to be a morally stabilizing influence as well as working in camp and even mounting guard when necessary.

Subsequent military recruitment in the Crusader States differed considerably from that of Crusading expeditions which originated in Europe. Most of the nobility of the Crusader States were from relatively modest knightly origins; the knights of the Middle East being known as *chevaliers de la terre* by friends, *poulains* (runts) by unsympathetic sources. During the 12th century the knightly elite had successfully negotiated limitations of these military obligations, particularly where expeditions beyond the frontiers were concerned. Members of this class could be involved in warfare as early as 15 years old and were still liable for active service until 60. The lack of agricultural land in the Crusader States also meant that the bulk of the military aristocracy soon lived in towns and thus formed a bourgeoise knightly class similar to that of Italy. Non-knightly troops included professional infantry and cavalry sergeants paid by the towns and the Church, most having been recruited from local commoners and visiting pilgrims, as well as siege engineer specialists from local populations. In an emergency a general feudal levy or *arrière ban* produced larger numbers of infantry sergeants and barely trained militias, including men from the indigenous Arabic-speaking Christian community and, in the north, Armenians. In the Crusader States urban militias also needed paying when operating outside their own immediate areas. The merchant class of the coastal ports similarly formed confraternities or 'brotherhoods' to defend their own walls.

Mercenaries were essential to the Crusader States in Syria and Palestine, a steady stream of these being much preferred to sudden hordes of uncontrollable Crusaders. By the late 12th century the Kingdom of Jerusalem was paying close attention to raising adequate funds to recruit and pay such professional infantry and cavalry, both from within the Crusader States themselves and from Europe. But these should not be confused with knights who were paid stipends via money fiefs since these were, at least in theory, still part of the feudal system of military obligation in return for fiefs of one sort or another.

By far the most important non-feudal military forces in the Crusader States of the Middle East were, of course, the Military Orders. Most Orders, such as the Teutonic Knights, recruited from a limited area but the two greatest Military Orders of the Templars and the Hospitallers attracted men from all over Western Europe. Nevertheless the majority still came from France. Some Orders also had a novitiate system for boys and abandoned children, as did monastic orders, but these were not obliged to enter the Military Order when they became adults at the age of 14 or 15. The Military Orders came to be seen as a good career for the younger sons of knightly families, particularly as they did not involve the same degree of 'renunciation of the world' as did the monastic orders. A regular supply of such younger knightly recruits would then be sent to the Crusader States by the Orders' dependent houses in Europe. Meanwhile visiting pilgrim knights also often attached themselves temporarily to one of the Military Orders while in the Holy Land.

# SARACEN FARIS

### INTRODUCTION

Soldiers of slave origin were the elites of most Islamic armies from the 11th to the 13th century but never formed a majority; the bulk of Muslim troops were free men. The professional cavalryman was generally known as a *faris* or 'horseman' in Arabic, a word that carried overtones similar to – though not identical with – the Western European knight.

### ORIGINS AND RECRUITMENT

It is in the nature of medieval history that much more is known about the upper echelons of societies and armies than about the ordinary soldiers. Yet this is slightly less true of Islamic civilization than of Christian Europe. Many leaders rose from the ranks, and some even founded ruling dynasties. Muslim culture, particularly in the 11th and 12th centuries, was one that recognized individual merit and respected the luck or 'divine favour' that enabled a man to win fame, fortune or power. At the same time, a soldier's ethnic or tribal origins could both open and close doors of opportunity.

Two camel-riders in bedouin Arab costume in a late 13th-century Syrian copy of the *Maqamat* of al Hariri. (British Lib., Ms. OR 9718, f.173r, London)

## CHRONOLOGY

| | |
|---|---|
| **1029** | Ghuzz Turks invade eastern Iran. |
| **1055** | Saljuq Turks conquer Baghdad. |
| **1086** | Saljuq Sultan replaces Arab princes of Iraq and Syria with Turkish governors. |
| **1092–6** | Saljuq civil wars. |
| **1095** | Byzantine Empire appeals to pope for help against Saljuqs. |
| **1097–9** | First Crusade invades Anatolia and Syria; Crusaders capture Jerusalem. |
| **1101** | Crusading armies defeated by Saljuqs of Rum (Anatolia). |
| **1101–8** | Saljuq civil wars and rebellions. |
| **1115** | Saljuqs defeated by Crusaders at battle of Danith. |
| **1122** | Caliph of Baghdad raises independent 'Abbasid army. |
| **1127–8** | Zangi appointed governor of Mosul; Zangi takes control of Aleppo. |
| **1144** | Zangi of Mosul retakes Crusader-held Edessa (Urfa). |
| **1146** | Nur al Din succeeds Zangi in Aleppo. |
| **1148** | Second Crusade defeated outside Damascus. |
| **1153** | Crusaders conquer Fatimid Ascalon. |
| **1154** | Nur al Din takes control of Damascus. |
| **1156** | Death of last Great Saljuq Sultan; fragmentation of Saljuq Empire. |
| **1163–69** | Five Crusader invasions of Fatimid Egypt. |
| **1169** | Saladin becomes governor of Egypt under Nur al Din. |
| **1174** | Death of Nur al Din; Saladin takes control of Damascus. |
| **1175** | Saladin defeats Zangids (successors of Nur al Din) at battle of Hama. |
| **1182–6** | Saladin takes control of Aleppo and Mosul. |
| **1187** | Battle of **Hattin**. |
| **1190–2** | Third Crusade retakes Acre; fails to re-conquer Jerusalem. |
| **1193** | Death of Saladin; start of fragmentation of his (Ayyubid) empire. |
| **1194** | Last Saljuqs of Iran overthrown by Khwarazmians. |
| **1218–21** | Fifth Crusade invades Egypt and is defeated. |
| **1220–2** | Mongols invade Transoxania, Iran and Afghanistan, and defeat Khwarazmians. |
| **1243** | Mongols defeat Saljuqs of Rum (Anatolia) at battle of Köse Dag. |
| **1244** | Jerusalem falls to freebooting Khwarazmian army. |
| **1245** | Ayyubid Empire reunited. |
| **1249–50** | Defeat of St Louis' Crusade against Egypt; overthrow of Ayyubid dynasty in Egypt; start of Mamluk rule. |
| **1256–8** | Mongols invade Iran and Iraq and sack Baghdad. |
| **1260** | Mongols invade Syria; defeated by Mamluks at battle of 'Ayn Jalut. |
| **1291** | Mamluks destroy remnants of Crusader Kingdom of Jerusalem. |

Sgraffiro-ware bowl showing a horseman in urban Arab costume, with a hunting bird on his wrist. The bowl is 13th century and from the Crimea, probably northern Syrian. (State Hermitage Museum, St Petersburg, Russia: photograph David Nicolle)

The defeat of the Arab leader al Basasiri by the Saljuq sultan Tughril in 1059 marked the end of Arab dominance in Syria and the rest of the Fertile Crescent until the area regained independence after World War II. The Fatimid Caliphate of Egypt was degenerating into a military dictatorship, and by the time the First Crusade appeared on the scene at the end of the 11th century, the rival Saljuq Turkish Empire was crumbling: several areas had been devastated; fortifications were in decay; some towns had been virtually deserted; whole provinces were infested with bandits; and most local Turkish governors were little more than tribal leaders. Yet the threat from Western European Crusades, and later from Mongols, meant that the first priority of each state was to maintain an effective army.

Under such circumstances a military career had obvious advantages. An elite of *mamluk* soldiers, purchased as slaves, trained and then freed, were extremely expensive, and although a ruler's *'askar* or personal regiment might consist of *mamluks*, the rest were normally mercenaries or *jund* soldiers who served for pay, pensions or grants of land. Middle Eastern military and civilian elites had been separate for several centuries and most soldiers were now recruited from the geographical and social fringes. They also retained a distinctive appearance, often reflecting their ethnic origins. The Turks wore long plaits similar to modern Rastafarian 'dreadlocks', and in Yemen many men wore their hair long, as the pre-Islamic Arabs had done. However, in most of the Muslim world men shaved their heads, long hair and extravagant moustaches being the mark of a professional warrior.

Individual city-folk did enlist, though most known examples come from the 10th century. One wealthy young man from Baghdad, for example, had ruined his reputation with drinking and music and so bought military equipment, two horses and two mules, grew his hair, learned to speak and behave like a mountaineer, ate garlic to give himself the required bad breath and served as a soldier for several years. Another account tells of a freed Greek slave who married his master's widow and enlisted as an elite soldier, but after suffering a snake-bite, he cut off his military moustache and retired as a religious ascetic. Early in the 12th century the famous Arab soldier and writer Usama Ibn Munqidh tried to persuade his tutor to become a soldier and fight the invading Crusaders, but the old scholar refused on the grounds that he was temperamentally unsuited.

Rough Turkish and Kurdish warriors were, in fact, tolerated as a necessary evil by the cultured Arab townsfolk of Syria and Iraq. Little information survives about ordinary soldiers and it is misleading to judge the ethnic composition of an army by its senior officers who tended to be Turkish or Kurdish.

A strong sense of group identity, or *sinf*, certainly existed among soldiers, often based on tribal origins. The sons of soldiers were still enlisted by some rulers, but were regarded as second best to men from peripheral tribal areas.

Arabs were proud of their reputation as hard-riding light cavalry able to endure greater hardship than most other troops; they dominated warfare in the real desert regions. Most wars were not, however, fought in deserts, but in the fertile cultivated parts of the Middle East, and usually for control of the rich trading cities. The tribal Arabs who served in the Ghaznavid armies of Afghanistan and north-west India were described as 'dare-devil riders', and as vital auxiliary cavalry in the Fertile Crescent (from Palestine through Syria and Iraq to the Persian Gulf).

The fortress-city of Shayzar in Syria remained an island of Arab-ruled territory with a largely Arab army. However, the main employer of Syrian Arab cavalry was the Fatimid Caliphate of Egypt. This service was also well paid.

Closely associated with Arab soldiers were the 12th-century *mawali* or 'clients'. Little is known about their origins, and although they attached themselves to a particular Arab tribe, their status was less than that of a warrior born into the tribe.

Like the majority of lowland bedouin Arabs, the mountain Kurds practised transhumance, migrating along fixed paths according to the season. Like the Arabs their military elites fought as cavalry, being known as 'rough jousters' riding 'shaven' horses, but whereas the Arab's typical weapon was the lance, the Kurds were known as swordsmen. The period of greatest opportunity for a Kurdish soldier was, naturally enough, under Saladin and his Ayyubid successors, who were themselves of Kurdish origin. Kurds offered themselves as individual mercenaries or came as tribal units which would then fight in distinct battlefield units.

The *Bayad wa Riyad* manuscript from Morocco or Andulusia, early 13th century. Music and poetry played a crucial role in the life of medieval Muslim civilization. (Vatican Library, Ms. Ar. 368, Rome, Italy)

Militarily much more important were the Turks, whether free Turcomans, detribalized Turkish professional soldiers or *mamluks* of slave origin. From early Islamic times the Turks had enjoyed a reputation as extremely effective warriors, and there were *Hadiths* or 'pious sayings' to support this: 'I have an army in the east which I call Turk. I set them upon any people who kindle My wrath.' One early 12th-century Arab poet described the Turks as demons in war, angels in peace. They were also famed as archers, for their eyesight and as armourers. But while Turcoman nomads were regarded as good soldiers, they were thought unruly, insisting on prompt payment of their wages, eager for a quick battle and unsuited to patient campaigning.

Armenians played a small, though significant, military role in the Muslim armies of the 11th and 12th centuries, despite being Christian. They were particularly prominent in Egypt, where part of the Armenian military elite and their families had emigrated after their homeland had been occupied by Byzantine Greeks and then by

Turks. Armenian regiments served the Fatimid caliphs loyally, and when they were finally disbanded by Saladin some individual soldiers migrated south to Christian Nubia where they joined a failed invasion of southern Egypt in 1172. Today it might seem strange that the Christian Armenians fought so enthusiastically for a Shi'ite Muslim ruler like the Fatimid caliph. However, like the Nubians and the Coptic majority within Egypt, they were Monophysite Christians and as such were regarded as doomed heretics by Greek Orthodox Byzantines and Catholic Crusaders.

The time when Berber soldiers could find guaranteed employment in the Middle East had passed; the Fatimid army had disbanded most of its Berber cavalry back in 1093, though some were still on strength, mostly from western Libya. At the same time, the majority of black African soldiers in the Fatimid army were of slave origin and fought as infantry, though there were also freely enlisted Nubians, Ethiopians and Arab bedouin from the south.

Clearly a soldier had many potential employers to choose from and men often served in several armies during their careers. Their choice would have been influenced by various factors: the wealth of an employer, religious affiliation and the employer's preference for a particular ethnic group.

However, the most important factor was whether other members of a soldier's family or tribe had already served with this or that employer.

The citadel and town of Shayzar in central Syria. (David Nicolle)

All these considerations had an impact on the size of the medieval Muslim army in which the recruit found employment. Some historians still suggest that, unlike Crusader leaders, Muslim rulers could always recruit more armies because of their huge manpower resources but this view fails to take account of the way in which armies were enlisted and the limited populations from which soldiers were drawn. The *Mémoires of Usama Ibn Munqidh* shed considerable light on the origins of leaders, officers and lower ranks in one small late 11th/early 12th century army, although the statistics must be treated with extreme caution:

## ETHNIC COMPOSITION OF ARMY OF SHAYZAR, LATE 11TH/EARLY 12TH CENTURY

| Rank | Origin of recruits |
| --- | --- |
| Governors, military leaders and senior officers (Shayzar and neighbouring states) | Arabs 18.4%, Kurds 5.2%, Turks 73.6% and slaves 2.6% |
| Cavalry and junior officers (largely Shayzar) | Arabs 44.4%, Kurds 41.6%, Turks 5.5%, slaves 5.5%, Christian Kurds 2.7% |
| Unspecified soldiers including infantry volunteers (largely Shayzar) | Arabs 50%, Kurds 21.4%, Turks 0%, slaves 14.3%, North Africans 14.3% (plus unspecified 'other North Africans') |

The recruitment policies of Turkish armies could also vary. According to a Jewish description of a Turcoman attack on Fatimid Egypt in the mid-11th century, the invaders included Turks, Armenians, Arabs, Greeks, various other Anatolians and even 'Germans' (probably meaning Europeans). The Saljuqs and their protégés enlisted Kurds and Daylamite mountaineers, though tribal Turcomans formed the bulk of their armies. As the Great Saljuq Empire fragmented, ethnically varied regional armies reappeared. The troops of previous Arab or Kurdish rulers may already have been absorbed into city militias, yet their descendants were still able to operate as regular soldiers.

The army of Turkish-ruled Damascus was both more important and more typical than that of Arab Shayzar. Here an individual soldier's career opportunities were certainly influenced by his ethnic background. Early 12th-century Damascus was a military state dedicated to *jihad* against the invading Europeans. Its army consisted of Turks, Kurds, Arab bedouin, urban militia and religious volunteers. Turks were most numerous, providing military leadership and guard units. The majority came from tribes in the Diyarbakir region of what is now south-eastern Turkey. The rulers of Damascus maintained close links with the region's local leaders and the men could be ordered to Syria if a Crusader threat loomed. A separate group – known as Turcomans rather than Turks – came from the same area but were

strictly volunteers who came of their own free will if the Crusaders threatened Damascus. Whereas Turks lived within the city, these Turcomans camped outside. The Kurds of Damascus included cavalry but never numbered more than a few hundred under a single Kurdish officer. Arabs are rarely mentioned in the regular army but frequently appeared on campaign, generally in logistical support.

The most successful among the small armies that emerged from the fragmenting Saljuq empire was that of Zangi and his son Nur al Din. Its leadership was Turkish and Kurdish; the troops were mainly Turcoman horse-archers and Kurdish close-combat cavalry. Most were professional *tawashi* cavalrymen, and they were backed up by bedouin Arab auxiliaries. It is worth noting that the muster-roll of a large Zangid army in Mosul in 1175 only included 6,000–6,500 cavalry. After Saladin united Egypt, Syria and the Jazira region, he could recruit larger armies than had been seen for many years. The bulk of these were freely recruited professionals, both officers and other ranks, and they were mostly Turks, with the Kurds being of secondary status and importance.

The last time an 'Abbasid caliph had had his own army was back in the 10th century, and the reappearance of a small but effective Caliphal army in the 1120s provided potential recruits with another employer. It also offered a military role to those whose religious convictions made them happier to serve the nominal head of 'orthodox' Sunni Islam rather than a 'heretical' Shi'ite Fatimid caliph or a secular leader whose commitment to Islam was only skin-deep. The revived 'Abbasid army was largely commanded by Turkish officers. It included Turkish soldiers but by 1193/4 it was mostly recruited from Iraqi Arab tribes and northern Kurds.

## TRAINING

Military standards had fallen by the mid-11th century, and the period of the Crusades was one in which Middle Eastern Muslim armies struggled to regain their lost professionalism and high morale. Even so, it is clear that traditions of training, battlefield control and tactics were – in theory if not in practice – far in advance of those seen in Europe.

The basic military skills of a *faris* were known as *furusiya*, a concept which also contained aspects of 'chivalry'. (Mere courage was known as *shuja'a*.) In the 9th century such skills included vaulting onto a horse's back without using stirrups, general riding ability, polo, archery at static and moving targets, and presumably the use of other weapons.

The military elite of the Crusader period were also expected to practise their skills constantly. Late 13th- or early 14th-century books on *furusiya* list the qualities required of a professional *faris* as: obedience to a superior officer; an ability to make correct military decisions; steadiness in adversity; horsemanship; nimbleness in attack; possession of good quality weapons and armour; and skill in their use. By then *furusiya* exercises reflected the Muslim military elite's traditional willingness to learn from any source, some exercises having come from Khurasan in eastern Iran, others from Byzantium, and a few from the Crusaders. They dealt with archery, use

**A LION HUNT**

'All of a sudden we were surprised to
see the lion rush past us like the wind
and go straight to one of our comrades
named Sa'dallah al Shaybani and knock
his horse to the ground with one blow.
I thrust my lance into the lion, hitting
it in the middle part of its body, and it
died on the spot.' (*Mémoires*, Usama
Ibn Munqidh)

Hunting served as a highly realistic
form of military training in the Middle
East, just as it did in medieval Europe.
Lions and other wild cats still roamed
Syria and Egypt in the 12th century,
and hunting them could be very
dangerous. Not only did it require
courage and skill with weapons, but also
great control over the huntsman's often
terrified horse. The lion also had to be

tracked and trapped before being killed
with a spear or sword. Other forms of
hunting included hawking – perhaps the
most 'aristocratic' sport – and chasing
the deer and wild asses of the desert.
Usama's *Mémoires* devote almost as
much time to these pastimes, and the
sometimes extraordinary adventures of
the huntsmen, as to recollections of war.
(Christa Hook © Osprey Publishing Ltd)

of the lance, sword and mace, wrestling, parade-ground skills, hunting, crossbow-
shooting, polo and horse-racing. Many of these 'games', as they were known, were
much closer to the British War Office *Cavalry Training Manual* of 1907 than to the
knightly skills being learned in medieval Europe. A professional *faris* was also
trained to fight on foot. A quote from one manual shows that the military elite saw

the importance of both cavalry and infantry, unlike the European knight who was prejudiced against infantry warfare:

> In some ways the horseman is superior to the infantry, in some ways the infantry is superior, and in other ways they are equal. But for strength of weapons, speed and striking power, if not for care and caution, in feigned retreat or in pursuit, the horseman is superior.

Whereas Fatimid cavalry largely fought with spear and sword, the first wave of Saljuq Turkish invaders relied on Central Asian horse-archery tactics of dispersal and harassment. Within two generations the Saljuq professional cavalry, though not the Turcoman tribal warriors, had largely reverted to a long-established Middle Eastern tradition of horse-archery, in which men shot volleys as close-packed units, often at rest. This system needed fewer spare horses and permitted the use of heavier armour. By the 12th and 13th centuries it seems that even in strongly Turkish areas like

Lustre-ware plate, 12th-century Egypt. A Fatimid nobleman or officer wears a massive turban indicating his status. (Museum of Islamic Art, inv. 13477, Cairo, Egypt; photograph David Nicolle)

99

Drawing on paper, from Fatimid Egypt, 11th/12th century. On the left a clean-shaven Turk in cavalry boots has a sabre hung from a belt with officer's pendants. On the right a turbaned Arab or Berber with a spear, sash and shoes wears a mail hauberk beneath his tunic. (Museum of Islamic Art, inv. 13703, Cairo, Egypt)

Azarbayjan and Anatolia the professional cavalry elite relied as much on spears, swords, maces and javelins as on archery.

The Muslim world had a long tradition of military theory, with writings dating back to the 8th century. Most of that written before the 12th century was for senior officers, and it sheds interesting light on military priorities. Greater emphasis was given to foot soldiers than cavalry, and the greatest of all to infantry archers. The counter-Crusades prompted a wave of updated military textbooks; some were purely theoretical, others dealt with *jihad*, army administration, broad strategy, narrow tactical considerations, specific skills or simply with military equipment. Some were apparently aimed at junior officers as well as commanders, and it is clear that high professional skills allied with extreme caution, avoidance of unnecessary casualties and a preference for wearing down a foe without resort to a major battle influenced the training and attitudes of ordinary soldiers.

According to an ideal system described in the *Siyasat Nama*, it took eight years to train a *mamluk* soldier. Although the reality was probably less, the Muslim military elite does seem to have been older – rank-for-rank – than their Crusader foes. The

schedule in the *Siyasat Nama* indicates training on foot first, then horsemanship followed by archery. After that a young soldier was allowed 'decorated' equipment. Later still he was entrusted with increasingly important duties.

The reality of training in Fatimid Egypt, at least where elite professional cavalry were concerned, was remarkably similar to the *furusiya* system of the later Mamluk Sultanate. Fatimid *hujra* barracks also served as training centres, and it is possible that here, as in the better recorded barracks of 10th-century Tarsus, retired warriors supervised the training of young soldiers. Cavalry skills focused on fighting horsemen and infantry, the use of and resistance to various weapons, striking different parts of the enemy and his horse, and ways of deceiving a foe. *Furusiya* exercises normally took place in a *maydan* or 'parade ground' which was also used as a camping area for an enlarged garrison or army. Larger cities, like Cairo, Aleppo and Damascus, had at least two *maydans*.

The Arab style of riding was closer to that of the Romans than that of the Central Asian Turks: it put great emphasis on long-distance endurance. The riding skills of professional soldiers were probably better than those of nomads, and the 'High Islamic School of Riding', which reached its peak in 12th and 13th century Egypt and Andalusia, was an amalgamation of Mediterranean and Persian methods. Here the rider used a saddle and 'seat' similar to that of modern horsemen. This was less tiring for himself and his horse than the riding style seen in medieval Europe. Books on horsemanship showed that a young horseman first learned to ride bareback, to

*Kitab al Baytarah*, 'Book of Veterinary Information'. A man wearing the fur-lined hat of the military elite trains a war-horse. (Topkapi Library, Ms. Ahmet III 2115, Istanbul, Turkey)

101

develop a really firm 'seat', and only then was allowed to use a wooden-framed saddle. He had his stirrups set further forward than in Europe, and though he rode in a sitting rather than straight-legged position, he certainly did not use the short stirrup leathers assumed by some historians; a Middle Eastern cavalryman rode with stirrups that would touch his ankle bone when his legs hung loose. Horses seem to have been trained to avoid spear thrusts, and a horse-archer's mount was trained to continue in a straight line, ignoring pressure from the rider's knees until it felt a pull on the reins.

Unlike the knightly elite of Europe, the professional Muslim cavalryman was expected to arm himself without the help of a servant. Training also included the use and maintenance of military equipment, where to keep it in camp so that it could be found in the dark, how to put on armour at night and how to take it off even while his horse was in motion. The Fatimid army of Egypt was greatly concerned with correct positioning in the ranks, discipline and the ability of cavalry squadrons to manoeuvre in unison. In later *furusiya* manuals, several manoeuvres look more like square-bashing than realistic fighting exercises. They were probably designed to strengthen team work, and to improve unit cohesion while riding at different speeds and wheeling in various directions.

### The Bow

Few unit exercises involved the bow; training in its use was largely an individual matter. The Middle Eastern tradition of horse-archery was based upon 'shower-shooting' in volleys, often while stationary. This tactic was more versatile than Central Asian horse-archery and needed less logistical backup. In the 10th century archers trained by shooting at a stuffed straw animal in a four-wheeled cart that was rolled downhill or pulled by a horseman. A fully competent 13th-century archer could reportedly shoot five arrows, held in the left hand with the bow, in two and a half seconds. Another five arrows were then snatched from a quiver.

Most archery training emphasized dexterity rather than accuracy. Nevertheless, a skilled archer was expected to hit a metre-wide target at 75 metres. (Closer-range archery training had a 60-metre training distance.) Training concentrated on three disciplines: shooting level, upwards or downwards, the latter two generally from horseback while moving. A horse-archer would probably have been able to loose five arrows at between 30 and five metres from an enemy when charging at full speed. He dropped his reins as he shot, but might use a strap from the reins to the ring-finger of his right hand to enable him to regain them quickly. The section on archery by al Tarsusi, the famous military author of the late 12th century who wrote for Saladin, offers the following advice to Muslim archers fighting the Crusaders:

When shooting at a horseman who is armoured or otherwise untouchable, shoot at his horse to dismount him. When shooting at a horseman who is not moving, aim at the saddle-bow and thus hit the man if [the arrow flies]

**MUSLIM HORSE-ARCHERS IN ACTION**
'If you wish to shoot and have a sword, drop the sword from your right hand, seize the wrist loop and slide it up the right forearm. Hold the bow and three arrows in your left hand. If you are on horseback and are also armed with a lance, push the lance beneath the right thigh. If you have a sword as well, put the lance beneath the left thigh. If a group of enemy halt out of range, disperse to shoot at them. If they come close, reassemble your forces. If you are near the enemy on a road, regroup to keep him on your left.' (*Murda al Tarsusi*, 'Book of Military Equipment and Tactics written for Saladin')
Documentary sources show that Muslim horse-archers used a variety of tactics including 'shower shooting' at a designated area or 'killing zone' rather than at an individual enemy. This was an essentially Persian tactic originally designed to cope with Turkish raiders from the Central Asian steppes in pre-Islamic times. The other most important form of horse-archery was Turkish in origin and involved shooting while the horse was in motion, either harassing an enemy from a distance or repeatedly charging and shooting. The aim was to get close, shoot at a range where the arrow would pierce almost any form of protection, then retreat out of range of counter-fire. (Christa Hook © Osprey Publishing Ltd)

too high and the horse if too low. If his back is turned, aim at the spot between his shoulders. If he charges with a sword shoot at him, but not from too far off for if you miss he might hit you with his sword. Never shoot blindly!

This advice was reflected in Fatimid traditions. The manual stated that if a horse-archer had a sword, he should dangle it from his right wrist by its hilt-loop while shooting. If he had a lance, he should put it under his right thigh unless he also had a sword, in which case the lance went beneath the left thigh. A group of horse-archers was advised to disperse around a bunched-up enemy but should reassemble if the foe came close. If encountered on a road, the enemy should be kept on the archer's left, but if this was impossible, the men should stay in line with their shields raised.

Shooting involved a sequence of skills: *itar* or stringing the bow; *qabda* or grasping the bow in the left hand; *tafwiq* or nocking an arrow in the string; *aqd* or locking the string in the right hand; *madd* or drawing back to the eye-brow, ear-lobe, moustache, chin or breastbone; *nazar* or aiming with any necessary corrections; and *itlaq* or loosing the arrow. Shooting was done in three ways: 'snatched' with the draw and release in one continuous movement; 'held' with a slow draw and a short pause before releasing; and 'twisted' with a partial draw followed by a pause then a snatched final draw and release. Men were advised to vary their techniques according to the tactical situation and to avoid tiring themselves.

Professional archers were trained to shoot from horseback, or standing, sitting, squatting or kneeling. They learned to shoot over fortifications and from beneath shields. There were several strengths of bow for different purposes, and they are distinguished by their draw-weights. A standard war weapon was from 50 kg up to a maximum of 75 kg. Three types of draw were used: the weak Mediterranean or European draw; the three-fingered *daniyyat* or Persian draw; and the powerful *bazm* or Turkish thumb-draw. A protective leather flap inside the fingers could be used with the Persian draw, and a protective thumb-ring with the Turkish thumb-draw.

## The Spear

A professional *faris* was trained to use his spear in a greater variety of ways than his European counterpart. In the long-established two-handed style, a rider slacked his reins as he lowered his lance-point, then dropped them as he struck the enemy. Such a thrust could pierce two layers of mail and come out the other side. Even so, Usama recommended the couched lance technique used by his Crusader foes, a style subsequently known as 'The Syrian Attack'. Later in the 12th century al Tarsusi advised cavalry to attack infantry with both spear and sword.

Other descriptions of cavalry combat mention the use of shields to parry rather than simply to obstruct a foe's lance blow. Among various spear exercises was the *birjas* game, where a charging horseman was expected to remove the topmost of a column of wooden blocks without knocking down any other blocks.

## The Sword

Sword fencing was also highly developed. Several detailed accounts of close combat from the 10th and 12th centuries illustrate the terrifying impact of a sword as well as the precision with which a fully trained *faris* could deliver a blow. On one occasion a Persian cavalryman charged into the midst of an Arab ruler's bodyguard

Cast-iron sword guard from al Rabadhah in Arabia, 8th/9th century. (King Sa 'ud Univ., Riyadh, Saudi Arabia)

and injured the enemy commander with carefully aimed cuts at his head, shoulder and elbow. An Arab cavalryman then struck at him, first severing the Persian's index finger – which suggests that this was over the quillons of his sword – then his middle finger. When the Persian dropped his sword the Arab promptly cut off his head. Sword exercises in *furusiya* manuals emphasized the strength and accuracy of cutting, but not thrusting. In one 'game' men on horseback rode past a line of green reeds, slicing sections off each reed in successive passes. As a result, the power of a good sword-cut could be devastating. To quote Usama:

> I had a fight with an Isma'ili [Assassin] who had a dagger in his hand while I had my sword. He rushed at me with the dagger and I hit him in the middle of his forearm as he was grasping the hilt of the dagger and holding the blade close to his forearm. My blow cut about four inches off the dagger-blade and severed his forearm in two. The mark of the edge of the dagger was left on the edge of my sword. A craftsman in our town, on seeing it, said: 'I can remove this dent.' But I said: 'Leave it as it is. It is the best thing on my sword.' The mark is there to this day.

Other cavalry training involved the use of cover and dead ground and the crossing of rivers; the ability to swim was considered second in importance only to literacy.

# GOD'S WARRIORS

## HOME AND BARRACKS

Medieval Islamic civilization, particularly among military groups, had great respect for individual worth and personal achievement. Attitudes were in many ways closer to those of the modern world than to those of medieval Europe. Overcoming natural cowardice, for example, was regarded as more admirable than feeling no fear. (Feeling no fear was often attributed to stupidity.) Military service was also considered to involve an element of personal humiliation through submission to orders, but at the same time, the military elite were also something of a social elite. As one Arab replied when taunted for his humble origins: 'My family line begins with me, yours ends with you!'

Protection of the weak by the strong was a powerful ideal and romantic ideals of honour, particularly among the Arabs, were remarkably similar to those of Western European chivalry. For example a cavalryman who felt that his honour had been tarnished by being struck by a second-rate soldier would charge among the enemy's ranks just so that he could return the blow. The beliefs and attitudes of the Turkish warrior classes were different: the Turks believed that they were destined to rule the world. Even after becoming Muslim, they continued to see themselves as a chosen people who had saved Islam in its hour of crisis.

The differing attitudes of Turkish, Persian and Arab soldiers were also reflected in their literary tastes. Tales of love and war written for the Turks had much in common with French *chansons de geste*, whereas Persian stories tended to focus on a lost imperial past, a clash of titanic heroes and the splendour of courtly life. The Arabic epic tradition, which reached its final form during the Crusades, showed deeper interest in human relations, the emotions of battle and the often tense relationship between men and women, with the leading character often being female. There were also elements of sex and violence: an enemy warrior-heroine with a 'bottom like a narcissus flower' finally succumbs to the hero, and, of course, falls in love with him.

Music played a very important part in the culture of Arab, Persian and Turkish military elites, but was regarded with deep suspicion by the religious leadership. Chess was associated with older and wiser warriors, and youngsters preferred faster, gambling games. The Saracen soldier's love of perfumes and flowers was seen as effeminate by the rougher Crusaders, but scents cooled a man in the heat of the Middle East, while flowers and fragrant leaves flavoured his drinks. Of course the Muslim warrior drank more than mere 'sherbet' – alcoholic beverages were widespread. A thick, sweet, slightly fermented juice made from dried grapes or dates was acceptable, and the Turks also drank a form of beer called *buzah*.

More is known about the social attitudes of the officer class than of ordinary soldiers. The Muslim elite was very concerned with etiquette: the correct way of eating; respect for age and women; and 'moderation in all things'. But where romance was concerned, they showed less restraint: pursuit of the fair sex was considered normal for a young man, though quite separate from the question of marriage. As Kai Ka'us, ruler of Gurgan, wrote for his son in AD 1082:

Carved ivory horn or 'oliphant' from southern Italy. It is in Fatimid style and was either made locally by Muslim craftsmen from Sicily or was imported from Egypt. Note the turbaned, mail-clad warrior near the top of the horn, armed with a sword and shield. Such huge and magnificent horns would have been prized possessions among the military elite. (Musée Crozatier, Le Puy, France)

Marry a woman of honourable family, because men marry in order to have a lady for the house and not to indulge in sexual pleasure. To satisfy your desires you can buy slave-girls in the bazaar, which involves less expense and less trouble.

The idea that the Muslim warrior's ideal woman was fat is also untrue. A beauty was described as slender like a cane or twig, with a pale face, long dark hair, large dark eyes, a straight nose, a small mouth, bright red lips, a small bosom, waist, hands and feet but wide hips. She was also highly sexed.

The significance of *jihad* and religious motivation may have become exaggerated but they were important. *Jihad* itself was never supposed to force conversion to Islam; it was intended to increase the power of Islam and to defend Muslims. The Crusader conquest of parts of Syria and the Holy Land was, in fact, received with apathy outside the areas immediately concerned. Yet the savagery of the newly arrived 'Franks' (Western European Christians) was noted, and some scholars who understood Crusader motivation worked for a revival of the *jihad* spirit. Once it did re-emerge, it was a Sunni or 'orthodox' Muslim phenomenon aimed as much against 'heretical' Shi'a Muslims as against the Crusaders. However, how much influence scholarly works on *jihad* had on ordinary soldiers remains unknown.

As far as the professional soldier was concerned the rules of war, or *siyar*, had been established back in the 8th century. They were rooted in religion, and any educated soldier knew them well. Basically they consisted of the rules of *jihad* (who could and could not be fought and under what circumstances), *'aman* (when and where safe-conduct should be offered to an enemy) and *hudnah* (the rules regulating truces). Sometimes such regulations were highly specific, dealing with the preservation of fruit trees and beehives. Among the most important practical regulations were those dealing with obedience to orders, keeping one's word – even to an enemy – not harming women, children, old men, non-military slaves or religious figures (unless the latter were spies), and causing no more devastation than was militarily necessary. Male prisoners could be killed or enslaved, though only for good reason, whereas female prisoners should be provided with transport into

12th- to 13th-century ewer from Iran. Inlaid metalwork would have been among the most prized possessions of a successful soldier. Such items have little value as bullion, being made of bronze with a tiny amount of gold or silver inlay, and would not have appealed to the average looting Crusader. But their exquisite craftsmanship made them valuable in the eyes of the educated Muslim elite. (British Museum, London, England)

captivity. Clearly Muslim soldiers and their commanders did not always live up to such high standards, but at least the *siyar* was there as an ideal – which is more than can be said for European warfare against non-Christians.

The back of a gold-inlaid polished steel mirror from early 13th-century Turkish Anatolia (modern Turkey), decorated with a horseman with a hunting hawk on his wrist. (Topkapi Mus., Istanbul, Turkey)

The Muslim soldier was also rather superstitious. Small totemic swords, magic daggers and written charms have been found in many areas, though very little is now known about how they were supposed to work. Astrology, the interpretation of dreams, and predictions were widespread and may have been particularly characteristic of the military – whose lives and careers were even more uncertain than those of ordinary men.

For several centuries the military elites of the Muslim Middle East had been firmly based in cities and towns. Even the Saljuq Turks soon settled into urban citadels and became, like their Arab and Persian predecessors, patrons of culture and religion. The core elites of their armies also lived within cities, though for several generations Turcoman tribal troops tended to live in tents beyond the walls.

In Fatimid Egypt the caliph's guard regiments had their *hujra* barracks within the palace grounds. Other regiments were sited elsewhere in the city, though none has yet been identified by archaeologists. The palatial houses of senior Fatimid officers were also defended by personal guards. Evidence from cities like Mosul in northern Iraq suggests that the tents of a large garrison could eventually have been replaced by houses, thus creating a new suburb with its own special markets and

Embroidered silk tomb-cover from Iran, late 10th century, considered by some scholars to be a forgery. This is an example of the richest fabrics produced in the Islamic countries at the time. (Mus. of Art, Cleveland, Ohio, USA)

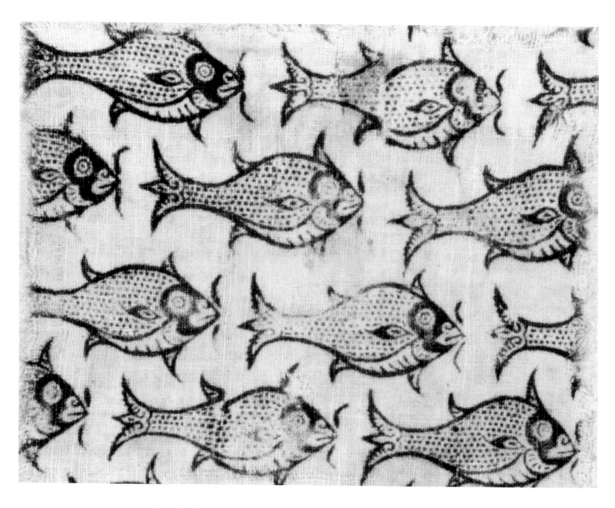

Printed cotton fabric from Fatimid Egypt, 10th–12th century. The technique of printing such large areas did not reach Europe for several centuries. (Mus. of Art, Cleveland, Ohio, USA)

other facilities. At the same time, even professional troops would gradually have acquired parallel civilian jobs.

Little is known of life within the *hujra* or barracks, but information from 10th-century Tarsus shows that some included their own armouries and workshops or even had shops underneath them and used the rents from these to support the volunteer soldiers who lived above. By the 14th/15th century the barracks of Egyptian *mamluks* had even developed as centres of literary endeavour, poetry and such, alongside the military training. In 11th-century Baghdad the most powerful officers lived in palaces overlooking the river, while over the road were barracks and mosques for their troops, and stables for cavalry horses.

Blocks of apartments and perhaps barracks which characterised great cities like Cairo had much in common with the towering tenements of ancient Rome. But most soldiers may have lived in private houses. This would be in keeping with the concern for privacy which lies at the heart of the Muslim way of life. Many ordinary city houses have been excavated by archaeologists, and, like Roman houses, they faced inwards, built around a courtyard. An extended family unit including several generations usually lived in one house and maintained close links with brothers, sisters, cousins, and clan or tribal members near and far. The *harim* or 'sacred area' was the women's domain, and the husband had his own room at its edge. The men of the house also needed a guest area for entertaining male visitors (women entertaining lady visitors within the *harim*). Family life was very close-knit, with business, education, entertainment and even amorous adventures taking place within a closed but extended family. The head of such a family might, like Usama Ibn Muqidh in AD 1154, find himself responsible for 50 people: men, women, his own and his brother's children, and various servants.

Marriage was a duty for a Muslim; not doing so for any reason other than health was sinful. The choice of a partner was generally left to the mother, a female relation or a professional female betrother. Cousins were seen as ideal spouses because their character would be well known, and such a marriage further strengthened family bonds. A man was permitted four wives, but it was considered better to have just one. The law insisted that each be treated exactly equally, even in the most private matters. Divorce was easier and certainly more acceptable than in Christian society and may have served as a counterbalance to an individual's initial lack of choice. Yet at the same time, Usama was shocked by the Crusaders' lack of sexual jealousy and by their lack of personal modesty.

Far from being isolated, Muslim women had access to public life – though the public world had no access to them. On at least two occasions the women of Usama's family seized weapons when Shayzar was attacked, and an 11th-century reference to a lady wielding great political influence 'because she won over the soldiers' wives' suggests that a soldier may have been something less than the master within his own house.

The bonds which kept the military classes together were quite distinct from family ties. *'Asabiyah* tribal solidarity was still strong, and played a very important role throughout the 12th century. It could link up with *'istina'*, the sense of obligation between soldiers and a 'patron' or commander who was seen as their foster father. In the 10th century the swearing of public mutual oaths of loyalty had been an important way of cementing the relationship between rulers, officers and men, but these were less important during the Crusader era. Gifts of clothes, arms, armour and horse harness enabled a leader to reward his followers, since status was shown by the richness of a man's dress and weaponry.

Medieval Middle Eastern costume was functional rather than formal; role, sex, religion and ethnic origin were indicated by the quality and colour of cloth and minor variations in the cut of clothes. The variety of dyes, patterns and fabrics was much wider than in medieval Europe, and elite troops wore magnificently distinctive dress, though not real uniforms. Professional Middle Eastern soldiers, though not North Africans, tended to wear Persian and Turkish rather than Arab costume when on duty. The most obvious items of dress were a double-breasted coat, a *hiyasa* belt incorporating decorative metal plates, and the *sharbush* stiff fur-edged cap with a triangular plate at the front. This could be replaced by a *qalawta* cap. In Saljuq Persia another elaborate cap for high-ranking military figures was the *dushakh*, which had a double-pointed shape.

Military jewellery ranged from the magnificent *hafir* or turban decoration of a ruler to the *siwarayn* or bracelets allowed senior officers and the *tawq* or necklace given to a successful commander. Ordinary officers wore what they could afford, and this, along with the fact that Muslim armies were normally paid in cash, explains the Crusaders' enthusiasm for stripping their dead foes.

Most cavalryman had only one war-horse, and a great deal of effort went into keeping it in peak condition. Mounts were normally tethered in an open air *mizalla* or paddock with a shaded shelter of palm leaves, but a surprise enemy attack could find the horses dispersed to pasture, as happened to Nur al Din in 1163. However, even a small castle like Shayzar had its *istabl* or stables for war-horses and pack animals. The animals were hobbled by three legs, rather than four as in Europe, and got their feed in nose-bags rather than mangers on the wall. Qualified staff, listed as military servants, looked after horse and harness, a stable-boy kept the place clean, a *sa'is* or groom looked after one or more animals and a *shaddad* or harnessman took care of the tack. A large stable might also have its own resident *baytar* or vet.

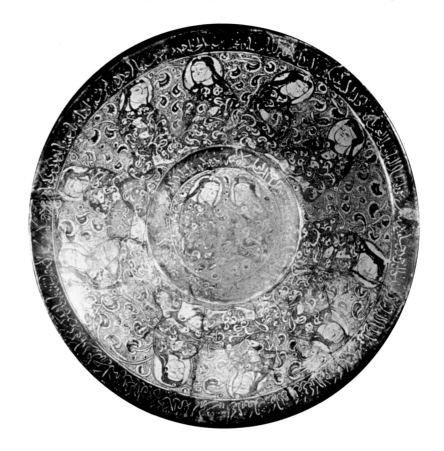

12th/13th-century lustre-ware plate from Iran. The potters of the Middle East learned much from China and then added their own techniques. Lustre-glazing gave pottery an almost metallic appearance. (Ashmolean Mus., Oxford, England)

Early 13th-century minai-ware bowl from Rayy in Iran. The man on the right carries a polo-stick in addition to his weapons. (Brooklyn Museum, inv. 86.227.60, New York, USA; photograph David Nicolle)

## MILITARY CAREERS

Known examples of military careers inevitably reflect the successful or literate elite, but in highly literate armies like those of the medieval Muslim Middle East, quite a lot of information survives about 'middle-ranking' soldiers.

The most detailed record of a 12th-century military career is that of Usama Ibn Munqidh, who was born into the long-established Arab warrior family which ruled Shayzar castle. At the age of 13 he saw his first Crusader assault on Shayzar. At 14 he began studying grammar, and at 21 he met a 'Frank' or Western European for the first time. Usama trained as a soldier, and witnessed a further four attacks on Shayzar, until at 24, the year his grammar tutor left, he took part in his first small battle against a Crusader force. At 31 his first surviving male child was born. At 35 Usama left Shayzar after quarrelling with the head of his family, and within a short time he enrolled in Nur al Din's army. Between the ages of 35 and 43 he took part in many campaigns against Crusaders, Armenians and fellow Muslims. Then he took service with the ruler of Damascus. At 49 Usama was entrusted with a diplomatic mission to Fatimid Egypt, after which he joined the Egyptian army and spent the next ten years fighting Crusaders in southern Palestine, going on diplomatic missions and getting caught up in the murderous politics of the declining Fatimid Caliphate. He then returned to Nur al Din whom he served for a further ten years, and eventually retired to the cultured Artuqid Turkish court of the Diyarbakir region where he concentrated on writing poetry, books of good advice and his famous *Mémoires*. At 79 Usama Ibn Munqidh was summoned back to Damascus by Saladin and became a respected teacher, supported by an *iqta'* 'fief' or estate near the town of Ma'arat al Nu'man. Usama died at the age of 93 – an astonishing age for the 12th century – and he was buried on the mountain overlooking Damascus.

On retirement a senior officer might be rewarded with the command of a town's police force or militia. Some were given low administrative ranks or simply retired to a frontier *ribat* for military volunteers. An injured or retired officer would normally lose his *iqta'*, but this could be replaced by a money allowance. The little information that survives about ordinary soldiers suggests that many retired as merchants, shopkeepers or owners of mule trains, while others became pillars of the religious establishment – even if only as local hermits. A certain Jawad, an expert swordsman in Shayzar, was met by Usama many years later:

> I saw him in Damascus. He had become a dealer in fodder and was selling barley and hay. He was old and looked like a worn-out water-bag, too weak even to keep the mice away from his fodder – much less keep away people.

The aged Usama wrote a poem on his own condition late in life:

> But now I have become like an idle girl who lies
> On stuffed cushions behind screens and curtains.
> I have almost become rotten from lying still so long,
> Just as the sword of Indian steel becomes rusty when left long in its sheath.
> After being dressed in coats of mail, I now dress in robes of fine fabric.
> Woe to me and to the fabrics!

## On Duty

The order of rank in 11th to 13th century Muslim armies varied and was flexible; individuals rose by merit and by luck from humble origins to the top echelons. One example was the 11th-century governor Anushtakin al Dizbari. He was a Turkish slave from Khuttal in Central Asia who took his name from his first owner, a Fatimid officer called Dizbar. After training in administrative and military duties, Anushtakin al Dizbari joined the Fatimid army, served in Syria and rose to become governor of Palestine around the age of 35.

Pay reflected rank, the status of the unit and the wealth of the ruler it served. Even so, soldiers generally earned more than skilled craftsmen – increasingly so up to the 13th century. In the Fatimid army, provincial garrison troops were paid directly by the Treasury in cash, as were soldiers listed according to their *hujra* barracks. Professional mercenaries were paid individually in cash by the government, while others received their pay via their officers. Such payments to the *jaysh* or army could have been every two, three or four months.

They generally seem to have been made at a special parade, and it is interesting to note that the Saljuq *Siyasat Nama* or 'Book of Government' strongly recommended a ruler to be present when his troops got their money so that he got the credit.

Smaller armies of the Fertile Crescent which emerged from the fragmentation of the Great Saljuq Empire were paid in a similar way. Regular soldiers in early 12th-century Damascus got a monthly *jamakiyah* or wage, and senior men were supported by *iqta'* fiefs as far afield as central Syria, central Lebanon and what is now southern Jordan. Nur al Din's *'askar* were not only paid but also equipped by him, though their weapons were kept in a government *zardkhanah* or arsenal to be distributed at the start of a campaign.

Payment in Saladin's army was similar to that of the preceding Fatimids and pay differentials between ranks could be immense. Junior recruits received little, but the biggest salary increases were from ordinary soldier to junior officer, and from high officer to men holding senior command. Professional cavalrymen also had a regular food allowance, usually as grain to feed their horses, and an additional payment was given at the start of a campaign, supposedly to cover additional active service costs.

A cavalryman's greatest expense was his war-horse, along with several cheaper baggage animals. The huge variations in price reflected the quality of animal: an ordinary horse in 12th-century Egypt was worth about three camels, a really fine-bred stallion 200 camels. A decorated harness could also prove expensive for officers. Although a soldier often received weapons free from the arsenal, their cost could be

The stables of Azraq castle in Jordan, built in AD 1236/7. (David Nicolle)

## TURKISH CAVALRYMAN.
## LATE 12TH CENTURY

(1) This figure has been given as many Turkish items of clothing and equipment as possible. He also wears his hair in the long plaited pigtail typical of tribal Turks. He wields a *latt* form of mace. The sabre was often carried using what would later be known in Europe as the Italian Grip, with the forefinger over the quillons. .

(1a) Detail of motif from woodblock printed cotton sash around waist.

(1b) Printed motif from cotton trousers.

(2a–d) Hypothetical exploded view of a sharbush hat based on later traditional headgear. Sewn segments of stiff felt with the upturned brim pronounced at the front (2a). Covering in red silk (2b) with a yellow silk 'button' on top. Fur lining (2c) only covering the brim. Peak decorated with a gilded and tooled leather 'plate' (2d).

(3) Interior of the shield showing the padded leather squab plus grip-straps

and a long guige to go around the neck.

(4a) Front view of the iron lamellar cuirass, laced to a felt jacket.

(4b) Rear view of the cuirass.

(4c) Detail of the interior of the jacket.

(4d) Three views of a single iron lame.

(4e) One simple version of lacing a lamellar cuirass using three laces for every row. The lower edging is here covered with a narrow strip of leather.

(5a) Decorated outer face of scabbard for a slightly curved sabre, without its bronze suspension points and chape.

(5b) Interior of one half of the scabbard. The outside would have a raised decoration, probably of gesso.

(5c) Sectional view of scabbard.

(5d) Fine leather covering for scabbard.

(5e) Undecorated inner face of the scabbard, with stitching to secure the leather covering.

(5f–h) Exterior, sectional view and interior of one bronze suspension point. These

consisted of two pieces riveted together.

(5i–k) exterior, section and bottom view of the bronze chape. This also consisted of two pieces of metal, apparently soldered together.

(6a) The blade of a slightly curved sabre.

(6b–c) Two halves of the wooden grip secured to the tang of the blade by rivets.

(6d) The upper rivet also secured a small bronze plate and a ring to which a wrist strap could be attached.

(6e–g) Inner, outer and sectional views of cast bronze quillons. These again consisted of two pieces of metal apparently soldered together.

(7) Exploded view of a *latt* form of mace, with a cast bronze head and wooden haft.

(8) Exploded and whole views of soft leather riding boots. These were buckled to a narrow belt beneath the tunic.

(9) Iron dagger and sheath worn in leg of right boot. (Christa Hook © Osprey Publishing Ltd)

deducted from his pay if they were lost. There is some evidence to suggest that troops also purchased their own equipment; this could range from a simple lamellar cuirass worth 'two sheep in autumn' to a senior officer's decorated military belt costing more than an ordinary soldier's annual pay.

Rulers might wear mail under their ordinary clothes as a precaution against assassination, but normal armour hung heavy on a man's shoulders and would only be put on just before going into action. The sequence for putting on cavalry equipment was basically the same as in Western Europe: first came a shirt or padded garment; then a mail hauberk and a cuirass, if worn; next came the sword-belt, a separate archery belt, a mace in its holder; then the shield and spear. Many Turkish warriors also seem to have hung amulets against the 'evil eye' from their body or weaponry. It was common to put a small dagger inside one's riding boot, and detailed evidence from two centuries later added a wooden spoon, a small leather bag for salt, a kerchief, a sharpening stone, eating knives, a comb in a case, a leather cup and a waterproof felt cape to the fully equipped cavalryman's kit.

Battles were infrequent, and the average Muslim cavalryman spent most of his time on other duties. A *tawashi* cavalryman in Nur al Din's army was expected to do a certain number of months' active service each year, though quite where is not known. While elite units would normally remain close to a ruler, this was not invariably the case. The *halqa* of Saladin's army was almost always near the Sultan, and the elite *jandariya* formed an Ayyubid ruler's guard in peace and in war. They also served as the Sultan's messengers, inflicted punishments and guarded arsenals and arms depots. *Jandariya* units could also garrison vital places in time of danger.

*Tawashis* first appeared as eunuchs in charge of military training, but by the 12th century they were an important cavalry force, usually stationed at the centre of an army and apparently never used as garrison troops. Under Saladin many *tawashi* elite horsemen appear to have been slave-recruited *mamluks*, while his *qaraghulam* or 'black *ghulam*' cavalry were of inferior status. The use of the term *qara* or black probably stems from the Turkish symbolic use of this word to denote low-born people of obscure origin as opposed to *aq* or white people of aristocratic birth – not black Africans.

Military reviews were central to a Middle Eastern soldier's duties. Men were drawn up for inspection in squadrons, 'alert and brave' and wearing their best if the ruler was to appear. In Fatimid Egypt the men often got special parade equipment from arsenals and treasuries, but observers also noted several cases of confusion, when troops did not know what to do or where to go, and they were sometimes given *madarij* papers explaining their precise position on parade. Reviews enabled troops to be assessed; the best were allocated to the ruler's own regiments, the average were sent off to garrison other cities, and the worst were used as provincial police.

More time was spent in tedious guard duties. In 11th-century Egypt the night garrison of the caliph's palace complex consisted of 500 cavalry and 500 infantry. Elsewhere the garrison of a 12th- or 13th-century city was responsible for guarding the wall, gates, citadel, parade ground and government offices. A strategic city like Mosul contained 1,500 cavalry and infantry in AD 1108/09, but other smaller towns to the north-west were garrisoned by just ten horsemen and an unknown number of foot soldiers. Garrisons also escorted merchant caravans between cities in areas infested with bandits.

## ON CAMPAIGN

Campaigns normally started in spring or autumn; late autumn and winter were unpopular as this was when auxiliary troops went home to plant winter crops. Winters could also be bleak and wet in Syria and northern Mesopotamia. Summer was often impractical because of the heat and dust, particularly in Iraq, and finding adequate drinking water for large numbers of troops could also be a problem in late summer. Many important operations were carried out by just a few hundred men, but in larger armies troops would be divided into tactical units, the smallest of which would have between 70 and 100 soldiers. On active service cavalry units of around 500 men were formed to mount an ambush, undertake reconnaissance ahead of the main army, form advance or rearguards or a banner-guard, protect the supply train or raid that of the enemy.

Marching was accompanied by military music from trumpets and drums carried on mules, and was used particularly in enemy territory to maintain morale. The later European tradition of military music clearly owed a great deal to that of the Ottoman Turks and their predecessors. A small army could cover 30 kilometres a day, which suggests that any infantry would also have been mounted. A large army

Among figures around the outer edge of this early 13th-century 'battle plate' from Iran are a retainer with a bow-case on his hip and a ruler carrying the animal-headed form of mace reserved for leading figures. (Freer Gallery of Art, inv. 43.3, Washington, USA: David Nicolle)

with a complete baggage train would not have covered such a distance since the train itself could include 7,000 merchants – from farriers for the horses to bath-owners for their riders – not to mention a field hospital.

Army doctors were expected to have an almost modern 'bedside manner' so as to reassure their patients; as Kai Ka'us advised his son in AD 1082:

> His person and dress must always be clean and he should wear pleasant perfume. When visiting a patient he must always look cheerful and untroubled, with pleasant words to encourage the sick. A doctor's heartening words to his patient increase the natural heat of his temperament [i.e. strengthen his powers of recovery].

Merchants of the *suq al-'askar* or 'army market' supplied food which soldiers bought with their wages. Little is known about what the men actually ate, though an interesting reference from 13th-century Turkish Anatolia mentions a soldier keeping an orange in his bowcase as a snack. Otherwise soldiers probably ate the same simple diet as other people, largely consisting of what is now called pitta bread, as well as assorted beans, dates, fruit, milk products, chicken and mutton. Vegetables were an essential and healthy part of every meal, for as the Arab proverb said: 'A table without vegetables is like an old man without wisdom.' Surviving medieval cookery books naturally reflect the tastes of the ruling elite rather than an army on campaign, but medieval Islamic cuisine was generally much simpler than the elaborate concoctions enjoyed by the European ruling classes. The following instructions for a simple egg dish come from a 13th-century Iraqi cookbook and could well have been a dish made in camp:

> Put some sesame oil in a frying pan. Celery leaves taken from their stalks are then chopped, added to the oil and fried. Then sprinkle over this sufficient amounts of cinnamon, mastic, coriander, and caraway. Next pour some vinegar into the mixture, as much as required, colouring with a little saffron. When the mixture has been heated, add a little salt then break the egg and add to it. Cover the pan until the egg is cooked and serve.
> (D. Waines, *In a Caliph's Kitchen*, London 1989)

The most vulnerable moment was considered to be the *nuzul* or 'halting' when an extended marching army congregated to set up camp. This was when elite cavalry units, however weary, had to watch for a sudden enemy attack. The camp itself consisted of concentric circles of tents round that of the leader, with guard-posts and a ditch around the perimeter. An elite cavalry unit would also be stationed up to a mile away in the direction of the enemy. The men were advised not to make fires as this attracted trouble, but if they were really cold they could dig a hole and light a hidden fire at the bottom.

## Battle and the Aftermath

Such caution inevitably influenced the conduct of ordinary soldiers. Most leaders realized that battles were won or lost in the minds of the combatants. Saladin, despite several defeats at the hands of the Third Crusade, never allowed his army to be destroyed, and eventually wore down his enemies so that the Crusade simply stalled. Even at the level of the common soldier, training emphasized checking thickets and hollows for potential ambushes while pursuing an apparently defeated foe. This was in stark contrast to the 'gung ho' behaviour of Crusader forces. In a full-scale battle, an identifying battle-cry was agreed before combat. The commander made his morale-boosting speech, usually of a religious nature, banners, probably associated with earlier Muslim heroes or Caliphs, were waved and men were ordered to stay close to their weapons until the fighting began. In general, Muslim officers showed great concern for the safety of their followers, as Usama again made clear during his first battle against a band of Crusaders:

وَكَادَ يَنْزِعُ زَرْعَ الْجِمَالَ النَّمِرَ وَأَنْشَدَ

الْحَجَ بَرَكْتَأْوَيْنَاوَأَدْلَجَا وَلَا أَعْيَانَكَ أَجْمَالًا أَجْدَأَ

The 'Freer Canteen', a large silver-inlaid bronze flask from the early 13th-century Jazira region, showing horse-armour. (Freer Gallery of Art, no. 41.10, Washington, USA; photograph David Nicolle)

They [the Crusaders] had been reinforced that night by sixty horsemen and sixty infantry. They drove us out of the valley and we retreated... Seeing us the Franks shouted aloud. Death seemed an easy thing to me in comparison with losing all those people under my command, so I turned back against one of their leading horsemen... and thrust my lance into his chest.

Theoretical works written for Saladin also emphasised the need to put only the best men in charge of assault troops or other important units. Military leaders were also warned not to neglect the interests of labourers and other non-combatants. The soldiers themselves were also reluctant to shed too much Muslim blood if they were fighting men of their own faith. Apart from religious considerations, late 11th/early 12th-century soldiers did not know who their future employer or ally might be and so wanted to avoid blood-feuds between families. On the other hand professional troops could fight even if their position was hopeless – just long enough to demonstrate their own military value before surrendering in the hope of being re-enlisted by the victor. On the other side, a commander should, according to al Harawi:

attempt to win over the hearts of [enemy] citizens, soldiers, officers and leaders by all possible means. He should communicate with them and offer the commanders and nobility whatever they want.

Tactics were the concern of the commander rather than the ordinary cavalryman. Although the Fatimid army relied primarily on infantry, in battle its heavy cavalry would be stationed behind the infantry, and light cavalry on the wings. Each cavalry squadron stood ready to charge through gaps in the infantry line which would open up, presumably when a signal was made. The horsemen would then try to strike the enemy in his flank, the cavalry in line formation, making limited attacks and withdrawals, with one unit replacing another so that none grew too tired. As al Tarsusi said in his military manual for Saladin:

> When it is the enemy's habit to charge en bloc and to rely on the shock impact of their detachments, as do the Franks and those neighbours who resemble them, this array is very effective because if one group of enemy attacks it can be taken in the flank and surrounded.

Syriac Gospels, mid-13th century, probably made in northern Iraq, showing the similarity between some Islamic military equipment and that of the European Crusaders. (Vatican Library, Ms. Syr. 559, f.135r, Rome, Italy)

On the other hand, the famous horse-archer cavalry of the Saljuq Turks suffered the most surprising reverses when pitted against early Crusader armies. By the late 11th century many Saljuq and regional armies had abandoned the old Central Asian tactics of dispersal and harassment, and reverted to time-honoured massed high-speed shooting by closely packed units of mounted bowmen. To be effective, however, this demanded a very high level of training, high morale and sophisticated logistical support, particularly to keep the cavalry supplied with arrows. The success of the First Crusade probably resulted less from a superiority of European armour and tactics than from a decline in military capabilities among the fragmented Saljuq armies.

Generally speaking, one of the most important roles of later 12th- and 13th-century Muslim cavalry was to separate an enemy from their baggage-train, and to pen enemy infantry against an obstacle and shower them with arrows while other units dealt with enemy cavalry. Selected marksmen could harass the foe before a general engagement – as was attempted at the battle of Arsuf in 1191. Tactical manuals suggested that sharpshooters try to bring down enemy leaders. Written records also show that an enemy's communications, as well as his morale, could be undermined by shooting or otherwise overthrowing his drummers or standard-bearers.

The Maristan or hospital of Nur al Din in Damascus, built in the late 12th century from the ransoms of Crusader prisoners. (David Nicolle)

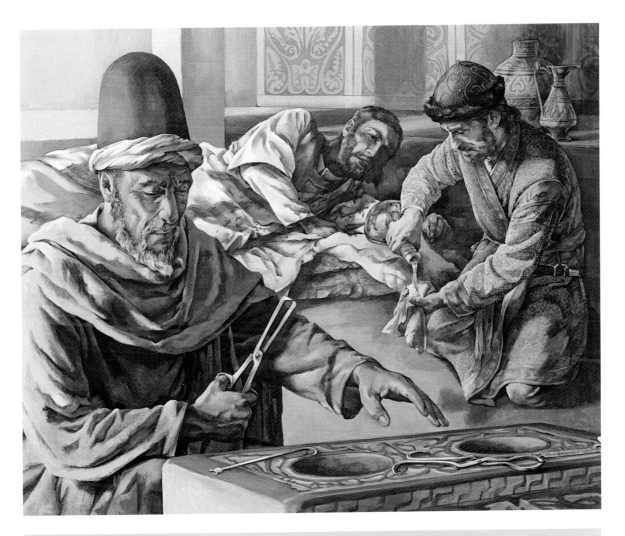

**TREATING THE WOUNDED**

'When they came near us I saw that the man in the middle had been struck across the centre of his face by a Crusader's sword... One half of his face was so loose that it hung over his chest and between the two halves was a gap almost the width of a hand-span... The surgeon sewed his face and treated it. The sides stuck together and the man recovered... He used to deal in beasts of burden and was thereafter nicknamed Ibn Ghazi The Slashed One.' (*Mémoires*, Usama Ibn Munqidh)

Muslim troops were fortunate in having far better medical backup than their Crusader opponents. Medicaments were mostly based on herbal extracts and distilled natural oils. Doctors or surgeons were highly respected professionals whose services were also in demand from the Crusader enemy. In fact the revival of medical science in Western Europe, mostly in Italy and Spain, owed more to what these countries learned from their Muslim neighbours across the Mediterranean than to any rediscovery of forgotten Roman or Greek medical knowledge. (Christa Hook © Osprey Publishing Ltd)

The dramatic power of horse-archers armed with composite bows should not obscure the fact that the weapon most feared by 12th- and 13th-century Muslim cavalrymen was the spear; horsemen were particularly reluctant to turn their back on an enemy so armed. Unlike the almost gentlemanly jousting by knights in High

Medieval Europe, the Muslim *faris* was trained to strike any vulnerable or exposed part of his enemy or his horse. Usama's *Mémoires* and fictional epics in Arabic, Persian and Turkish are full of cases where men struck each other in their unarmoured legs or wounded an opponent's horse in any way possible.

If a spear broke or a man was thrown from his saddle, he usually drew his sword. The last fight of Aibak al Akrash (one of Saladin's best men) near Acre shows how a soldier would struggle on in the hope of a comrade coming to his rescue. According to Saladin's biographer, Baha al Din, Aibak's horse was killed under him so he put his back against a rock and kept the Crusaders at bay until his quiver was empty. Then he fought with his sword until finally overwhelmed by sheer numbers. Baha al Din described the death of another Muslim champion, Ayaz the Tall, later in the same campaign: 'He dismounted to pick up his lance and was trying to remount his restive horse when the Franks swooped down and killed him.' The death of this hero was also recorded by the anonymous chronicler of Richard the Lionheart's Crusade, who commented on the Muslim champion's great spear: 'heavier than two of ours, to which he gave the name Aias Estog'. One wonders how the chronicler knew. Did the wounded Ayaz speak to his enemies before he died or was one of his comrades captured? Other references indicate that swords were generally unable to penetrate armour, though they could inflict appalling injuries on unprotected parts of the body; for this reason the armour-breaking mace was a popular weapon among Muslim cavalrymen.

Poets described the sound of an army at rest as like the waves of the sea, while the noise of battle consisted of the rattle of armour and harness, the clatter of swords, the crash of maces, the whistling of arrows, the twang of bows and the shouts of men. When it was all over, the men took off their armour, their eyes circled with dust, and, if victorious, set about sharing the spoils. *Ghanimah* or loot usually went to the unpaid volunteers. Other more specific, and probably more valuable, booty was divided according to a strict system of *fay*: one-fifth went to the commander to cover administrative costs, and the rest went to the soldiers – more to cavalry than infantry because of their greater expenses.

In the euphoria of victory, even elite Turkish troops could revert to the pagan practice of collecting enemy heads and dangling them from the saddles of captured horses as happened after the fall of Acre in 1291. Usama mentions a short-sighted Kurdish soldier named 'Annaz who came home with his own brother Badr's head as a grisly trophy, claiming that it was a Crusader he had slain. In reality he, like others, had been beheading corpses after the battle, and once the truth was known this man fled, never to be seen again. Sometimes enemy dead were left to rot or thrown down a well and covered with lime and earth.

Wherever possible the Muslims' own dead would, of course, be given a proper burial. This was to be done on the day of death, for as the Prophet Mohammed said: 'When any one of you dies, you must not keep him in the house but carry him quickly to his grave.' The body would be washed, its ankles or toes tied together, hands placed on the chest, wrapped in white cloth then placed in a grave on its right side with the face turned towards Mecca. Soldiers, it seemed, often carried their own shrouds on campaign.

Burial ceremonies were simple, in keeping with Islam's lack of pomp. Someone would remind the dead man's spirit of the answers he must give the angels Munkar and Nikar before entering Paradise. There were various beliefs about what happened to the dead man's soul: some said that it remained in the body until the morning after the burial; others thought that the souls of *jihad* martyrs slept in the crops of green birds which ate the fruits and drank the waters of the rivers of Paradise until the Day of Judgement.

Unlike medieval Christianity, Islam made no virtue of unnecessary suffering, and Muslim civilization developed the most advanced medical services seen before modern times. In the Aleppo citadel during Saladin's reign, there was a resident doctor on a fixed salary who was famous for his skill at amputations. (Generally speaking, Muslim doctors disapproved of drastic surgery unless absolutely necessary.) There was also special osteological equipment to deal with dislocated joints and fractured bones, ranging from rack-like frames for setting dislocated hips or shoulders to complex soothing ointments to reduce inflammation. Muslim doctors also performed complex operations using sophisticated surgical instruments such as saws, tongs, tweezers and drills. Cauterization was used to remove infection around wounds, to seal amputations and to remove tumours. The religious preoccupation with cleanliness must have helped reduce the risk of infection, but Muslim doctors also inherited knowledge of medicinal drugs from the Greeks, Romans, Persians, Indians and even Chinese, as well as making their own discoveries. Usama's *Mémoires* include stories of men recovering from horrific battle injuries with remarkably few cases of infection; included in these was the case of Numayr al 'Ahharuzi:

> The Frank struck him with a sword on the side of his face and cut through his eyebrow, eyelid, cheek, nose and upper lip so that the whole side of his face hung down to his chest... He arrived in Shayzar in that condition. There his face was stitched together and his cut was treated until he was healed and returned to his former condition, except that his eye was lost for good.

After a battle there would be prisoners. A strong sense of shared interest meant that captured Muslims would normally be well treated. Rulers and commanders followed the well-established tradition of generosity to defeated foes in the hope of turning them into supporters or allies. This did not normally apply to Crusader or Mongol prisoners; they would have to be ransomed if they were to escape slavery. The humiliation of prisoners was common, though mutilation was rarer. In 1157, for example, Crusader prisoners were paraded through Damascus in full armour, carrying their own flags and riding their own horses. Somewhat earlier Usama recorded how the Christians put out the right eye of a Muslim prisoner before exchanging him, so that he could not look around his shield in battle. On the Muslim side, Zangi cut off the thumbs of captured fellow-Muslim crossbowmen so that they could no longer shoot weapons that were considered particularly terrible.

## ARMS AND ARMOUR

Status was indicated by the quality or decoration of equipment and a man could be publicly rebuked for wearing a sword belt above his rank. Individual troops seem to have decided what their equipment should be, but they clearly had to have enough to pass muster on parade, and to be able to appear in light or full equipment depending on their duties. Elite warriors and champions had decorated arms, armour and horse harness, and guard units sometimes wore plumed head-dresses, enamelled or gilded belts, and silvered or gilded maces. Beneath such decoration Muslim cavalry kit had certain consistent features and there is little real evidence that they were lightly equipped. Indeed, Arab troops could have been mistaken for Crusaders until they were quite close. According to 12th- and 13th-century Syrian and Egyptian sources, basic kit was a helmet, a mail hauberk, leather or padded leggings, riding boots, sometimes spurs, a sword, a mace, an axe, a dagger, a small knife, a spear, sometimes a javelin, a shield and, for the wealthy elite, a lamellar cuirass.

Archaeological evidence suggests that one-piece iron helmets were made from the 8th century, and these may have been the *baydah* or 'egg' helmets. The earliest surviving so-called 'turban helmet' with its bulbous, pointed and often fluted shape

*Kitab al Tiryaq*, 'Book of Antidotes', Iraq AD 1199. Three men, perhaps a retired *amir* with two young Turkish retainers, find poisonous snakes in a water jar. (Bibliothèque Nationale, Ms. Ar. 2964, f5, Paris, France)

Painted ceramic bowl from Raqqa, late 12th/ early 13th century. Everything about the rider's equipment is typically Islamic except for his Byzantine-style shield. (Staatliche Museum, Berlin, Germany)

comes from the mid-14th century but pictorial evidence from Egypt and elsewhere suggests that it was known 200 years earlier. Segmented helmets of simpler construction were used, as were leather helmets. Although the mail *coif* was commonplace, mail aventails attached to helmets had long been popular and were adopted in Western Europe shortly afterwards. There is also evidence of masked or visored helmets in some Turkish areas by the 13th century.

*Dir'* or mail hauberks were usually worn beneath another garment, often two at a time. The quilted *jubbah* could contain a layer of mail the same as the hot and heavy *kazaghand,* a garment which spread to Europe as the *jazerant*. The *jawshan* or lamellar cuirass was more typical of Persian and Turkish than Arab areas, though it rose in popularity in Syria and Egypt in the 12th and 13th centuries. It could be made of hardened leather lamellae but was often of iron, clattering so loudly that it was considered unsuitable for stealthy warfare. Several references in Usama's *Mémoires* show that horsemen took the risk of removing their armour to make themselves faster or more agile. Carelessness could also lead to injury, as when Usama's father was in such a hurry that he failed to notice that his servant had

131

not secured one side of his *jawshan*; as a result a javelin struck him a nasty though superficial wound across the front of his chest.

The most important protection for a horseman was his shield. These varied from the large round *turs* to the elongated *tariqah* used by Crusaders, the smaller round leather *daraqah*, the spiral cane and cotton Turkish *kalkan*, the huge leather *lamt* of North Africa and the flat-based elongated 'Genoese' *januwiyah* used by infantry. In some regions shields covered in iron segments were used, but most were simply covered in leather or animal skins or painted.

The most striking offensive weapon was the recurved composite bow. Its shape and construction gave it a draw or pull equal to that of the much larger European longbow, but it could achieve twice the range – weight for weight. Unlike the simple longbow, the wood, horn and sinew construction meant that its pull started stiff but then eased out, reducing tension as the archer took aim. It also had much greater 'potential energy' at the moment of release than a European longbow; in other words much less of its power was lost as a result of drag, friction or the inherent inflexibility of the bow itself. From the 11th century the old Hun-style composite bow was gradually ousted by the newer Turkish form with its smooth rather than angled shape. This was slightly harder to draw, as it lacked some of the lever action given by the angled 'ears' of the old bow, but it gave a more efficient energy transfer when shot. It was also smaller and easier to use on horseback.

Muslim archers had developed a remarkable variety of highly specialized arrowheads for use against different targets. The 13th-century *Adab al Harb*' 'Art of War' by Fakhr-i Mudabbir stated that 'fish-backed' or 'ball-shaped' arrows should be used against mail or lamellar armour and most shields, the 'little spade', 'spinach', 'willow leaf', 'noodle' or 'duck's foot' against quilted soft-armour, an arrowhead of 'tempered steel' against a man in iron armour, and a 'course winged' or 'little spade' against an unprotected enemy. The rest of their equipment consisted of two spare strings for each bow and two thumb-rings for each string – more useful at long range as they tended to reduce accuracy at close range. The *nawak* arrow-guide was sometimes also used on horseback. It was a groove or channel containing a short *husban* dart the length of between a third and a hand's breadth. Groove and dart were pulled back together, and the dart was released to slide down the groove. The *nawak*'s great range and the virtual invisibility of its dart made it a useful sniper's weapon.

Almost all cavalry were armed with some form of spear, and various types of javelin were still used by fully trained cavalry in the later 13th century. A soldier's most prestigious and usually most decorated weapon was, however, his sword. Arab straight *sayf* swords descended from the Roman *gladius* continued to be used well into the 14th century – largely by infantry – as did a variety of longer, straight, double-edged cavalry swords. Quite when curved sabres were adopted by Muslim horsemen remains uncertain. The weapon had been developed in Central Asia by the late 8th or early 9th century and spread across most of the Muslim world in the wake of Turkish mercenaries, slave-warriors and conquerors. It remained more characteristic of Turkish troops than of their Persian, Kurdish or Arab comrades for several centuries.

Carved ivory plaque,
Fatimid Egypt or Iraq,
11th–12th century. Not
all hunting was done on
horseback, even by the
cavalry elite. (Bargello
Museum, Florence, Italy;
photograph David Nicolle)

Maces had been used for several centuries and those mentioned in Fatimid sources were up to one metre long. Al Tarsusi's treatise on weaponry lists various types, some made entirely of iron, others with an iron or bronze head that was 'toothed', flanged, smooth, cucumber shaped or consisted of rings. The mace seems to have had almost mystical significance for the Turks, probably stemming from the ancient Turkish paganism. The full equipment of a mid-13th-century Turkish champion was described in the *Danishmandname* by 'Arif 'Ali Toqati:

First of all he dressed in an embroidered shirt which was embroidered with gold.
Over this shirt he put on a coat of mail in which the links were of gold or were riveted with gold.
At his waist he belted a sword, a precious gift which even the Shah of Kashmir had not seen even in a dream.
He belted on also a quiver, Oh my beloved, one which only the Khakhan [pre-Islamic Turkish emperor of Central Asia] had power to see.
Next he placed his mace in its holder and on his arm he put a Chinese shield.
In his hand he put a spear so sharp that if it struck an enemy it shattered him to pieces.

The dagger was a more prosaic weapon, though regarded as versatile and as a last line of defence. The large *khanjar* was the most common and the slender *yafrut* was used only by Berbers. Another cavalry weapon was the *tabarzin* or 'war axe'. Other types, for use on horseback or on foot, were the *najikh*, which had a point or hammer at the back, and the somewhat obscure *durbash*. Tribal Turks and invading Mongols used lassos, and these were greatly feared even by highly trained professional Muslim cavalry.

Horse armour was known to Muslim cavalry during the early medieval and Crusader period and seems to have been more widely used than in Europe, at least until the 13th century. Early horse armours were usually called *tijfaf*, a word that reflected their felt construction though some incorporated mail, lamellar or scale defences as well as rigid protections for the horse's head.

### Manufacture and Maintenance of Equipment

The main arms industries of the Muslim world were located in forested regions on its fringes, close to iron-mining areas; most were far from the main centres of population and military power, but the great cities of the Middle East had arms bazaars where soldiers could buy equipment or have damaged kit repaired. Major campaigns led to acute shortages, with agents trying to buy weaponry far afield, and armourers at home working overtime. Great efforts were also made to recover the equipment of dead enemies. Usama described one of his *kazaghands* as being made from two mail hauberks, the longer one being of Crusader origin, the shorter of Muslim manufacture.

## HORSE HARNESS

(1) Arab horse harness developed from a fusion of the bedouin style and the traditions of the Mediterranean and Sassanian Iran. It was associated with what has become known as 'The High Islamic Riding School' which in turn contributed to medieval, Renaissance and modern European riding styles.
(1a) Detail of pattern from thick woven woollen saddle blanket.
(2) Bronze harness pendant.
(3) Bronze bridle attachment.
(4) Bronze trefoil strap linkage.
(5) A complete bridle consisting of leather cheek, brow, neck and chin straps, a broadened nose band covered with a panel of embroidered silk, a bronze curb bridle and a twisted scarf.
(6) The wooden saddle frame or 'tree' had a broad strap supporting the seat, two leather-padded wooden panels on each side of the horse's spine, and

attachments for breast and crupper-straps, and for girth and stirrup leathers.
(6a) Rear view of the cantle showing the 'tunnel' beneath the seat.
(7) Complete saddle with partial leather covering. Padded seat, tooled leather or embroidered fabric flaps, canvas girth, knotted stirrup leathers and bronze stirrups.
(8) The Turkish tribal horse harness was simpler. Here the saddle is removed but a shaped horse blanket is held in place by a secondary girth. The knotted tail and neck tassel are typically Turkish.
(8a) Simple Turkish bridle consisting of plain leather straps and an iron snaffle bit with long cheek-pieces or psalions. Separate leather collar decorated with pierced bronze medallions and a henna-stained horsehair tassel in a bronze holder.

(8b) Top view of the hinged mouth piece.
(8c) Detail of bronze buckle.
(8d) Detail of a bronze collar medallion.
(9) The wood-framed saddle was basically the same as that in the Arab saddle, though the pommel was typically tilted forward.
(9a) Rear view of cantle.
(9b) Front view of pommel.
(9c) Basic saddle with rounded leather skirt and cloth-covered leather flap.
(9d) Complete saddle including quilted fabric seat, decorative cloth panels front and rear, plain leather breast- and breeching-straps.
(9e) Detailed front and side views of silver-inlaid bronze stirrups for use with soft riding boots.
(9f) Detail of pierced bronze medallion used as a harness or breeching-strap linkage. (Christa Hook © Osprey Publishing Ltd)

The early 12th-century so-called *mihrab* or prayer niche from Gu Kummet, near Sinjar in northern Iraq, was probably a door. It is unusual in being decorated by carved niches including warriors armed with a variety of weapons. This form of decoration was based on Syriac churches and monasteries in northern Iraq, many of which had comparable carvings of saints and monks. (Nat. Museum, Baghdad, Iraq)

The military challenge of the Crusades, along with the willingness of Islamic civilization to learn and experiment, led to some strange weapons being invented, though most did not get beyond the prototype stage. Al Tarsusi in his book on weapons refers to several weird ideas, ranging from crossbows fixed inside shields to multiple crossbows inside revolving wooden frames. Some of these ideas resurfaced in southern Spain and Venice a century or so later.

Arab, Persian and Turkish smiths used early forms of decarbonized steel for their best helmets, swords and spears. There was a passionate interest in sword typology: scholars drew up complicated family trees to illustrate the relationship between various forms. The slender *qala'i* blade, for example, was two and a half fingers wide and four to five spans long, and the broader *salmani*, four fingers wide and four spans long. A surviving 9th- to 11th-century sabre excavated at Nishapur in Iran is, in fact, 3.5 cm (two fingers) wide and 71.5 cm (three and a half spans) long excluding the lost hilt.

Sword typologies also dealt with materials and whether they had been forged from a single ingot, built up of layers, cast in a mould or cut from a sheet. European swords were pattern-welded from hard but brittle 'male' iron. More flexible Asiatic blades of *fuladh* steel were made from soft 'female' iron treated and forged in various ways.

The first forging was done at a much higher temperature than was possible in Europe, being nearer to white-hot than merely red. Blades were then beaten from the steel compounds, and the resulting weapons were characterized by a beautiful surface pattern called *firind* – now known as 'watering'. Surviving examples contain much cementite (iron carbide) which makes metal hard but brittle. Other chemicals were also added during a process of alternate heatings and quenchings, and the result was a blade with the hardest metal along the cutting edge but which was also astonishingly flexible and virtually unbreakable.

The making of a complete sword and its accoutrements required the skills of a smelter, a forger, a smith, a temperer or sharpener, a hilt maker and fixer, a scabbard wood shaper, a tanner for the leather covering of the scabbard, a scabbard ornamenter, a chape-maker and a belt stitcher – probably in some sort of production-line. Indeed, surviving bronze matrices for making moulds to mass-produce parts of the hilt and scabbard have been found.

The manufacture of the composite bow was almost as complicated as that of a sword-blade. Various stages were influenced by the weather, and it could take one or two years to complete. Different types of wood, glue, horn and sinew were used in different regions, depending upon their availability and the climate in which the bow was used. For example, Far Eastern bowyers used bamboo wood, spinal sinew and fish glue, Central Asians ram-horn, Indians and Middle Easterners water-buffalo-horn and sinews from an animal's Achilles tendon. Bows also came in different sizes and strengths depending on whether the weapon was for hunting, training or war. The 13th-century *Adab al Harb* described the widely used Khwarazmi bow from Central Asia as having a short limb and long ear, and a thick bow-string of horse-hide. It was considered inaccurate and wobbly. The Parvanchi, Ghaznachi, Karuri and Lawhuri bows of Afghanistan and Pakistan were preferred by marksmen.

Most arrows were made from poplar or willow, the former being heavy for short range, the latter light for long range. Arrows made wholly or partly of reed gave the greatest range of all. Since arrowheads were of the tanged type a hole had to be bored in the shaft unless it was of reed. One 13th-century archery text specifies that a man's arrows should be as long as the distance between the top of his shoulder to the tip of his middle finger, or from armpit to the tip of the forefinger, or from elbow to elbow when the fists were held together.

Al Tarsusi's book on late 12th-century weaponry gives instructions on how to make hardened leather *jawshans* and *khud* helmets. Contrary to popular opinion, hardened leather was not 'boiled in oil', which would simply have made it softer, but

Crossbow mounted inside a shield. The crossbow incorporates an angled composite bow. (Bodleian Lib., Ms. Hunt 264, f.117, Oxford, England)

**OPPOSITE**
The Church of the Holy Sepulchre in Jerusalem, constructed by Emperor Constantine I (d. 337) over the reputed site of Christ's empty tomb, is the central shrine of Christianity. This is a 15th-century view of the church, with the Dome of the Rock behind. The artist has exaggerated the height of the buildings in proportion to their width, but the general design is reasonably accurate. Built by Caliph Abd al-Malik between 688 and 691, the Dome of the Rock was probably designed deliberately to mimic the Church of the Holy Sepulchre, hence the close resemblance between the two buildings. But whereas the central part of the Church is circular, the Dome of the Rock is octagonal. (BL MS. Egerton 1070 fol. 5: by permission of the British Library)

was treated in oil before being shaped in a mould where it was probably hardened and waterproofed with wax. Leather armours also lent themselves to decorative gilding.

Ordinary soldiers were responsible for the maintenance, repair and appearance of their kit; a man was expected to clean his mail in a noxious but effective mixture of ash, dung and oily sediment. He also attended to the rawhide or silk lacing system of his lamellar cuirass, checking for any rot, wear or holes and fixing minor problems himself.

OPPOSITE
A view inside the Aqsa
Mosque in Jerusalem.
Called 'the Temple of
Solomon' by Westerners,
the mosque was the
original headquarters of
the Templars, given to
them by King Baldwin II
of Jerusalem in 1120.
(David Nicolle)

# KNIGHT TEMPLAR

## INTRODUCTION

The Templars were religious men who followed a religious lifestyle based on prayer, and who also vowed to defend Christians and Christian territory against non-Christians. They formed a religious order, an organization acknowledged by the Catholic or Latin Church as having special rights and duties in society. Members wore a distinctive uniform, known as a habit, and lived a communal lifestyle in the properties belonging to the Order. They followed a Rule, approved by the pope, which set out their daily routine and lifestyle. The Templars' contemporaries saw them as skilled and fearless warriors who played a leading role in the defence of Christendom against its enemies. The Order was set up in 1120 and was dissolved by the pope in 1312.

The Templars began in the wake of the First Crusade. After Crusaders had captured the city of Jerusalem in July 1099, some warriors from Western Europe stayed in the city. One account states that a group of these warriors began to follow a religious way of life in the Church of the Holy Sepulchre, built on the reputed site of Christ's empty tomb, the most important shrine of the Christian faith. However, as pilgrims on their way to the Holy Sepulchre came under attack from Muslim bandits on the road to Jerusalem, these warriors decided that the new Kingdom of Jerusalem needed fighters more than it needed men who simply prayed. So they formed a military religious brotherhood and vowed to use their military skills to protect Christians. Military religious brotherhoods or confraternities were not a new idea: some warriors who had taken part in the First Crusade had formed brotherhoods to fight together and share booty, while in Western Europe military religious brotherhoods of knights had formed to protect monasteries from marauding bandits.

In January 1120 the little group of warriors went to the Church council at Nablus, which all the clergy of the Kingdom of Jerusalem attended, and asked for official Church approval for their new group. The clergy agreed, and the King of Jerusalem, Baldwin II, gave them his palace in the former Aqsa Mosque on the Temple Mount in Jerusalem. The Western Europeans in the Holy Land (known as 'Franks' to the Muslims) called this building 'The Temple of Solomon', and so the new group became 'the Order of the Temple', and its members were called Templars. To be a true religious order of the Church, the group also needed the approval of the pope. This came in January 1129, at the Church Council of Troyes in north-eastern France.

The Templars not only defended pilgrims in the region conquered by the Crusaders, which the Western Europeans called Outremer ('the land overseas'), but also helped to defend the borders of the new crusader states against hostile neighbours, both Muslim and Christian. In the West, some rulers saw that the Templars could play a useful role in defending their territories too against non-Christians. So the Templars were given frontier land to defend in the Iberian Peninsula and in Eastern Europe. Other landowners, well away from the frontiers, gave land endowments to the Templars to support their work of protecting Christendom. So while the Templars' main military operations took place in Outremer and the Iberian Peninsula, all across

RIVAL MILITARY ELITES · KNIGHT TEMPLAR

Aerial view of Jerusalem from the east in 1917, showing the walled city. The city's size had changed little since the 16th century when the walls were rebuilt by Suleiman the Magnificent (1520–66). In the foreground is the Temple platform (Haram al-Sharif) with the Dome of the Rock in the centre and the Aqsa Mosque to the left. The Templars' buildings can be seen attached to the Aqsa Mosque and to the east of the mosque; these were demolished in 1938–42. (Bayerisches Hauptstaatsarchiv, Abt. IV: Kriegsarchiv. BS-Pal. 779: © Bayerisches Hauptstaatsarchiv)

what is now Europe Templars were running farms and engaged in commercial operations to raise funds to support their Order's work on the frontiers.

The chief officer of the Order was the master, who was elected by the brothers at the Order's headquarters in the East, called 'the convent'. As the Order's territorial possessions grew, the brothers developed a devolved structure. The Order's lands were divided into provinces, each with a manager called a 'grand commander' to oversee it. Within each province the Order's property was organized around 'commanderies' (or preceptories, to use the Latin term), each administered by an official called a commander. The typical rural commandery was effectively a large farmhouse where a few brothers could live, with perhaps a chapel and accommodation for travellers, and extensive farm buildings. The commandery acted as a central administrative base for the Order's property in a certain locality. Outlying properties, called *camerae* or chambers, might be let out to tenants or run by a single brother. The commander of each commandery was supposed to pay a certain portion of its annual income, called a *responsion*, to the provincial grand commander, who sent the money to the Order's headquarters in the East. The provincial grand commander would hold annual meetings called chapters – the usual term for a meeting of members of a religious order – at which the commanders would present their accounts and pay their *responsions*. The Order held general chapter meetings every few years, to which all the grand commanders came with the *responsions* from their provinces. These general assemblies also appointed new officials and passed ordinances. So although the brothers were scattered across Christendom, they kept in touch with headquarters through the system of chapter meetings, and also through regular newsletters sent from the brothers in the East to the brothers in the West.

The Order of the Temple was the first of the military religious orders set up to defend Christendom, but many others followed. After the Templars received official Church recognition in the 1120s the Order of the Hospital of St John of Jerusalem, which housed and cared for poor pilgrims in Jerusalem, also began to finance military protection for pilgrims. The Teutonic Order was founded in Acre in the late 12th century, while other military religious orders were founded in the Iberian

The Templars were entrusted with the care of fortresses in troubled areas of Christendom, where the ruler could not trust the secular lords; and they built fortresses of their own in order to protect their property. This is their fortress of Vrána in modern Croatia, showing the south-east tower and ditch. (Lelja Dobronic)

Peninsula and in north-eastern Europe. These organizations followed the Templars' original concept of serving God through fighting those who attacked Christians, and some of them followed the same religious rule as the Templars. The Templars also helped to inform Christians in Western Europe about events in the East and encouraged them to send aid and to support their fellow-religionists. Although they ultimately failed to save Outremer, through their military skill and dedication they prolonged its existence.

The Order came to an end in the early 14th century. After the loss of Outremer to the Mamluk Sultan of Egypt in 1291, the Templars set up their headquarters on the island of Cyprus, hoping to organize a new crusade. But in 1307 King Philip IV of France accused them of heresy and witchcraft. The charges were certainly false, but the Order fell victim to the French king's own financial and political problems. The trial of the Order was indecisive, and Pope Clement V announced that the charges were unproven, but the Order's reputation was so damaged that he dissolved the Order and gave its property to the military religious Order of the Hospital to carry on the Order's vocation of defending Christendom. In the Iberian Peninsula, where the military religious orders' vocation of defending Christian frontiers against Muslim attack was still very much alive, and with increasing Muslim piracy along the coasts, new military religious orders were set up using the property of the former Order of the Temple.

## RECRUITMENT AND ADMISSION

There were many different sorts of people in the Order of the Temple. Because the Order's central function was to protect Catholic Christians, the most important members of the Order were the warriors. The higher-status warriors were knights, who had received this status in some sort of formal or semi-formal ceremony. When the Templars first began, in 1120, the concept of knighthood was still fluid and many knights were not of high social status. But by the time the Order was dissolved in 1312 knightly status had become socially important in the Christian West, and only brothers whose parents came from knightly families were allowed to enter the Order as knights.

Warriors who were not knights were called *servientes* in Latin or *sergents* in French, generally translated as 'sergeants' but literally meaning 'servants'. They supported the knights on the battlefield, but not all of them were warriors. The same term was applied to brothers of the Order who did not fight but who served the Order as craftsmen or labourers.

The Order also had priest-brothers, who served the spiritual needs of the members, hearing confessions, celebrating mass, and praying. In Europe there were also some sisters. There were one or two nunneries under the Order's supervision, as well as some women called 'sisters' living near to or in male houses of the Order, who had made religious vows and followed a religious lifestyle, but who were segregated from the brothers of the Order. The role of these sisters was to give spiritual support to the warriors by praying for the work of the Order. They were

## CHRONOLOGY

| | |
|---|---|
| **1095** | First Crusade called by Pope Urban II. |
| **1099** | Jerusalem captured by First Crusade; Kingdom of Jerusalem established. |
| **c. 1119** | Knights connected to the Church of the Holy Sepulchre in Jerusalem found a religious brotherhood to fight Muslim bandits in Kingdom of Jerusalem. |
| **1120** | Clergy of the Church Council at Nablus agree that the new brotherhood is a valid religious order; brothers are given King Baldwin II of Jerusalem's palace in the former Aqsa Mosque: 'the Temple of Solomon', and become Templars. |
| **1128** | Countess Teresa of Portugal promises the Order of the Temple the castle of Soure on the Muslim frontier of Portugal. |
| **1129** | Council of Troyes; The Order of the Temple receives papal approval and the Latin religious rule of the Order is established. |
| **early 1130s** | Bernard, abbot of Clairvaux, writes 'In praise of the new knighthood' for Hugh de Payns, master of the Order of the Temple, to encourage the new Order. |
| **1131** | Templars given border stronghold of Granyena by Count Ramon Berenguer III of Barcelona. |
| **1134** | King Alfonso I of Aragon dies, bequeathing his kingdom to the Templars, the Hospitallers and the canons of the Holy Sepulchre. |
| **1136–7** | Templars established in the Amanus March, the frontier area north of Antioch in Syria (now Antakya, Turkey). |
| **1137** | Templars given extensive lands in Essex, England, by Matilda of Boulogne, Queen of England, niece of Godfrey de Bouillon and Baldwin of Edessa. |
| **1139** | Pope Innocent II issues 'Omne datum optimum', a papal bull containing a set of religious privileges for the Templars, enabling them to operate more efficiently. |
| **1143** | Agreement between Count Ramon Berenguer IV of Barcelona, ruler of Aragon, and the Templars whereby the Templars commit themselves to the war against the Muslims in Aragon in exchange for the gift of certain castles and lands. |
| **1144** | Pope Celestine II issues 'Milites Templi', a papal bull containing a set of religious privileges for the Templars; followed by the bull 'Milites Dei', giving further privileges, issued by Pope Eugenius III a year later. |
| **1147–9** | Second Crusade. |
| **1149–50** | Templars given the strategic castle of Gaza in southern Palestine. |
| **1153** | City of Ascalon (now Tell-Ashqelon, Israel) captured by the Franks of the Kingdom of Jerusalem. |
| **1163–9** | King Amalric (Amaury) of Jerusalem invades Egypt. |
| **1177** | King Baldwin IV of Jerusalem defeats Saladin at the Battle of Montgisard. |

The Templars' castle of Monzón, Huesca, in the kingdom of Aragon. The Order received the castle from Count Ramon Berenguer IV of Barcelona as part of the settlement made between the Order and Ramon when he became ruler of Aragon. The young King James I of Aragon was brought up here until the age of nine, when he left to form his own court. The Templars of Monzón resisted a royal siege from the end of 1307 until 1 June 1309, at the time of the trial of the Templars in Aragon. The outer fortifications of the castle were reworked in the 17th and 18th centuries. (Joan Fuguet Sans)

| | |
|---|---|
| **1179** | Saladin is victorious at the Battle of Marj Ayun and destroys the Templars' castle of Vadum Iacob in northern Galilee. |
| **1187** | Battle of **Hattin:** Templars lose their headquarters in Jerusalem. |
| **1189–92** | Third Crusade. |
| **1191** | Templars establish new headquarters at Acre (now Akko, Israel). |
| **1191–1216** | Intermittent war between Templars and King Leon of Cilician Armenia over the Amanus March. |
| **1204** | Fourth Crusade captures Constantinople (now Istanbul, Turkey). Templars are given some land in Greece. |
| **1217–21** | Fifth Crusade: campaigns in Palestine and Egypt. |
| **1218** | Templars and some Crusaders build Castle Pilgrim (now 'Atlit in Israel), south of Acre. |
| **1228–9** | Crusade of Frederick II: part of Jerusalem recovered by treaty, but not the Temple Mount where the Templars' original headquarters had been. |
| **1229–30** | King James I of Aragon captures Muslim-held Balearic Islands; his forces include Templars. |
| **1230** | Templars receive their first properties in Bohemia (now the Czech Republic). |
| **1233** | King James I of Aragon invades Muslim kingdom of Valencia; his forces include Templars. |

| | |
|---|---|
| **1237** | Templars are heavily defeated trying to recover their castle of Darbsak in Antioch from the Muslims of Aleppo (now Halep in Turkey). |
| **1239–40** | Crusade of Theobald of Champagne and Navarre. |
| **1240–1** | Crusade of Earl Richard of Cornwall. |
| **1240** | Templars begin to rebuild their castle of Safed in northern Galilee. |
| **1241** | Mongols invade Hungary and Poland, defeating the Christian defensive forces, including local Templars. |
| **1244** | Jerusalem falls to the Khwarezmian Turks. Palestinian Franks are heavily defeated by Egyptian forces in alliance with the Khwarezmian Turks at Battle of La Forbie. |
| **1248–54** | Crusade of Louis IX of France: campaigns in Egypt and Palestine. |
| **1250** | Crusaders defeated at Battle of al-Mansurah in Egypt and many Templars are killed. |
| **1260** | Mongols defeated by the Mamluks of Egypt at Battle of Ain Jalut. |
| **1266** | Sultan Baybars of Egypt captures the Templars' castle of Safed. |
| **1268** | Baybars captures Antioch. |
| **1270** | Louis IX's Second Crusade, to Tunis. |
| **1271–2** | Crusade of the Lord Edward of England. |
| **1274** | Second Council of Lyons discusses a new crusade, which never sets out. |
| **1289** | Sultan Qalawun of Egypt captures Tripoli (now Tarabalus in Syria). |
| **1291** | Acre captured by al-Ashraf Khalil, son of Qalawun: the end of the Latin Kingdom of Jerusalem. Templars evacuate Castle Pilgrim, Sidon and Tortosa (now Tartus in Syria) and move their headquarters to Cyprus. |
| **1302** | Templars lose Ruad (now Arwad) island, off Tortosa, to Sultan Al-Malik al-Nasir Mohammad of Egypt. |
| **1306** | King Henry II of Cyprus ousted by his brother Amaury de Lusignan, lord of Tyre. Templars support Amaury. |
| **1307** | Templars in France are arrested on the orders of King Philip IV. |
| **1310** | King Henry II of Cyprus returns to power and puts Templars on Cyprus under close arrest. |
| **1311–12** | Church council held at Vienne, France. |
| **1312** | Pope Clement IV abolishes the Order of the Temple in the bull 'Vox in excelso'. He issues the bull 'Ad providam', transferring the Order's property to the Order of the Hospital of St John of Jerusalem (the Hospitallers). |
| **1314** | Two of the leading Templar officers, James of Molay the master of the Order, and Geoffrey of Charney, commander of Normandy, are burned at the stake at Paris. |
| **1316/17** | Ayme d'Oselier, marshal of the Temple, and other Templars on Cyprus die in prison with other leading opponents of King Henry II of Cyprus. |
| **1319** | Order of Montesa established in the kingdom of Valencia. The new Order receives the property of the former Order of the Temple and of the Order of the Hospital in Valencia. The Order of Christ is established in Portugal, with the property of the former Order of the Temple. |

## AN ADMISSION CEREMONY IN THE 1280s

The ceremony takes place just after sunrise in the chapel of a commandery of the Order in north-western Europe, in the chancel, before the altar. Here three brothers are being admitted; fashionable young noblemen dressed in secular clothes, they are kneeling on the floor before the *receptor* or receiver, the local provincial commander of the Order, who is asking them questions to ascertain whether they can be admitted into the Order. The provincial commander, a knight-brother, is wearing the white mantle of the Order. In his hands he holds a small book containing the rule and statutes of the order, from which he is reading the questions that applicants must answer: Are they married? Do they owe anyone money? Are they anyone's serf, or slave? On his right is the chaplain of the commandery, who will recite prayers at the conclusion of the ceremony. On his left stand two sergeant-brothers as witnesses and assistants; one is holding in his arms two white mantles and a brown mantle, which the *receptor* will place around the newly admitted brothers' shoulders when they have given their vows. The walls of the chapel are richly decorated with scenes from the life of the Blessed Virgin Mary, a patron of the Order; the new brothers will be making their vows to 'God and Lady St Mary'. The Templars' chapels were always sumptuously decorated: as a Cypriot merchant commented during the trial of the Order, the Templars' churches were better decorated than those of any other religious persons in the world. (Wayne Reynolds © Osprey Publishing Ltd) never expected to fight; they followed a lifestyle like that of traditional nuns. In addition, there were various associate members, men and women, attached to the Order who made regular donations and possibly hoped to join the Order in the future, but had not taken full religious vows.

The vast majority of the Order's members joined as adults. The rule of the Order stated that children should not be received as members. Although some children were brought up within the Order's houses (for example, because their parents had died and entrusted their children to the Order's care), they were not obliged to join the Order when they grew up. The founders of the Order intended that only adult men who were able to fight should join the Order. Most men joined in their mid- to late 20s, but a significant minority joined in their teens, and a few joined as early as ten years old. At the other end of the age spectrum, some joined as old men, after a career as warriors and administrators in secular society. They would not normally fight for the Order, but ended their days peacefully in one of the Order's houses in the West. It was also possible for men to join the Order for a short period as 'brothers for a term' and then return to their homes and families.

The Templars' commandery of Arville, Loir-et-Cher, France. Many Templars were admitted into the Order in Western Europe, in the chapels of small local commanderies such as this one. They would then be sent wherever the Order needed them. (Joan Fuguet Sans)

The 12th-century circular nave of New Temple church, London, showing the tombs of noble knights who were associate members of the Order. Many nobles supported the Order by becoming associate members, and were received as full members on their deathbed. They made the Order a large donation in their will and were buried within one of the Order's churches. The circular design of the nave of New Temple church was based on the Church of the Holy Sepulchre in Jerusalem. This late 19th-century drawing, based on a photograph by J. Clerk, Q.C., shows the interior of Temple church before it was burnt out by incendiary bombs on the night of 10 May 1941. (T. Henry Baylis, *The Temple Church and Chapel of St. Ann: An Historical Record and Guide*, London: George Philip, 1893, frontispiece)

Every person who joined the Order had their own motives. It was rare for members to record exactly why they joined the Order, but sometimes it is possible to guess. The obvious and overwhelming reason for joining the Order was to help to protect the Christian holy places in Outremer. Christians believed that these were the places where Jesus Christ had lived, died and risen from the dead. So they thought it was essential that these sites be protected from non-Christians who, Christians believed, would defile them with their presence; and that Christian pilgrimage to them should be secure. As the Templars formed a religious Order, Latin Christians believed that service in the Order would wipe out sins and put a person right with God, so that on their death they could go straight to Heaven. In addition, death on the battlefield fighting the Muslims was martyrdom, and would win immediate entry to Heaven. As this was an era when life could be very short and uncertain, people in general were very anxious to ensure their wellbeing after death, even though they could do little to improve their circumstances in life. A glorious death on the battlefield, which would win them lasting fame, was better than an obscure death from sickness or starvation.

Many men who joined the Templars joined because they had been on pilgrimage to the Holy Land and seen the brothers fighting courageously against the Muslims, or because they had seen members of the Order travelling around Europe, preaching about the Order's work on the frontiers of Christendom and asking for charitable donations. Other events could prompt a man to make the decision to join.

Some men joined the Order to escape a difficult situation at home, for example after the death of a much-loved wife. In the early 1130s a French knight named Guy Cornelly, from the region of Dijon, joined the Order because his wife had been struck down by leprosy. He entrusted his wife and daughters to the care of the abbot and monks of Dijon, giving them his land to support them, and then went to Jerusalem to fight in the service of God until the end of his life. Other warriors might join as an act of penance for their sins when they were in fear of death: one medieval account stated that Gerard de Ridefort, master of the Temple 1185–89, had joined the Order when he was very ill in Jerusalem.

Other motivations were more mundane. Warriors joined the Order for a worthwhile career, if they had no inheritance or other means of supporting themselves. Members of the Order had the opportunity to exercise authority and win promotion, so that men of relatively poor background and low status in society could win considerable power and influence. To outsiders, life in the Order seemed very comfortable: brothers were guaranteed clothing and regular meals, by contrast with the uncertain life of many warriors in the secular world. At the trial of the English Templars in 1309, Brother Hugh of Tadcaster said that he used to be employed as key keeper (*claviger*) by the Order, and had asked to be admitted to the Order. Some men were drawn to join the Order because members of their family were already in the Order; others might join because their employer joined the Order and they joined with him as comrades or as servants. It is also likely that some men joined because they wanted to travel and to see the holy places.

It was not to the Order's advantage to admit men who might change their minds when they had actually experienced life within the Order, and so the Order's Rule specified that an applicant to join the Order should not be admitted immediately, but should wait for a time while the brothers assessed his motivation, and while he

The fortified commandery of St Eulalie de Cernon, Aveyron, France; a local centre for recruitment of personnel and production of food to be sold or exported to the East. Like other religious houses in the locality, the commandery was fortified as protection for the Templars and their tenants against local lawlessness. (Joan Fuguet Sans)

learned about the Order's Rule and regulations. Then, if he was found suitable and still wished to join, he could be admitted. However, because the Order frequently suffered heavy losses on the battlefields of Outremer, this regulation was soon abandoned, and applicants for membership who seemed suitable were admitted to full membership immediately.

In the early years of the Order the brothers would not accept men who had been excommunicated – cut off from contact with the Christian Church because of

The chapel of the Templars' commandery at Metz in Upper Lotharingia (or Lorraine) in the Rhineland. Templar commanderies usually had their own chapel, where the brothers could worship without disturbance from outsiders. Chapter meetings would be held in the chapel, as few houses had a separate chapter house. The chapel has an octagonal floor plan, possibly reflecting the design of the Church of the Holy Sepulchre. Alternatively, it may have imitated the palatine chapel built at Aachen for Emperor Charlemagne at the end of the 9th century. That building itself copied the church of San Vitale in Ravenna, built in the 6th century by Emperor Justinian to imitate Emperor Constantine I's ecclesiastical buildings in Constantinople. (Jochen Burgtorf)

their crimes – but outsiders saw the Order as a good place to reform criminal knights and actually encouraged them to join. Bernard, abbot of the great Cistercian abbey of Clairvaux in east-central France, who was a supporter of the early Templars, wrote in the 1130s that robbers, homicides and other criminals went to fight the Muslims in the Holy Land, and this was a double blessing: their neighbours were delighted to see them leave, and the Franks of the Kingdom of Jerusalem were delighted to have their help. Law courts in the West sent condemned knights to the Holy Land to fight in defence of Jerusalem: for example, in 1224 Pope Honorius III told the master of the Temple to receive a knight, Bertran, who had killed a bishop, into the Order for seven years to do penance for his crime. The presence of such men in the Order, who had joined not because they had a religious vocation but as a punishment for serious crimes such as murder, must have made for a discipline problem. The lists of penances included in the 'judgements' and customs of the Order include examples of brothers fighting between themselves, killing Christian merchants or stealing from Christians. The punishments given for these crimes in the Order's regulations – flogging and/or life imprisonment – seem severe, but were necessary in order to keep discipline.

Although it was against Church law to charge a fee for admission into a religious order, most religious orders expected applicants to make a financial contribution to their order when they joined. During the trial of the Templars, a few brothers said that they had paid a fee to join the Order of the Temple. This fee was a *passagium*, which was intended to pay the new member's expenses on his journey to the Holy Land – a similar fee was paid by men who joined the Order of the Hospitallers. One brother in England, Roger of Dalton, said that he had paid 60 marks, the equivalent of 40 pounds.

There was a set ceremony laid down for the admission of brothers into the Order. This was included in manuscripts with the Order's Rule, statutes, customs and judgements, and was used by brothers responsible for receiving new members. At the trial of the Order of 1307–12 it was alleged that the admission ceremony always took place in secret and at night, but many brothers stated that the ceremony usually took place at or after dawn. This could be a time of convenience – before the many duties of the day began – or a symbolic time, symbolizing entrance into a new life in the religious order. Some brothers said that no outsiders were present at the ceremony, but one English brother, Brother William Raven, stated that in addition to various Templars around a hundred outsiders were present when he was admitted. Admissions were generally conducted by the provincial commander and usually took place as part of a chapter meeting in the chapel of the local commandery. But any suitable room could be used: the English brother William of Scotho said that he was received in the dormitory.

Before the candidate for admission was brought into the chapter meeting, two or three of the older brothers talked to him about the regulations of the house, its work, its hardships and its discipline, to make sure that he was aware of what he was committing himself to. If he still wanted to join, they asked him if he had any commitments in the outside world: whether he were married, had promised to join a different religious order, whether he owed any money, whether he was physically fit; and they asked him to confirm that he was legally free. If he could confirm that no one had any claim on him, the admission could proceed.

The applicant for admission then came into the chapter meeting and formally requested to be admitted to the Order. The president of the meeting would explain to him that although to outsiders life in the Order appeared comfortable, he would have to obey orders, go where he did not want to go, and do what he did not want to do.

> You only see the outer surface. On the surface you see that we have fine horses, beautiful equipment, drink and eat well and have fine robes, and it seems to you that you would have an easy life. But you do not know about the harsh commandments underneath the surface…

The examples of 'harsh commandments' would reflect the applicant's station in life: knights would be told that they would be sent to far-off countries, but not necessarily the ones they wanted to see (such as Armenia instead of Acre), while sergeants (servants) were told that they would be given low-status jobs such as looking after the pigs. The applicant was warned that the only good reason for joining the Order was to escape the sinful world, do God's work and do penance for his sins. He would have to be a slave of the Order.

If he was still happy to proceed, the applicant was sent out of the chapter meeting to pray, and the brothers discussed his case. If they were willing to receive him, he was brought back in and again cross-examined on whether he had any outside commitments which might allow outsiders to make a claim on him after he joined the Order. He was warned that if he was found to have lied he would be evicted from the Order.

If his answers were satisfactory, he was asked to promise to 'God and St Mary' (the Virgin Mary), to obey the master of the Order, to be celibate and live without personal property, to keep the traditions and customs of the Order, help to conquer the 'holy land of Jerusalem', to never leave the Order except with the permission of the master and convent, and to never be 'in a place where a Christian could be wrongfully deprived of property'. When the applicant had promised all these things, the president of the meeting welcomed him into the Order and placed the Order's mantle on his shoulders, fastening the laces that held it on. At this point the applicant might also receive a woollen cord to tie around his waist as a symbol of chastity, and a soft cap in the style usually worn by religious men. The chaplain brother said a prayer, and the president and chaplain gave the new member the kiss of peace. While the new brother sat on the floor like a medieval pupil before his teacher, the president read out a summary of the rule and customs of the Order to him and told him to ask any questions that he might have. Finally he dismissed the new brother with a blessing.

After being received into the Order the new brothers did not necessarily stay in the commandery where they were received, but were sent where they were needed. Brother Roger of Dalton was received at the Templars' house at Balsall in Warwickshire in 1305 and then sent to Denney in Cambridgeshire, where he was put in charge of a 'grange', an outlying farm under the jurisdiction of the commander at Denney. In contrast, Brother Robert de la More, a knight received into the Order at Temple Dinsley in Hertfordshire in around 1304, was sent overseas to Cyprus.

Not all those admitted to the Order were sent to the military front in the East. Many brothers were retained in the West to administer the Order's properties and accumulate the supplies needed to support the Order's operations in the East. This barn at the commandery of Temple Cressing in Essex, England, shows the scale of the Templars' huge agricultural operation in Essex. It would have stored grain produced on the Templars' estates, that could either be sold locally or exported by ship to the East. (Nigel Nicholson)

Probably new brothers who were already trained warriors were sent straight to Outremer, while those who were experienced administrators were kept in Europe to manage the Order's estates.

Each brother was allowed to have one squire, to help look after his horses and equipment, and to assist him on the battlefield. Some squires were employed by the Order, but some served in the Order unpaid as a religious service 'for charity' for a short period. Others were members of the Order who had been admitted as sergeant-brothers. The Order also employed mercenaries. The Order's regulations refer to *turcopoles*, lightly armed cavalry employed by the Order and under the command of an official called the *turcopolier*. Mercenaries would be employed as the Order required them and were paid at the current rate they would expect from any employer.

Although the brothers often fought alongside Crusaders, they were not themselves Crusaders. Crusaders took temporary vows, but members of the military religious orders took vows for life. Although if they could not settle in the Order they could ask their superiors to allow them to transfer to another religious order, they were expected to move to a stricter religious order. Any brother who ran away from the Order would be pursued, brought back to the Order and punished as a deserter from Christ's cause.

## BELIEF AND BELONGING

The Templars were all Catholic Christians, and followed the religious beliefs of their day, but because they were warriors rather than literary men, they wrote very little about themselves. To get an impression of their own beliefs we have to rely mainly on what other people wrote about them or for them. We can also consider the Templars' art – such as frescoes in their churches in Western Europe – and some of the evidence given during the trial of the Order, 1307–12. Because of the methods used during heresy trials at that time to ensure that the accused confessed to the accusations, the confessions made by the Templars in France would now be regarded as 'unsafe', and no modern court would accept them. However, information that they gave which was not a confession may be reliable, particularly when it is supported by other information from outside the Order.

This evidence shows that the Templars' beliefs were like those of the other knights in Western European society at the time: deeply held and straightforward. Although churchmen had traditionally doubted whether men who shed blood and killed others could please God and be admitted to Heaven, the warriors had no such doubts. Epic literature produced for reciting to warriors in the nobles' castles and halls depicts the role of the warrior in society as noble and glorious, and fighting as part of his duty to God. Indeed, fighting was depicted as being much more valuable to God than the monks' duty of praying, because warriors defended Christians and Christian territory and so, in a manner of speaking, protected God. According to this warrior viewpoint, when the Crusaders captured Jerusalem and the holy places in

The cult of St George was widespread in the medieval West. This 12th-century tympanum from the parish church of St John the Baptist in Ruardean, Gloucestershire, is a particularly fine example of veneration for this warrior saint, who appears to be wearing early 12th-century armour: a pointed helmet with nose guard, and a chain mail hauberk with broad panels to protect the legs. As they were drawn from a secular society that celebrated fighting for God, it is not surprising that the Templars also venerated St George. (Nigel Nicholson)

The Blessed Virgin Mary was held in great respect and love by Catholic Christians in the Middle Ages. Mary and her son Jesus were regarded as patrons of many religious orders, including the Order of the Temple, and many of the Templars' churches were dedicated to Mary. New brothers made their vows to God and to Mary, and the brothers kept chastity in Mary's honour. This is the statue of the 'White Virgin Mary' and Christ Child in the Templars' church at their commandery of Villasirpa, at Palencia in Castile, Spain. ( Joan Fuguet Sans)

the First Crusade they were recovering Christ's territory, as was their duty as Christ's warriors. The Templars' own Rule depicted the Order as a re-creation of knighthood, in which knights served God rather than their own interests: 'this religious order represents the flowering and resuscitation of the order of knighthood'. But in fact the knightly literature of the time indicates that many knights believed that they were already doing this; joining the Templars would be a way of taking a step yet further in virtue. When the brothers joined the Order of the Temple they took vows to 'God and Our Lady Saint Mary', the Virgin Mary, mother of Jesus. As medieval Christians believed that the Virgin Mary is queen of Heaven, they believed that, like queens on earth, she would intercede with the king (God) on behalf of his subjects. Outsiders gave donations to 'God, the Blessed Virgin Mary and the Order of the Temple', and many of the Templars' churches were dedicated to the Virgin Mary.

Like other medieval Catholic Christians, the Templars also venerated other saints. St George was important, as (according to legend) he was a military man who also served God, and he had been tortured and killed by non-Christians for refusing to give up his Christian faith. The Templars could have looked to St George as an example of how they should live their lives, serving God as military men and refusing to give up their Christian faith even if they were captured and tortured by the Muslims. The Templars had a statue of St George in the chapel of their castle at Safed in Galilee, which was destroyed by the Muslims after they captured the castle in 1266.

An important focus for medieval Christians was holy relics – physical remains of the saints. These could be objects that had belonged to the saint or parts of the saint's body. All religious orders collected holy relics, both as a focus for their own members' faith and also to inspire the faith of outsiders. The Templars also collected relics, such as (they claimed) the body of the great Greek saint Euphemia of Chalcedon.

The Templars would not have been very well educated, and would not have understood the complex theological debates that were then going on in the universities of Western Europe, but they knew some popular Bible stories. In England, in the third quarter of the 12th century, an anonymous cleric produced a translation of the Book of Judges in the Old Testament for the Templars to use. This tells how the children of Israel defended the Holy Land that they had captured with God's help. There is an obvious parallel between the situation described in the Book of Judges and the Templars in the Holy Land in the 12th century, defending the Holy Land that they believed the Crusaders had captured with God's help. Some other religious works were translated for the use of the English Templars, including an account of the coming end of the world. Medieval Christians believed that the world would end because of a figure called 'the Antichrist', the opponent of Jesus Christ. Some Christian writers believed that Mohammed, the great prophet of Islam, was the Antichrist. Some also believed that the Crusades and the recapture of the holy places in the First Crusade were part of the 'End Times' and the coming of Christ's kingdom. But before Christ could return, the Antichrist and his forces, the Muslims, must be defeated. Therefore the Templars, champions of Christendom against the Muslims, were in the front line of the war against the Antichrist and needed to be well informed on the subject. A poem about the Antichrist warned them that they would be persecuted and face great dangers, and that they must stand firm in their faith and believe that if they were victorious they would be rewarded by Christ.

All of you, hear my advice! Be of great heart and undertake boldly to do good, and God will help you. If you deserve the highest place, He will give it to you. May God grant through His grace that we may be among the first, but if not, at least among the last. Amen.

Modern veneration of relics: the relics of the martyr St Euphemia in the Patriarchal Church of St George, Constantinople (Istanbul). The relics are housed in a 19th-century silver casket covered in a white cloth decorated with red, as a symbol of martyrdom. To the left of the casket stands the icon of the saint. Behind the casket can be seen the magnificent iconostasis, dividing the nave of the church from the sanctuary, decorated with images of the Virgin Mary, Christ and the saints. Although this is a Greek Orthodox church rather than Catholic, the Templars' relics would have been similarly housed. (J. M. Upton-Ward)

We might expect the brothers to have produced their own history books to teach brothers about the history of the Order, to raise morale and encourage a community spirit within the Order, but they do not seem to have done so. Instead, some oral accounts of the Order's history and past glorious deeds circulated among the brothers. Friends of the Order told some anecdotes about the brothers' brave deeds, and during the trial of the Order some brothers referred to stories about the Order's beginnings. As the brothers were not well educated and were men of action rather than men of study, it would not really be surprising if they preferred to recite tales about the Order's history rather than read books about it.

Many of the stories told about the Templars indicate that the brothers believed that they were fighting for God, and that if they died in battle for God they would go straight to Heaven. In 1139 Pope Innocent II, setting out the religious privileges that the Order of the Temple would have (such as being able to build chapels and employ priests), wrote: 'Like true Israelites and warriors most equipped for divine battles, truly on fire with the flame of Christian love, you fulfil in your deeds that gospel saying: "Greater love has no man than this, that a man lay down his life for his friends"' – words echoed by many other popes after him. The martyr-saints venerated by the Templars, such as St George and St Euphemia, would have encouraged them to give up their lives in Christ's service. Outsiders, such as an anonymous pilgrim who was in the Holy Land sometime between 1167 and 1187, described the Templars riding fearlessly into battle and dying for Christ. Jacques de Vitry, bishop of Acre from 1216 to around 1228, told a story to encourage the Templars:

> You should always be prepared to shed your blood for Christ, that is to say, to lay down your lives for God with desire and the sword, following the example of a certain knight of Christ who when he saw the great number of Saracens, began to speak out of his great faith and the joy of his heart, and to say to his horse: 'Oh Blackie, good comrade, I have done many good days' work by mounting and riding on you; but this day's work will surpass all the others, for today you will carry me to eternal life.' After this, he killed many Saracens, and at last fell himself, crowned in battle with fortunate martyrdom.

It is difficult to know whether all Templars really did believe this. Probably not all were as determined as this, but stories like these and the saints that were held up as examples to the brothers indicate that they were encouraged to believe it.

Tempelberg church, near Lebus in north-eastern Germany. Bishop Henry of Lebus donated the tithe, or tenth of produce, from this church's lands to the Templars in 1244. The fabric of the church dates mainly from the 13th century, though it was rebuilt in later times. (Jürgen Sarnowsky)

Medieval religious artists loved symbolism and word play. A common example was the use of the symbol of a lamb with a cross to represent Jesus Christ, the *agnus Dei* (lamb of God). This fine example, showing the lamb lying down with two lions, possibly a biblical allusion, is from a 11th-century tympanum from the parish church of St Mary, Upleadon, in Gloucestershire, England. (Nigel Nicholson)

There were several occasions when the Templars' readiness to advance into danger looked like rashness to other Christians, and while martyrdom might have been a good spiritual move, in terms of military strategy it could be disastrous. Sometimes the Templars and the other military religious orders opted for the strategic, cautious approach – and were then criticized by Western commentators who thought that they should have been bolder.

The leaders of the Order apparently also encouraged a particular image of the Order. They claimed that it was especially responsible for the defence of Christendom, and if the brothers had to abandon their posts, the whole of Christendom would be destroyed by their enemies. This would have made the Templars more confident in themselves, but would have made them appear arrogant to outsiders.

The Order's seals showed various symbols that were important to the Order, such as two knights on one horse, a domed building, and a lamb. In the Middle Ages, when most of the population could not read or write, a seal was fixed to official documents instead of a signature, as a visual and physical sign that the document had been approved. The symbols on the Order's seals reminded members of the Order of its purpose, as well as advertising the Order's work to outsiders who had business with the Order, or saw the Order's seal in the course of their work. The problem with such symbols is that they have to be interpreted, and outsiders were not always sure what the symbols meant. The lamb was obviously 'the lamb of God', Jesus Christ, to whose service the Order was dedicated. The dome would have represented the dome of the Church of the Holy Sepulchre, the central shrine of Christendom where the first brothers of the Order had originally met and which the Order protected. But outsiders were not sure what the two knights on one horse represented: one contemporary wrote that it was a reminder that when the Order began it was so poor that the brothers could only afford one horse between two; another wrote that it represented the charity of the Order: one knight had rescued another whose horse had been killed in battle. The former seems more likely.

In their day-to-day lives, the Templars' distinctive habit, with the red cross on the left breast of the mantle, would have encouraged a feeling of identity among members of the Order. The surviving frescoes in their chapels in the West sometimes show scenes of warfare in the Holy Land, which would have reminded the brothers of the true function of their Order. Some of the Order's churches and chapels were built with a circular nave, a visual image of the circular central part of the Church of the Holy Sepulchre that would remind the brothers and outsiders of the Order's work in the Holy Land. Other military religious orders and returning pilgrims and Crusaders also built churches with circular naves as a symbol of the Holy Sepulchre.

The Templars' weekly chapter meetings in houses with four or more brothers would have fostered a sense of community, while the provincial and general chapter meetings enabled the leaders of the Order to keep the different parts of the Order in touch with each other. In the 13th century an official was appointed with overall command of the houses in the West, presumably to improve administrative efficiency; in the middle of the century this responsibility was divided between two 'visitors', who were to go around the Western houses, checking their procedures and practices. This would have encouraged the brothers in individual houses to see themselves as members of a larger organization.

The fact that brothers travelled between Outremer and the West should have encouraged a feeling of identity throughout the Order. In fact, by the early 14th century it seems that only a small proportion of the brothers ever actually went to Outremer, and some witnesses in the trial of the Order actually thought that brothers were sent to Outremer as a punishment, rather than to carry out the central purpose of the Order. As communications were slow and erratic, it must have been difficult for the leaders of the Order in Outremer to keep the brothers in the West accurately informed of military policy. In the Iberian Peninsula, where the brothers helped to push forward another frontier with the Muslims, and in Eastern Europe, where there were other non-Christians threatening Christian territory and where the Templars were often introduced simply to bring in colonists and cultivate unused land, the local Templars must have found it difficult to remember at times that their original vocation had centred on the far-off Holy Land.

**TOP**
Images produced by the Order: the lead seal of Brother Bertrand de Blancafort, master of the Temple, from a charter of 27 April 1168, showing two knights on one horse. Although its meaning was unclear, this was the best-known image of the Order. Outsiders variously believed that the image symbolized the poverty of the Order in its early days, or the brothers' charity in helping other knights on the battlefield. (Staatsarchiv Amberg, Kloster Waldsassen U 7/1; © Staatsarchiv Amberg)

**BOTTOM**
Reverse side of the same seal, showing the cupola of the dome of the Church of the Holy Sepulchre. This image was important for the Order because it had originally been set up by knights who had been lay members of the religious community at that church, and its overriding purpose was to protect the Church of the Holy Sepulchre as the central shrine of the Christian faith. (Staatsarchiv Amberg, Kloster Waldsassen U 7/1; © Staatsarchiv Amberg)

## TRAINING

The Templars' Rule, statutes and customs do not give any specific instructions about training. There are references to the master giving permission to the brothers to race horses or joust. The regulations warned brothers that when they jousted they should not throw their lances, because of the risk of injury. They were not allowed to hunt – traditionally a way of practising horsemanship – partly because it was a secular pastime and partly because of the risk of serious injury. The Order's regulations also refer to brothers riding out for pleasure, but the brothers' daily timetable, which was based on the monastic daily timetable first drawn up by St Benedict of Nursia for his abbey at Monte Cassino in Italy in the 6th century, makes no mention of military

**OUTSIDE A SMALL TEMPLAR FORTRESS IN OUTREMER, 1230s**
Two Templar knights, armed, mounted on horseback and carrying lances, charge each other in a practice joust. They wear no coverings over their chain mail, like the Templars in the frescoes in the Templars' church at San Bevignate in Perugia, Italy, painted in the 1240s. Their commander, dressed in the Templar knightly habit of white mantle over dark tunic, stands appraising their technique with a critical eye. Beyond the jousters, watching them with interest, stand two assistants: one sergeant-brother, in his dark habit, and one servant of the Order. Each holds upright in his arms, butts resting on the ground, a bundle of four spare lances for the jousters. The splintered remains of two broken lances lie on the sandy ground near the jousters, the result of an earlier joust. (Wayne Reynolds © Osprey Publishing Ltd)

training. Presumably the brothers were supposed to fit their military training into any part of the day when they were not occupied praying in chapel or attending a chapter meeting: for example, during the morning between the services of tierce and sext (at 9.00 am and midday respectively) or in the afternoon after the service of nones at 3.00 pm and before dusk.

This absence of organized training was the custom in the medieval West. It was not usual in the 12th and 13th centuries for commanders-in-chief in Western Europe to oversee the training of their troops; it was the individual's responsibility to

A 12th-century fresco from the Templars' chapel at Cressac-sur-Charente, France, showing a single knight charging on horseback with couched lance. Although the literature of the time took the skill for granted, effective handling of the lance on horseback in battle required daily practice. (Picture: M. Debès. Hurault phot., reproduced from *La Peinture murale en France: le haut moyen âge et l'époque romane*, by Paul Deschamps and Marc Thibout: Collection Arts et Historia, Éditions d'histoire et d'art, Librairie Plon, Paris 1951, p. 137, plate LXVII (1))

organize his own training. The Templars' regulations assume that brothers who entered the order as knights or as fighting sergeants would already be trained warriors, who would be practised in the use of the couched lance from horseback and in fighting with a sword from horseback and on foot, and who would have experienced military action in Europe before coming to the Holy Land to fight for the Order. The regulations imply that, as active warriors, the brothers would be eager to race their horses and joust, and that the master's responsibility was not to initiate such exercises but to regulate them so that they did not damage themselves or their horses.

The Templars' regulations also refer to their using crossbows, which could be fired from horseback or on foot. The Templars would have learned how to use these weapons before they joined the Order. Again, if they were to use them effectively in military action they would have had to practise in peacetime, but the Order's regulations say nothing about arrangements for such practice, only that the brothers used to bet 'on the draw of a crossbow'. Perhaps they were shooting at targets and betting on the outcome. The regulations tried to limit what they could wager, rather than forbidding them to bet altogether, implying that an outright ban would have been impossible to enforce.

The statutes of the Order do set out how the brothers were to march together and engage in battle, but do not state that the brothers should practise this before going into battle. Contemporary writers record the Templar warriors charging all together in a tightly packed *eschielle*, or squadron, against Muslim battle lines, breaking through them and scattering the Muslim forces to right and left, enabling the other Christian forces to follow them into the midst of the enemy. Conducting a charge in this manner, with horses close together, moving at the same speed and with precision, would require considerable practice. The fact that contemporaries commented on the Templars' charge, and that the Muslims feared their charge so much, indicates that they were well practised at it. Western knights were not renowned for charging in a tightly knit wedge and in a disciplined manner, so it seems more likely that this skill was learned after brother knights had joined the Order. It is uncertain whether repeated battle experience would be sufficient to learn

## THE TEMPLARS' DAY ACCORDING TO THE RULE OF THE TEMPLE

| Time | Service in Chapel (if house has one, otherwise hall) | |
|------|------|------|
| at night | Matins in chapel | Brothers to join in prayers<br>Brothers then go and check horses and equipment and speak to their squires<br>Sleep until dawn |
| c. 6am | Prime<br>Mass (or after sext) | |
| c. 9am | Tierce | |
| c. 12 noon | Sext<br>Mass (if not heard earlier) | Afterwards repair armour and equipment, make tent pegs, tent posts or anything necessary<br>Followed by lunch: knights sit at first sitting; sergeants at second sitting; clerk to read aloud while they eat<br>Go to chapel and give thanks: 'Go to their posts and do the best that God instructs them' |
| c. 3pm | Nones<br>Vespers for the dead<br>Vigils for the dead | |
| dusk | Vespers<br>Compline | Followed by supper<br>Followed by a drink<br>Check horses and equipment, speak to squire if necessary |
| dark | Bed | |

# GOD'S WARRIORS

Two bearded Templars playing chess, showing their dark woollen monastic-style tunics, soft religious-style hats and white woollen mantles, and the red cross on the left breast of the mantle. This image, from a manuscript of King Alfonso X of Castile's *Libro de Ajedrez, dados y tables*, shows the Templars as courtiers rather than as warriors. Templars in commanderies or on the frontier of Christendom would not normally have the leisure for board games. The Order's regulations specified that they should not play chess or backgammon. (Biblioteca del Monasterio de El Escorial, MS. T. I 6, fol. 25: © Patrimonio Nacional, Spain)

this manoeuvre, or whether the brothers would have practised their tightly disciplined charge along with their racing of horses and jousting, with the master's permission. The latter seems more likely, but we do not know for sure.

The Templars' leading members were knights, whose typical mode of fighting was on horseback and their typical weapons the sword and the lance. The Order's statutes refer only to mounted warriors in battle situations, implying that foot soldiers were of little importance to the Order. Those sergeant-brothers that were not armed could fight if they wished (presumably on foot), but no instructions were given for them in the statutes. The statutes state that the commanders could buy Turkish arms (presumably lighter than Frankish arms) to give to the craftsmen sergeant-brothers, which indicates that the ordinary sergeant-brothers could be expected to fight. But the statutes do not explain what their role would be.

A great deal of the Order's military activity consisted of fast-moving raids across enemy territory, in which mounted warriors had the advantage of speed and manoeuvrability: foot soldiers would have slowed down the raiding force. So it is possible that the Order made relatively little use of foot soldiers on the battlefield, instead choosing to mount its support troops as light cavalry and mounted archers.

## APPEARANCE AND EQUIPMENT

The Order's Rule of 1129 set out how the Brothers should dress when not on military duty. The emphasis was on practicality and simplicity. An official called the *drappier*, or draper, was responsible for ensuring that the brothers in the East were issued with the necessary clothes. Thirteenth-century manuscript illustrations show that the brothers' basic peacetime dress was similar to that of monks. They wore a long tunic of dark cloth or *cappa*, belted at the waist and reaching to their ankles, with tight-fitting sleeves. Some pictures show the tunic having a hood of the same dark cloth. On their heads they wore the dark-coloured soft cap that was typical of religious men in the period. They wore ordinary shoes on their feet, without any decoration or fashionable designs. A particular distinguishing mark of all male members of the order was that they wore a beard and kept their hair respectably short, although this was long by early 21st-century standards, covering their ears.

Over the long tunic the brothers wore a mantle, a light-weight cloak, also called the 'habit' as it was the distinguishing dress of brothers of the Order. Knights wore a white mantle, symbolizing purity. The sergeants wore a mantle of black or brown cloth. Because, as he and they believed, the brothers fought and died in the service

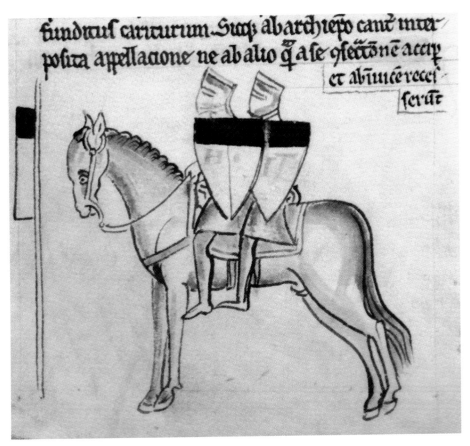

An outsider's view of the Order: two Templars on one horse, fully armed and showing the Order's black and white shield, with a black section above and white beneath. This drawing, based on the image on the Order's seal (see page 164), appears in the *Chronica majora* or 'Greater Chronicle' of Matthew Paris, chronicler of the abbey of St Albans in England. It represents the most common outsiders' view of the Order: religious warriors united in the service of Christ. (Corpus Christi College 26, p. 220: © the Master and Fellows of Corpus Christi College, Cambridge)

# GOD'S WARRIORS

A group of Templars on
the tomb of Don Felipe
in the Templar church
at the commandery of
Villasirpa (Palencia).
The carving clearly
shows their characteristic
beards, religious-style
soft, dark-coloured hats,
long, dark tunics and
white mantles with the
red cross on the left
breast. They appear
here as part of a noble
household, surrounded
by other members of
Don Felipe's entourage.
The presence of Templars
in many noble and
royal households was
a testament to their
reputation for piety,
integrity and efficient
financial management.
(Joan Fuguet Sans)

of God and to protect other Christians, Pope Eugenius III (1145–53) allowed them to wear a red cross on the left breast of their mantles, symbolizing martyrdom. They were not allowed to add fancy decorations to their mantles, but they were allowed to have their winter mantle lined with sheepskin for extra warmth.

Under their tunics, the brothers wore a shirt, which was normally of wool, but they were allowed to wear linen in summer because of the heat of the Middle East. Over this shirt, around their waists, they wore a simple belt made of a woollen cord, which symbolized chastity. They also wore breeches of woollen cloth, and woollen leggings or *chausses* on their legs. At night they were expected to sleep in their shirts, breeches, belts and shoes. Undressing completely would be a form of self-indulgence, a giving-in to physical comfort that was not appropriate for either religious men or for disciplined warriors. Religious men were not to pamper themselves, and warriors had to be ready to get up and fight at any moment of the day or night.

The Order's hierarchical statutes, dating from before the loss of Jerusalem in 1187 and perhaps from around 1165, list the armour that was to be issued to the knight-brothers. Under their armour they wore a padded jerkin or *haubergeon*, which itself acted as an additional layer of protection against enemy blows. Over this they wore a long-sleeved chain-mail hauberk with chain mail to cover the hands and with a chain-mail hood or *coif*. They also wore iron *chausses* (chain-mail leggings). Over their hauberk the knights wore a white surcoat, which kept the hot sun off their metal armour and allowed them to display the symbols of the Order, to distinguish them from other troops on the field of battle. In 1240 Pope Gregory IX wrote that the knights used to wear white *capae* or *cappae*, monastic-style tunics, over their armour, so this 'surcoat' was probably a *cappa*. Wearing a monastic tunic over their armour would enable the brothers to recognize each other on the battlefield and distinguish them from other warriors, but it did restrict their movements.

On their head, over the *coif*, the knight-brothers wore a helm or helmet – in the 1160s this would have been open-faced, but 13th-century manuscript illustrations and the fresco in the Templars' church of San Bevignate in Perugia, dating from the 1240s, show the Templars wearing fully enclosed helmets. Alternatively, they could have a *chapeau de fer*, or kettle-hat, a conical iron helmet with a wide brim to deflect enemy blows. Their feet were covered with chain mail. As with their 'peacetime' clothes, the Templars' armour was to be plain, without the gilding and decoration with jewels and precious metals that was common in this period. Unlike secular knights, they had vowed to give up personal wealth, and they were not fighting for their own honour but for the honour of God and their Order.

Their weapons were the standard weapons of Western knights in the period. They would carry a sword, the long broadsword of the period, and a shield. The fresco in the church of San Bevignate shows one Templar carrying a triangular shield, with the Order's white-and-black arms and a black cross (rather than the Order's usual red cross). Twelfth-century frescoes in the Templars' church at Cressac-sur-Charente in France show warriors riding out to fight wearing white surcoats over their armour with crosses on the breast and carrying kite-shaped shields. Because the shields show

This knight depicted on his tomb in the parish church of St Mary the Virgin in Bishop's Frome, Herefordshire, is believed locally to have been a Templar. In fact there is nothing in the effigy to support this theory. However, his armour is typical of the late 13th-century European knight, with the triangular shield and the long sword hanging from a leather sword belt around his hips, and this is the sort of armour that Templars of his day would have worn. (Nigel Nicholson)

various different designs it is not certain that these are all Templars, although the crosses on their white surcoats suggest that they may be. The brothers were also issued with a lance, three knives of different lengths (a dagger, a bread knife and a small knife) and a 'Turkish' mace. The lance, made from wood – ash wood was preferred, as it is both strong and flexible – varied in thickness and in length, but an average cavalry lance would be around four metres long (13 feet). The Order's regulations also refer to the brothers having crossbows and 'Turkish' arms other than maces, which had been captured in battle or purchased locally. As the Turks were fast-moving, lightly armed horsemen, presumably these were lighter weapons than their Western counterparts.

The Order's regulations contain no details about the crossbows that the Order generally used. We might guess that the brothers preferred to use the best weapons available, and that therefore by the late 12th century they would be using composite horn bows rather than wooden bows, as the former were lighter and smaller than the latter. The advantage of a crossbow over a simple bow was that it could be used effectively by a comparative novice and was much more powerful than the simple bow. In a siege situation, or where a large group of crossbowmen were operating together on a battlefield, the crossbow could be devastating, for it could pierce chain mail. But drawing back the string of a crossbow, locking it in place with a 'trigger' and placing the arrow or bolt in position, ready to shoot (the process was called 'spanning') was more difficult and time-consuming than drawing a simple bow. In the 12th and 13th centuries as crossbows became stronger, new and more effective methods of spanning them were developed: the crossbow was given a 'stirrup' into which the user could place one foot, while the bow string was held on a hook suspended from a belt around the user's waist. To span the bow, the user gripped the hook and pulled while pressing down with the foot in the stirrup. It is reasonable to assume that the knight-brothers and sergeant-brothers would operate crossbows in siege situations or when they had to fight on foot.

The Order's later regulations say nothing about the Templars' battlefield 'uniform', but in around 1240 Pope Gregory IX wrote to the Templars on the subject. Although the pope was no warrior himself, as God's representative on Earth (as the Latin Christians believed) he was responsible for the wellbeing of the Order, which was dedicated to God's service. He also had the authority to approve changes to the Order's regulations and customs, which included the armour that they wore in battle. In place of the *cappa*, which impeded their hands and arms and made them more vulnerable to their enemies, the pope allowed the brothers to wear a large supertunic over their armour, with a cross on the breast. It is not clear what this looked like, as the contemporary fresco in the Templars' church of San Bevignate shows the Templars without any coverings on their armour, but it was probably a sleeveless surcoat.

According to the Order's statutes, the armour of armed sergeant-brothers covered less of the body than that of the knights. Presumably they were given a padded jerkin to wear under their armour. Their chain-mail shirt had no sleeves, their chain-mail leggings had no foot coverings (so that they could walk more easily, and therefore fight on foot), and they wore a kettle-hat rather than a full helmet. They wore black surcoats, with a red cross on the front and the back. Their weapons were apparently similar to those of the knight-brothers, but as they were under the command of the *turcopolier* on the battlefield – who also commanded the lightly armed mercenary troops called *turcopoles* – they were presumably more lightly armoured than the knight-brothers, and would have ridden lighter horses.

The most important piece of equipment for a knight was his warhorse. Even though he might dismount to fight, the warhorse gave him status, speed, manoeuvrability, and extra height in battle. The Templars' rule and statutes laid down how many horses each brother was allowed to have; ideally a knight required more than one warhorse, in case his first was killed in battle, and he would also require a riding horse and pack horses. The knight-brother could have up to four horses: two warhorses (*destriers*), a riding horse (*palfroi*) or mule and a packhorse (*roncin*). He had at least one squire to assist him. The sergeant-brothers had one horse each and no squire, but sergeant-brothers holding military commands such as the under-marshal and the standard-bearer could have two horses and one squire to assist them.

# GOD'S WARRIORS

Frescoes from the Templars' church at Cressac-sur-Charente in France, showing fighting men. Those on the upper level date from the 12th century. They have crosses on their surcoats and may be Templars, although their shields do not carry the Templars' black and white arms but show various designs. Those on the lower level date from the 13th century and do not appear to be Templars, but show knights riding together in a tightly massed group as the Templars would have done. (David Nicolle)

A riding horse could be a gelding or a mare, but a warhorse had to be a stallion. The fictional literature of the 12th to 15th centuries suggests that medieval war-horses could be very tall, but the evidence of archaeology and medieval art indicates that in fact horses were not over 15 hands high (five feet to the shoulder), so that the knight would have stood shoulder to shoulder with his warhorse.

The horses' equipment, like the brothers' armour, was to be plain and undecorated, and the brothers were not allowed to adapt it to their own preference (for example, shortening the stirrup leathers) without permission. The Order's 12th-century statutes refer to the horses' bridles, saddles and girths, stirrups and horse blankets. Each brother and each squire was allowed one saddlebag, in which to carry their drinking cups, flasks, bowl and spoon and other personal equipment, as well as a leather or wire mesh bag for carrying chain-mail shirts. There is no reference to armour for the horses; this did not become common in any case until the late 12th century. The Templars' horses in the San Bevignate fresco, dating from the 1240s, have horse-coverings with the brothers' arms – black and white with red and black crosses – but they do not seem to be wearing metal horse armour. This would make them more vulnerable to enemy weapons, but also quicker on their feet than horses

174

weighed down by metal armour. When the Templars were arrested in Cyprus in 1308 and an inventory was made of their armour and weapons, the Order had armour for both men and horses.

The marshal of the Order had control over all the weapons and armour of the Order. All gifts, bequests and booty of this type were to be handed over to the marshal. Although much of the Order's equipment must have come from gifts and from booty, the Order also had workshops where equipment could be made. Brothers were not allowed to take things from these workshops without permission. The marshal also controlled the horses. The horses used by the Order in the East would usually have been the heavier Western European warhorses rather than the lighter horses used by the Muslims. When horses arrived from the West the marshal had to inspect them, and he was responsible for allocating horses where they were needed. Brothers were not allowed to request a particular animal, but they could return a horse that was unsuitable. The fact that the Order's statutes specify that the marshal could buy male and female horses suggests that the Order also bred its own horses, but whereas the Teutonic Order had organized stud farms there are only passing references in the Templars' statutes to putting horses to stud.

The brothers were responsible for the care of their own horses and weapons. They were not to exhaust their horses, and were to ensure that they were properly fed. They were not to try out their swords by hitting them against a hard object, such as an anvil, in case they broke, and they should not throw their equipment about, as it might be damaged or lost. If they lost a weapon they would be punished: section 157 of the Catalan version of the Order's Rule and Judgements tells how one Brother Marlí, who lost a sword and a bow through carelessness, was expelled from the Order. Similarly, a brother who killed, lost or wounded a horse or mule was in danger of being expelled from the Order 'at the brothers' discretion' (section 596 of the Rule). Although the Order had vast possessions in land, its expenses in equipment and personnel were very high, and it could not afford to lose money through carelessness and irresponsibility.

## LIVING CONDITIONS ON CAMPAIGN

In the peaceful West and away from the frontier with the Muslims, the Templars lived in houses very similar to contemporary manor houses, including various agricultural buildings, a hall, a dormitory where the brothers slept, lodgings for travellers who were passing by and perhaps a chapel. These houses were not enclosed like traditional monasteries, because the brothers had to come and go, overseeing their farms and other businesses, collecting rents and charitable donations for their work in the East. Brother Roger of Dalton spent his whole career in the Order administering a 'grange' attached to the Order's commandery of Denney in Cambridgeshire, England, and never attended any of the Order's official meetings. After the Order of the Temple was dissolved in 1312 he went to a monastery in the diocese of Ely. He then worked as an administrator for the Hospitallers, looking after their house at Ashley in Cambridgeshire, where he was still working 26 years later.

The chapel of the
Templars' castle of
Gardeny in the kingdom
of Aragon. The Templars
were given the site of this
castle in 1149, as a reward
for their assistance in the
Christian conquest of the
city of Lleida. The first
mention of the castle
they constructed there
dates from 1156. Gardeny
was not one of the castles
that defied the order for
the arrest of the Templars
in 1307, but some of
the Templars from
Gardeny joined the
rebels at Monzón.
(Joan Fuguet Sans)

On the frontier and in areas without a strong authority to keep law and order, the Templars lived in fortified buildings. Their castle at Vrána in Croatia is an example. On the frontiers with the Muslims they were given castles to garrison, such as the castles of Gardeny, Miravet and Monzón in the Iberian Peninsula and in Outremer Baghras, to the north of Antioch, and Safed in Galilee. They also built their own fortresses, such as Castle Pilgrim ('Atlit) to the south of Haifa in the Kingdom of Jerusalem. These fortresses would enclose the brothers' living quarters and chapel, so that they could carry on their religious lifestyle, but would also include military buildings such as stores for weapons and workshops. The fortresses would also require lodgings for mercenary troops and other warriors who were assisting the Order but who were not members. So that the brothers could carry on with their daily religious timetable without distraction, the living quarters would have to be arranged so that the Templars were segregated from the other warriors within the castle. The concentric castle design which the military religious orders and the Franks in Outremer began to use from the mid-12th century onwards suited the Templars well because it allowed them to have their own religious buildings in the central part of the castle, cut off from the rest of the garrison, who could be housed in an outer ward.

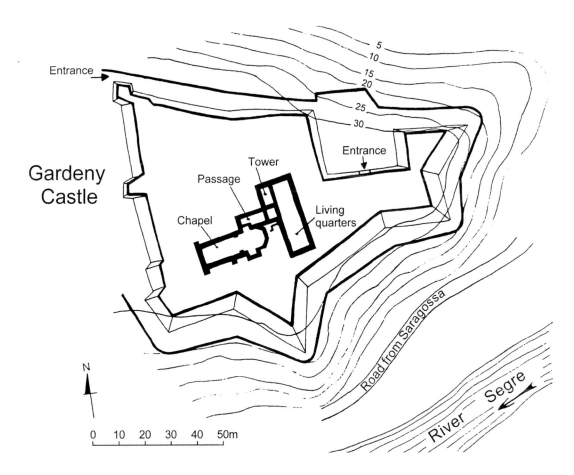

For the most part detailed figures for personnel in these castles have not survived, but in the 1260s a supporter of the Templars wrote a description of the Templars' rebuilding of their castle of Safed, which records that the peacetime garrison there totalled 1,700 persons, which rose to 2,000 in time of war. On a daily basis in peacetime, the castle required 50 knights, 30 sergeant-brothers, with horses and weapons, and 50 *turcopoles* with horses and weapons. There would also be 300 crossbowmen, 820 people involved in manual work and other duties, and 400 slaves – as this totals only 1,650, presumably these are rough figures. The garrison consumed over 12,000 mule-loads of wheat and barley annually.

Although the Templars produced a good deal of food on their estates in Outremer much of their grain would have been brought from the West. The Templars in Outremer imported large quantities of grain by sea from Sicily. The Order owned a few ships of its own, and also hired ships as and when they were needed.

The Templars' regulations, included in manuscripts of their Rule, laid down their daily timetable (see page 167). When they were not praying in the chapel they should be busy with some other useful work: seeing to their horses, instructing their squires, mending armour and equipment or making tent pegs. They were

Plan of Gardeny castle after a plan of the 19th century showing the buildings essential to the Order: the living quarters, chapel and a defensive tower, surrounded by concentric walls. The basic plan of the castle – upper enclosure containing the living quarters, surrounded by a concentric enclosure at a lower level – dates from the time of the Templars, although part of the upper enclosure wall and most of the lower enclosure wall were reconstructed by the Hospitallers in the 17th and 18th centuries. (Joan Fuguet Sans)

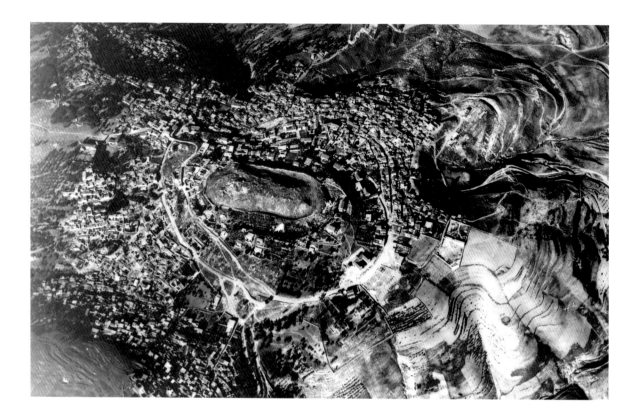

Aerial view of Safed castle in northern Galilee (now in Israel) in 1917. The Templars built a castle here in the 12th century. In 1188 it fell to Saladin after a long and bitter siege, and remained abandoned until 1240, when it was returned to the Templars in a peace treaty. The bishop of Marseilles persuaded the Templars to rebuild it. It fell to siege by Sultan Baybars in 1266 and the Templar garrison was massacred. The site is now a park with woodland, and the ruins can no longer easily be seen from above. (Bayerisches Hauptstaatsarchiv, Abt. IV: Kriegsarchiv, BS-Pal. 520; © Bayerisches Hauptstaatsarchiv)

expected to put their work down when they heard the bell ring for chapel, unless they were in the middle of an essential task that could not be left. They generally had two meals a day, one in early afternoon and one at dusk, with a drink before they went to bed; but in Lent and on fast days they had only one meal, in the middle of the afternoon. Unlike traditional monks they were allowed to eat meat at meals, as they had to keep up their strength for fighting. The Order's regulations mention the brothers eating beef, mutton, cheese, fresh and salted fish, bread and green vegetables, and drinking wine. From archaeological excavations of their properties in the Holy Land, such as the Red Tower, we know that they also ate pork.

Training would have to be fitted into their day at an appropriate point. They retired to bed when it was dark, sleeping two to a room with a light always lit, as was normal practice in monastic orders. They got up at night to attend the service of Matins in the chapel, but then went back to bed and slept until dawn. This meant that in winter they would have a long night's sleep, but only a short sleep in summer. Possibly, like traditional monastic orders, they had an additional sleep in the afternoon in summer (like the modern siesta).

The brothers had promised when they joined the order that they would not own any personal property, they would not have sexual relations with anyone, and they would obey orders given to them by their commanders. Daily instructions were handed out in chapel before services. If the order was clearly unreasonable the brothers were allowed to refuse to obey; otherwise they should say: 'De par Dieu' – 'for God's sake, I will do it', and go and carry out instructions. Although it would have been difficult for warriors who were used to organizing their own lives to accept the authority of another, the standard of living within the Order was better than that for most poor warriors of the time. Bishop Jacques de Vitry wrote about a man 'who never in his whole life in the outside world laid his head on a pillow'. He entered the Order of the Temple, and quickly became used to a life of comparative luxury. When he was without a pillow one night because the linen cover was being washed, he disturbed the whole convent with his muttering and complaining. Other poor brothers, said Bishop Jacques, got ideas above their social station after entering the Order and, given some ordinary task like guarding the gates, became very proud and took advantage of their post to insult visitors and passers-by.

By contrast, when they were out on campaign the brothers were expected to live a rough life in the field. The Order's statutes set out how the brothers were to behave when they were out on campaign.

The master of the Order was in supreme military command, but could not begin a war without the consent of the central convent: the senior officials of the Order and the military brothers at the Order's headquarters. But according to section 106 of the Order's statutes: 'the marshal of the convent shall call the brothers to arms and give them orders wherever the master is', and the brothers were not to start loading baggage for a campaign or mount themselves until they had heard his order given. When they were commanded to mount, they should mount and ride slowly with their troop, with their squires behind them, and take up their position in the line of march. The Order's standard-bearer or *gonfanier* would lead the Templars' forces, carrying the Order's piebald (black and white) banner. In Old French the banner was known as the *gonfanon bauçant,* which means 'the piebald banner'. The brothers rode at a walk or an amble, each knight with his equipment on his packhorse in front of him. At night they should ride in silence; during the day they could talk to each other, but should be careful to ensure that their packhorses were in front of them, so that they knew where their baggage was and did not lose it. They were not supposed to break the line of march to water their horses, unless they happened to pass running water in peaceful territory, when it would be possible to let their horses drink without breaking up the line. This was because if the army became divided during the march it would be in danger from enemy ambush.

Campaigning in the Holy Land had many problems. During the Third Crusade, the Crusaders discovered that the coast road south of Haifa had not been kept up, and was so overgrown with plants that neither foot soldiers nor horses could get past. The army had to take an upland route where the vegetation was sparser. In summer campaigns it was often difficult to find water, as the rivers dried up. It might be necessary to dig for some time into a river bed before finding good water. In contrast, the endless winter rain made armour rust and food rot, while pack animals

slipped in the mud and could not get up again. In addition to all this, there was the danger from enemy attack while on the march.

The Templars' and Hospitallers' discipline on the march made them a highly valued part of a Crusader army. During the Second Crusade, the French Crusaders marched across Asia Minor, through mountainous country, constantly harassed by Turkish raiders. The Crusaders suffered serious losses, but the Templars, who marched in disciplined order, were able to defend themselves. The Crusaders' leaders decided to put the Templars in charge of discipline on the march. Under the Templars' command, the Crusaders learnt to hold their position in the march and to stand firm if they were attacked. In 1191, during the Third Crusade, on the march south from Acre to Jaffa, the Templars and Hospitallers were put in charge of the vanguard and rearguard, the most dangerous positions for an army on the march.

When the time came to camp for the night, the *gonfanier* would decide where to set up the Order's camp, and the command would be given to make camp: 'Make camp, lord brothers, on God's behalf' (Rule, section 148). The chapel tent would be placed in the centre, with the marshal's tent, the tent where meals were served and the tents of other commanding officers. The brothers' tents would be pitched around these. Announcements were made to the brothers by a public crier, who camped next to the *gonfanier*. If the alarm were given because the Muslims had broken into the camp, the brothers near the break-in were to repel the enemy, while the other brothers were to go to the chapel to receive their orders. So, when the Muslims broke into the Crusaders' camp during the siege of Damietta in 1219, throwing the Crusaders into confusion, the Templars drew up their squadron and charged the Muslims, driving them out of the camp. Oliver of Paderborn, school master of Cologne, an eyewitness of the siege, wrote:

> The spirit which fell on Gideon stirred up the Templars. The master of the Temple with the marshal and rest of the brothers who were present made a charge through a narrow exit and manfully turned the unbelievers in flight... Thus the Lord God saved those who hoped in Him, through the virtue of the Templars and of those who worked with them and committed themselves to danger.

While in camp, or while in a castle in wartime, the brothers were not allowed to go out without permission, in case of ambush. Nor were they allowed to go out foraging or to reconnoitre on their own initiative. A lone horseman was very vulnerable to attack. Bishop Jacques de Vitry recounted an anecdote of a Templar caught in a Muslim ambush who saved himself by making his horse leap off the cliff road into the sea (the horse died, but he survived). Even a group of Templars together could be in danger of being overwhelmed by superior forces. During the Third Crusade, some Templars rode out as a protective escort for a group of squires who were cutting grass for horse fodder. They were ambushed by a larger Muslim force and almost overwhelmed. The Templars were able to hold off their attackers by dismounting and standing back to back to fight, each man covering his neighbour, but if they had not been rescued by a larger troop of warriors from the crusader camp they would all have been captured or killed.

**OPPOSITE**
The Templars in the East produced much of their own food from their own estates, and processed it for their own consumption. This is the Templars' mill at Da'uk, on the Nahr Kurdaneh or River Belus to the south of Acre, which ground the wheat produced on the Order's estates in the area for use by their headquarters at Acre. (Denys Pringle)

**CAMP SCENE DURING A TEMPLAR EXPEDITION INTO MUSLIM-HELD TERRITORY, 1240s**

The tents are arranged with the chapel tent in the centre and the knight-brothers' tents around the chapel tent. A priest-brother stands outside the chapel tent, talking to the marshal.

The marshal's tent is next to the chapel tent. The banner outside it is the banner shown in the fresco in the Templars' church of San Bevignate in Perugia, Italy, dating from the 1240s. The mess-tent stands beyond the marshal's tent: note the plume of smoke from the fire. Two Templar knights, companions and assistants to the marshal, check their kit in the opening to the marshal's tent. In front of the nearest tent, a Templar sergeant and his servant check his weapons and a sergeant-brother leads a warhorse whose coverings bear the Templars' arms. (Wayne Reynolds © Osprey Publishing Ltd)

The Templars' camp itself was not closed to outsiders, as the brothers were allowed to entertain other Christians in the army. The army could carry its own food in its baggage train, but the statutes also refer to gifts of food being made to the brothers by outsiders while they were on campaign. Careful arrangements were made to ensure that every brother received fair rations and no one went hungry. Left-overs were distributed to the poor. Two knight-brothers received the same as three *turcopoles*, and two *turcopoles* received the same as three sergeant-brothers. The rationale behind this seems to have been that those who were most heavily armed and of highest rank received the most food. But in any case they were not expected to eat everything that they were given, as the poor expected to be fed from what was left.

When the time came to move off from the camp site, the brothers could take down their tents and pack them up with their basic equipment, but should not start to load the baggage on to their horses or mount themselves until the marshal gave the order. Before moving off, they should check the camp site carefully to ensure that nothing was left behind.

When the brothers were going to engage in battle, the marshal would command them to form into *eschielles* or squadrons. Section 102 of the Order's statutes laid down that 'When they are established in squadrons, no brother should go from one squadron to another', unless they got separated from their original unit in the confusion of the fighting on the battlefield. They were not to break ranks or charge without permission; the only circumstance in which they could move out of line was to go to rescue a Christian from the Muslims. The *turcopolier* lined up his *turcopoles* and the sergeant-brothers in the squadron with the knight-brothers. The sergeant-brothers drew up in close formation behind the knight-brothers and should follow them, in support.

A depiction of a battle at Damietta during the Fifth Crusade, from Matthew Paris's *Chronica majora*. The Templars played an important role in the crusade. In battle they were first on to the field and last to retreat, and defended the rest of the crusader army if it was routed by the enemy. (Cambridge, Corpus Christi College MS. 16, fol. 54v: © the Master and Fellows of Corpus Christi College, Cambridge)

The marshal, as the military commander of the Order, would lead the Order on the battlefield, but if the master was present he would normally lead. A pilgrim who was in the Holy Land sometime between 1167 and 1187 described how the Templars engaged battle, all together and singing a psalm as a battle cry:

> Their bicoloured standard which is called the 'bauçant' (piebald) goes before them into battle. They go into battle in order and without making a noise, they are first to desire engagement and more vigorous than others; they are the first to go and the last to return, and they wait for their Master's command before acting. When they make the decision that it would be profitable to fight and the trumpet sounds to give the order to advance, they piously sing this psalm of David: 'Not to us, Lord, not to us but to your name give the glory', couch their lances and charge into the enemy. As one body, they rampage through the ranks of the enemy, they never yield, they either destroy the foe completely or they die. In returning from the battle they are the last and they go behind the rest of the crowd, looking after all the rest and protecting them. But if any of them turns their back on the enemy or does not act with sufficient courage, or bears weapons against Christians, he is severely disciplined.

The brother who broke rank, wrote this eyewitness, lost his mantle and had to eat on the floor with the dogs for a year.

Military brothers who ran away from the battlefield would be expelled from the Order, although non-military brothers who were acting only as support troops were allowed to retreat from the battlefield if they saw that there was nothing they could do to assist. Brothers who went over to the Muslims were also expelled from the Order forever. A slightly more lenient punishment was to take away a brother's habit. He could ask to have his habit restored to him after doing penance. A brother could lose his habit for striking another brother or another Christian, for threatening to desert to the Muslims, for killing or losing a slave, or for killing or maiming a horse. The same punishment was inflicted for undertaking an unauthorized raid against the Muslims, if it led to the Order suffering a defeat, with brothers dead and captured. A brother who was carrying the Order's banner in battle would lose the habit if he lowered the banner to charge, because the brothers followed the banner in battle, and if it were lowered it indicated that the Order had been defeated. Punishments could include beatings, and periods of fasting on bread and water. Brothers who had committed severe crimes would be put in chains and imprisoned, where they sometimes died. The Order's Rule includes a number of examples: one Brother Jacques de Ravane, commander of the palace of Acre, was put in prison because he made a raid on the Muslims without permission (section 610); while one Brother George the mason, who deserted to the Muslims and was brought back by force, was put in prison and died there (section 603). However, the Order never imposed a death penalty, nor condemned brothers to mutilation. As a religious order the Order would not shed the blood of its own members.

Brothers' offences were discussed and judgements decided in the weekly chapter meetings in each commandery. Serious cases were brought before the provincial chapter once a year; if they were very serious, they were brought before the Order's general chapter meeting, which met once every few years. The brothers were not allowed to discuss the decisions of the chapter meeting with outsiders. This was normal in religious orders, but may have annoyed the relatives of brothers who had been punished, when they did not know the full details. The Order's discipline helped it to win its military reputation, but some outsiders thought that it was unreasonably strict.

## EXPERIENCE OF BATTLE

The Franks of Outremer and the neighbouring Muslims maintained hostilities by frequent raids against each other rather than constant battle. Likewise in the Iberian Peninsula the Templars were generally involved in raids on Muslim territory rather than full-scale battle, which occurred only rarely. The brothers were also involved in the defence of fortresses, and in sieges of Muslim-held fortresses.

The Templars took part in raids or *chevauchées* initiated by the king or other secular lords, as well as organizing their own raids on enemy territory. On their own raids, they would often be joined by other Christian forces. The purpose of these was to terrify the enemy, to undermine the enemy's position and to enrich themselves by carrying off booty, such as cattle and sheep, and prisoners. Other expeditions were intended to intercept Muslim raiding parties and destroy them. Some raids were successful, but others were not.

Archbishop William of Tyre, in his history of the Kingdom of Jerusalem written between 1170 and 1184, described a raid against an invading Turkish force near Hebron in 1139. The raid was led by the Templar Master, Robert de Craon, and a secular knight named Bernard Vacher carried the king's banner. The Turks won a decisive victory. In the mid-13th century Matthew Paris, monk and chronicler of the Benedictine abbey of St Albans in England, recorded in his *Chronica majora* or 'Great Chronicle' and in his 'History of the English' an attack by the Templars and Hospitallers on the castle of Darbsak in 1237. This castle in the Amanus March to the north of Antioch had been held by the Templars before Saladin captured it in 1188. The Templars hoped to recover it, but rode into an ambush and were heavily defeated. According to Matthew Paris, the Templars had been warned of the ambush and some wanted to turn back, but the commander of Antioch, William of Montferrat, refused to take their advice. This account may or may not be true, but it gives us some insight into how military decisions were made in the Order: the commander of the expedition took advice from other brothers, but made the final decision himself.

Some raids were more successful. For example, the contemporary *Annales de Terre Sancte* recount that in June 1264 the Hospitallers and Templars went on a raid from Acre to the area of Ramla and Jaffa to recover the castellan of Jaffa, who had

**THE TEMPLARS' CAVALRY CHARGE, MID-13TH CENTURY**

Led by the marshal, carrying the banner, the Templars charge in a unit, so close together 'that an apple thrown into their midst would not hit the ground without touching a man or horse'. Lances are couched, shields across chests, legs braced in stirrups, body braced against saddle bow and reins released ready for impact. Immediately behind the marshal comes a group of five knights under the commander of the knights, who carries a second banner furled around his lance. If the marshal's banner should fall, he will unfurl his banner as a rallying point for the brothers. Behind them, half-concealed by the dust raised by the charging knights, the *turcopolier* waits with the Templars' sergeant-brothers. With them the rest of the Christian army waits in line, ready to follow the Templars into the breach in the enemy's lines: there is a squadron of Hospitallers, and squadrons made up of various Christian pilgrims from overseas. The different arms shown are hypothetical. (Wayne Reynolds © Osprey Publishing Ltd)

been captured by the Muslims. They raided as far south as Ascalon, where they encountered a Muslim force 300 strong, led by two *amirs*. They defeated this force, killing 28 of the Muslim warriors and the two *amirs*, and returned to Acre with much booty.

Not surprisingly, the Templars became involved in fighting while they were escorting Christian pilgrims around the holy places in Outremer. According to the pilgrim Theodoric, who was in the Holy Land between 1169 and 1174, the Templars and Hospitallers escorted pilgrims to the River Jordan and watched over them while they bathed in the river, in imitation of Christ's baptism in the Jordan. He also mentioned the Templars' castle of Quarantene nearby, and many other castles on the road from Jerusalem to Acre from which the Templars and Hospitallers guarded the road for Christian travellers. In around 1163 two eminent nobles from Poitou in western France, Geoffrey Martel, brother of the count of Angoulême, and Hugh le Brun of Lusignan, were on pilgrimage in the Holy Land. Having visited the holy places around Jerusalem they set out north to Antioch, with an escort of Templars led by the famous English nobleman Gilbert de Lacy, who had joined the Order of the Temple after a distinguished military career in the West. The party came under attack from the forces of Nur al Din, ruler of Damascus, but the Templars defeated the attackers and drove them off.

In battle the Templars, with the other military religious orders, acted as shock troops, charging in a compact body to break up the enemy's lines. One eyewitness account of the battle of Montgisard in 1177 described the effect of the Templars' charge on the enemy:

Odo [de Saint-Amand] the Master of the Knighthood of the Temple, like another Judas Maccabaeus, had 84 knights of his Order with him in his personal company. He took himself into battle with his men, strengthened by the sign of the cross. Spurring all together, as one man, they made a charge, turning neither to the left nor to the right. Recognizing the body of troops in which Saladin commanded many knights, they manfully approached it, immediately penetrated it, incessantly knocked down, scattered, struck and crushed. Saladin was smitten with admiration, seeing his men dispersed everywhere, everywhere turned in flight, everywhere given to the mouth of the sword. He took thought for his own safety and fled, throwing off his mail shirt for speed, mounted a racing camel and barely escaped with a few of his men.

The Templars' discipline and courage won them a great reputation both among the Muslims and in the West. In the early 13th century, Guiot de Provins, a poet turned Cluniac monk, wrote of them:

The Templars are most doughty men… it is the order of knighthood. They are in great honour in Syria; the Turks fear them greatly, they are like a castle or a wall against them; they will never flee in battle. Faith! So it would give me great grief if I entered their order, because I know that I would flee, I could never wait for the blows! I don't think I am crazy to say this, because they fight too fiercely. I will never be killed, if it so pleases God, for the sake of winning prestige or displaying boldness – I would much rather be a coward, and alive, than dead and the most esteemed man in the world.

9

3

2

1

7

6

8

5

10a

10c

10b

4

WAN.04

**KNIGHT TEMPLAR OF AROUND 1170**

The knight is dressed much as a European knight of the period would dress, except that his armour and weapons are plain and undecorated, for use rather than for show. His equipment is that laid down in the Order's statutes, compiled in around 1165, and carried by the knights depicted in the 12th-century frescoes in the Templars' church of Cressac-sur-Charente, France.

He wears a chain-mail shirt or hauberk (1) with long sleeves and handcoverings, and a chain-mail *coif* or hood covering his head and chin. The hauberk is slit front and rear so that he can ride a horse. The *coif* forms part of the hauberk. The front flap, the *ventaille* or 'ventilator' which covers the chin and mouth, can be untied for comfort, or laced closed above the left ear (2). In the detail, note the leather lace around the head to which the helmet is laced. On his head, over the coif, he wears a one-piece rounded metal helmet with a nasal piece to protect his nose (3). This is tied securely to the band around his coif with leather laces.

On his legs he wears iron chain-mail *chausses* or leggings (4) over cloth leggings. The chain mail laces up the back of his leg. On his feet he wears chain-mail shoes with iron spurs on his ankles (5).

Over his armour he wears a white woollen *cappa* with a red cross on the breast (6). The *cappa* is slit front and rear so that he can ride a horse. This *cappa* is based on the brief description by Pope Gregory IX in 1240, combined with the evidence from the frescoes in the Templars' church at Cressac-sur-Charente. The sleeves are tight-fitting and there is no hood. The correct position of the cross is unclear from the evidence. Archbishop William of Tyre recorded that the Templars wore a red cross on their mantles only; 13th-century pictures of Templars in their habits show the cross on the left breast of the mantle (that is, over the heart) and do not show the Templars' battlefield surcoats. The frescoes in the Templars' church at Cressac-sur-Charente show a cross on the right breast or the centre of the surcoat, or no cross at all; but in fact these knights may not be Templars. In action, a cross on the left breast would be hidden by the shield, but a cross on the right breast or in the centre of the chest would lose its symbolism because it would not be over the heart. In this plate the author has compromised by putting the cross on the left breast. It is possible that the Templars' battlefield *cappae* were pure white, without any cross.

This knight has a curved triangular shield slung across his shoulders, painted with the Templars' black-and-white insignia (7). The frescoes at Cressac-sur-Charente do not show this design; the earliest visual evidence of it is the drawings produced in the mid-13th century by Matthew Paris, chronicler of the Benedictine Abbey of St Albans in England. At this knight's left thigh, a sword is suspended in a plain leather scabbard from his plain leather swordbelt (8). He holds an ash-wood lance with an iron tip in his right hand.

Under his armour he wears a padded jerkin or *jupeau d'armer* (9) which covers his body, arms and upper legs. Under this he wears woollen breeches (10a), woollen leggings on his legs (10b), and a white linen shirt (10c). (Wayne Reynolds © Osprey Publishing Ltd)

Guiot summed up the problem that the Templars faced from their own side: they themselves were well disciplined and would not run away in battle, but they could not always rely on the rest of the Franks to support them. At the siege of Ascalon in 1153, according to an eyewitness account recorded in the Low Countries, the Templars were the first to break into the Muslim-held city. They fought their way into the central square and made a stand there, but the rest of the Frankish force failed to follow them and they were all killed. At the battle of Hattin (see Part One), according to a contemporary letter to the master of the Hospitallers in Italy, the rest of the Franks did not follow the Templars when they charged Saladin's army, and the Templars were surrounded by the Muslim troops and killed or captured. In a battle outside Acre on 4 October 1189, according to one contemporary writer, the Templars charged Saladin's forces, but went on too far ahead for the rest of the Crusader army to follow them, and were surrounded and cut to pieces. Another contemporary wrote that as he described their deaths he wept at the thought that so often the 'holy legion of the Temple' bore the danger of battle alone.

Although the shock of a well-judged charge could enable the Templars to defeat a numerically superior army, there was a limit to the advantage that discipline could give over numbers. At the Spring of the Cresson on 1 May 1187 a small force of Templars and Hospitallers was defeated by sheer weight of numbers.

A depiction of the siege of Damietta during the Fifth Crusade: attacking the city from boats on the river. Note the different weapons being used by the attackers: staff slings, bows and an iron flail. Water-borne assaults were as dangerous for the attacker as for the attacked: the Templars were involved in one such assault in which their ship ran aground and all aboard were drowned. From Matthew Paris's *Chronica majora*. (Cambridge, Corpus Christi College MS. 16, fol. 55v: © the Master and Fellows of Corpus Christi College, Cambridge)

On the battlefield, brothers were supposed to remain with the Templars' banner. Those who became cut off from the main Templar force and could not get back to the banner should join another contingent of the Christian army, such as the Hospitallers. Brothers who were wounded should not leave the field without permission of their commander. Yet occasionally the Templars' discipline failed. After a successful cavalry charge the squadron was supposed to re-form to charge again, but the Templars did not always succeed in re-forming their ranks. At the battle of Marj Ayun in 1179 the Templars, led by Master Odo de Saint-Amand, and the Franks under King Baldwin IV, charged some scattered groups of Muslims, catching them by surprise and dispersing them. Count Raymond III of Tripoli and Master Odo, believing that the battle was won, took up a position on a hill overlooking the battlefield, while the infantry plundered. Then Saladin arrived with his main army in battle order. The Franks were taken by surprise and defeated. The king and Count Raymond escaped, but Master Odo was captured and died in prison.

As the Templars normally formed part of any large expeditionary force against the Muslims in Outremer or the Iberian Peninsula, they were frequently involved in sieges of fortified cities and of smaller fortresses. Although raiding could wear down the enemy, only the capture of fortresses could win control of the land. Contemporary commentators described the Templars' leaders giving military advice during sieges, and the Templars taking part in assaults. Apart from the siege of

Ascalon in 1153, the Templars took part in the unsuccessful siege of Damascus in 1148, the unsuccessful siege of Harenc (or Harim) in 1177, the siege of Acre in 1189–91 and two sieges of Damietta in Egypt, 1218–19 and 1249. At Damascus and Harenc the defenders paid the Frankish besiegers to lift the siege, and the Templars were later blamed by Westerners for having advised the besiegers to accept the money rather than pressing on to take the fortress. The commander of the besieging force had to weigh up the costs of continuing the siege, and whether he had sufficient supplies to continue, against the advantage of finally capturing the fortress – and whether he would be able to hold it if he did so. In both of these cases it appears that the commander decided to cut his losses, and the Templars, with their extensive experience of warfare in the East, agreed with him.

At Acre in 1189–91, and at the siege of Damietta of 1218–19, the Templars played an active role in the besieging force. They built siege engines which could bombard the walls of the fortress. At Acre they were reported to have a *perière*.

A siege scene from an early 14th-century manuscript, showing a counterweight *trebuchet* about to be shot. The man on the far left is about to pull the rope which releases a key to shoot the weapon. The *trebuchet* is shown much smaller than reality. The Templars used a counterweight *trebuchet* at the siege of Damietta during the Fifth Crusade. (BL MS. Add.10294, fol.81v: by permission of the British Library)

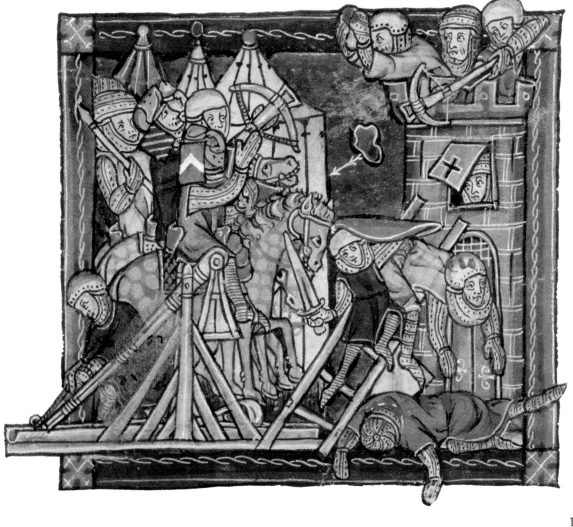

191

Technically this was a term for a traction stone thrower operated by several men giving a sharp tug on ropes attached to a pivot, but as it was described as causing considerable damage to the massive walls of Acre, it may have been a more powerful machine such as a counterweight *trebuchet*. At the siege of Damietta of 1218–19 they had a powerful counterweight *trebuchet* that had been given to them by the duke of Austria. Contemporary commentators do not tell us whether the Templars' own engineers – sergeant-brothers within the Order – constructed, maintained and operated these engines, or whether they hired engineers and workers to do this.

At the siege of Damietta (an important fortified port near the mouth of the River Nile) in 1218–19, the Crusaders prepared ships to cross the river and attack the walls of the city. One of the Templars' ships was caught in the current and thrown close to the enemy bank, where the enemy attacked it with grappling irons and Greek fire. The Templars on board fought back bravely, but at last the Egyptian forces succeeded in boarding the ship to fight the Templars hand-to-hand. The ship was holed – observers did not know whether the Egyptians or the Templars did this – and went to the bottom of the river, drowning everyone on board. Oliver of Paderborn wrote:

And just as Samson killed more dying than he had previously when alive, thus also these [Templar] martyrs dragged more with them into the whirlpool of water than they could have killed with the sword.

As owners of many fortresses, the Templars often had to defend their fortresses against siege by the Muslims. 'Imad al Din, Saladin's secretary, described the Templars' fortresses as impregnable and like lairs of wild animals. Although the Templars' castles in the Kingdom of Jerusalem fell to him, usually only after a long siege, in July 1188 Saladin was unable to capture the Templars' tower at Tortosa. Their castle of Darbsak in the Amanus March surrendered after a siege of 11 days, after Saladin's forces had mined one of the towers of the outer rampart. Baghras surrendered after a long bombardment. 'Imad al Din, who was stunned by the castle's strong position, was amazed that the Templars ever gave in, but Saladin's offer of terms – allowing the Templars to withdraw to Antioch in peace – had been a powerful incentive to surrender. In 1266 Sultan Baybars of Egypt persuaded the Templar garrison of Safed to surrender the castle with a similar promise of 'life and limb', but then had the defenders seized as they left the castle and executed.

The Templars did not always defend their fortresses to the death. If they judged that a fortress could not be held against a besieger and that there was no hope of relief, they would surrender it quickly. Archbishop William of Tyre described how King Amaury of Jerusalem (1163–74) entrusted a cave fortress in Transjordan in the Kingdom of Jerusalem to the Templars. When Nur al Din's general Shirkuh came to attack it the Templar garrison surrendered without waiting for relief, and the king hanged them as traitors. It is not clear why the Templars did not wait for aid to come.

When the Franks were defeated by the Muslims in battle, those left alive who failed to escape were taken away as prisoners. When the French Crusaders were defeated at Gaza in 1239, the scene depicted here, the Templars and Hospitallers were blamed for not giving more assistance to the Crusaders, despite the fact that they had advised the Crusaders against making their disastrous expedition. On the left, the Crusaders flee the field; on the right, captives are taken away to prison in Egypt. From Matthew Paris's *Chronica majora*. (Cambridge, Corpus Christi College MS. 16, fol. 133v; © the Master and Fellows of Corpus Christi College, Cambridge)

Baghras Castle, now in Turkey. The Templars were given the castle during the 1130s, but after a hard-fought siege they surrendered it to Saladin in 1188. Saladin had abandoned the castle by 1191, when it was taken over by Leon, ruler of Cicilian Armenia. The Templars tried to recover their castle, but Leon refused to give it up; the two parties did not make peace until 1216. In 1268 the Templars abandoned the castle as they knew that it could not be held against Sultan Baybars. (David Nicolle)

In 1268 when the Templar castle of Baghras came under siege by Sultan Baybars of Egypt (who had just captured the city of Antioch), one Templar brother took the initiative, went out of the castle and began to negotiate surrender terms. The experience of Safed had clearly taught the Templars that Baybars was not a general who would look kindly on defenders 'wasting his time' through a long siege. The commander of Baghras wanted to defend the castle and the brothers agreed with him, but the mercenaries said that they would leave, as they did not want to die. The commander and brothers discussed the matter and decided that they were very unlikely to be relieved because Antioch, to which they would normally have looked for help, had already fallen to Baybars. So they agreed to surrender the castle, but to destroy everything before leaving and go to the neighbouring castle of Roche Guillaume and repair it. The terms of surrender were agreed and they retreated, but they did not complete the work of destruction before their departure as planned.

Meanwhile, in Acre the master of the Order, Thomas Bérard, had heard that Antioch had fallen and Baghras was under siege. Knowing that the castle could not hold out and that he could not send relief, he sent a brother to order the garrison to surrender the castle and retreat to Roche Guillaume. When the messenger arrived he discovered that this was what they had done. But nonetheless the commander and brothers of Baghras were summoned before the Order's chapter meeting at the Order's headquarters in Acre, because they had surrendered before receiving the command to do so and because they had not destroyed everything before departing. The master and convent eventually decided that the commander and brothers of Baghras would not be expelled from the order for disobedience or for causing the Order loss, but they would have their habits taken away for a year and a day.

There were, then, occasions when even the Templars, brave warriors as they were, had to retreat. The non-fighting sergeant-brothers, if they saw that the brothers were losing and there was nothing they could do to help, were allowed to withdraw with the Order's equipment, so that it would not fall into enemy hands. The fighting brothers were not allowed to withdraw as long as the Order's banner was upright. Any brother who retreated before the banner was lowered would be expelled from the Order. The Templars were (as the anonymous pilgrim wrote before 1187) generally the last to retreat from a battlefield, and with the brothers of the other military religious orders they protected the rest of the Christian forces while they withdrew. Their casualties were always high when the Franks or the Crusaders were defeated. As in the case of Jacques de Vitry's story about the Templar and Blackie the horse, some Templars deliberately tried to become martyrs. A contemporary account of the aftermath of the battle of Hattin told how a Templar called Nicholas, who had been captured by the Muslims and was condemned to be executed with the other brothers of the military religious orders, encouraged the other Templars to meet their martyrdom bravely.

If they were not executed by their Muslim captors, Templars captured on the battlefield would be imprisoned awaiting ransom. Some contemporaries reported that the Templars would not pay ransoms, except for a belt and a knife, which seems to be a way of saying that fighting was their ransom and if they were captured they would die rather than pay. But by the mid-13th century the Order of the Temple seems to have accepted that it was best to ransom brothers who were captured in battle. The Catalan translation of the Templars' Rule states that brothers who had been captured should not wear their habits in prison, and if they were released they could not put their habits back on until they had spoken to the master – as if they ceased to be brothers of the Order through the shame of imprisonment.

Unlike the Hospitallers, the Templars did not have a large institution for the care of the sick and wounded, but they did have their own infirmary at their headquarters, where the sick and elderly were cared for. The infirmarer could give the brothers in the infirmary permission to have themselves bled (which was regarded as a cure for many illnesses), but they had to have the master's permission to have wounds treated or to take medicine. The Order had no medical experts of its own; if brothers were ill, a physician had to be employed to care for them.

When brothers died on the battlefield, the Order would try to recover the bodies to give them Christian burial, but this would not always be possible if the Order had been defeated. Brothers' graves were not necessarily marked; graves on Templar sites with effigies of knights are usually the graves of associate members of the Order. The Order would celebrate a service called 'Vespers for the dead' in chapel every afternoon at which the brothers prayed for the souls of dead brothers. When a brother died, a mass was said for his soul, prayers were said for the next seven days, and a poor person was fed with meat for 40 days, for the sake of the dead brother's soul. Prayers would be said and a poor person fed for the soul of any associate of the Order who died or was killed while serving in the Order. However, the Order did not promote any of its dead brothers as saints. All brothers were spiritually equal within the Order and none were honoured above the rest.

# CONCLUSION

The supposed military arrogance of the European knightly elite had already been blamed for the failure of the Second Crusade in the middle of the 12th century. While efforts were made to change this on a personal level, the unwillingness of Western European Crusaders to heed the advice of residents of the Crusader States continued. Meanwhile attitudes towards Crusading were already changing, with some European scholars now suggesting that the sword was not the best way to confront the challenge posed by Islam.

Another phenomenon which is, even today, widely unrecognized was the large number of Christian warriors who either served as mercenaries in Islamic armies or who converted to Islam and 'turned renegade' after capture. They included men whose lands had been overrun following Saladin's victory at Hattin, and even some members of the otherwise highly motivated military orders. Perhaps the widespread belief that the justice of the Christian cause could be proved by the sword was itself a double-edged weapon, convincing Christian knights, sergeants and others of the injustice of their cause through their own defeat in battle.

Saladin succeeded in defeating and almost destroying the Crusader Kingdom of Jerusalem. He then contained the massive threat posed by the Third Crusade. Thereafter it became almost an article of faith amongst the Islamic rulers, military leaders and peoples who lived around what remained of Crusader territory, that Saladin's successes were largely a result of his unification of the Crusader States' Islamic neighbours. In reality there was far more to Saladin's successes than this. Yet the idea of the overriding importance of *tawhid* or 'Unity' took such deep root that it remains to this day. *Tawhid* has constantly been invoked by Israel's Arab neighbours in their struggle to contain what they perceived as a 'Zionist threat' – even while the rivalries of Arab leaders tore the Middle East apart. More disturbingly, perhaps, the term *tawhid* is still invoked by groups of fanatics and extremists in an effort to justify unjustifiable actions. The word *jihad* has, of course, already suffered a similar fate in the vocabulary of the Western World.

**OPPOSITE**
The military history of Cairo is summed up in this photograph taken from the Muqattam Hill. Closest to the camera is 'The Army Mosque' built for Badr al Jamali, the Armenian commander-in-chief of the Fatimid armies in AD 1085 and still within a prohibited military compound. Beyond stands the great Cairo Citadel built for Saladin surmounted by the massive mosque of Muhammad Ali built in the early 19th century. (David Nicolle)

196

# APPENDICES

## APPENDIX ONE

### THE BATTLEFIELDS OF THE 1187 CAMPAIGN TODAY

Saladin's campaign of 1187 ranged over five countries – Syria, Lebanon, Jordan, Israel and Egypt, the Israeli-occupied sections of what may yet become a fifth country – Palestine – plus the Israeli-occupied portions of Syria. Nevertheless, most of the sites involved are quite easy to visit and the Horns of Hattin themselves lie next to an hospitable *kibbutz* which includes a first-rate hotel.

Tal 'Ashtarah and Tasil where Saladin's army mustered lie south of the little town of Nawa in the fertile Province of Dara'a south of Damascus. Unfortunately this is only ten kilometres from the Syrian–Israeli cease-fire line, within a UN-policed area which even Syrian citizens need permits to enter. These can be obtained in Damascus but can take several days. Busra, like all other regions, towns and castles in Syria, welcomes visitors. No part of Jordan is subject to permits though before trying to visit the spectacular cave-fortress at Ayn Habis it is advisable to check with the authorities as the caves actually overlook a sensitive frontier.

Four-wheeled drive vehicles are not necessary in Syria or Jordan though a car with good ground clearance is advisable when using unmade roads. Taxis are cheap and abundant throughout this part of the world whereas hire-cars are expensive. Local bus services are cheaper still but only link the main villages. Good hotels are found in Damascus, Dara'a, Irbid, Amman, Karak and Petra, adequate *funduqs* (small hotels for local travellers) being found in all small towns. Most of the Lebanese castles and cities involved in Saladin's campaign lie in the turbulent south of the country, and at the time of writing travel in this area could still be considered hazardous. Otherwise the same type of transport and accommodation are available as in Syria and Jordan. The same applies in Egypt except that a four-wheeled drive vehicle is strongly advised when one leaves the surfaced roads in Sinai.

The main sites of the 1187 campaign lie in Israel, occupied East Jerusalem, the West Bank and Gaza Strip. In Israel proper travel can, to the surprise of many Western visitors, be more difficult than in the neighbouring Arab countries. Most holiday-makers stick to the beaches or carefully sanitized visits to major archaeological sites. But those who go off the beaten track find settlements and small towns where strangers, other than those visiting relatives, are rare. While the main tourist centres have excellent hotels, the countryside lacks small hostelries comparable to the *funduqs* of neighbouring Arab countries. There are, however, camp-sites and *kibbutzim* which offer excellent though sometimes expensive accommodation. Political temperatures were high in the occupied territories at the time of writing but otherwise the same information concerning types of vehicle, public transport and accommodation apply as in Syria or Jordan. Saladin's army only transited the Golan Heights, though it camped for one night outside the now dynamited village of Khisfin. Unlike the other tense occupied territories, the Golan is quiet for the simple reason that the inhabitants were expelled at gunpoint in 1967.

The battlefield of Hattin lies at the eastern edge of *kibbutz* Lavi and is easily approached by a track which turns north off the main Haifa–Tiberius road (Route 77) just east of the Horns of Hattin. Almost all the villages that featured in the campaign were destroyed by the Israelis following the 1948 War and their

All that now remains of the village of Hattin, destroyed by the Israelis in 1948, is a minaret among the tangled bushes around Hattin spring. The Arab village itself is largely buried beneath the expanding Tiberius city rubbish tip from which this picture was taken. (David Nicolle)

The marshy area known as Al Qahwani (Cavan) to the south of Lake Tiberius, seen from Khirbat Aqaba on the Israeli-occupied Golan Heights. The town of Tiberius is some distance to the right on the far side of the lake. The old road which Saladin's army followed goes straight ahead to the flat lands where they camped on 27 June before crossing the Jordan. (David Nicolle)

inhabitants expelled. The people of Tur'an survived, however, as did those of Ayn Mahil overlooking what were the Springs of Cresson. Saffuriyah Castle is still there but nothing remains of the village except for fragments of houses amid the trees. Lubiyah now consists of scattered rubble overgrown with thistles and surrounded by the trees of a memorial park while Nimrin has also been obliterated. The tomb of Nabi Shu'ayb, however, has become a flourishing shrine for the Druze sect. In front of it stands a car-park laid over a rubbish tip which is itself gradually swallowing up the abandoned remains of Hattin village. To the south Kafr Sabt, where Saladin established his headquarters, has again been replaced by an Israeli settlement. Tiberius of course remains, though its main mosque now appears to be a storeroom for a neighbouring café. The so-called Crusader Citadel north of the old town is an 18th-century structure, but recent excavations to the south have uncovered what are believed to be a Crusader church and part of the walls of the original Arab-Crusader town.

200

# APPENDIX TWO

## MUSEUMS AND COLLECTIONS CONTAINING SARACEN ARTEFACTS

Muslims did not place artefacts in the graves of their dead. The Middle East has suffered many invasions that have destroyed or dispersed treasured relics, and modern archaeology has only recently begun to study Islamic civilization in detail. Consequently very little arms and armour survives from the medieval Middle East, and much of what does exist is in private collections. Where illustrated manuscripts and other pictorial sources are concerned, Western domination of the Muslim world during the 19th and early 20th centuries meant that many of the greatest libraries were pillaged. As a result, with a few notable exceptions, the finest collections are now in Europe, Russia and North America.

### Armenia
Yerevan: Matendarian Library (manuscripts)

### Egypt
Cairo: Bab al Nasr city gate (carvings)
Museum of Islamic Art (wood-carving, manuscript fragments, ceramics, metalwork, ivories, textiles, arms, armour, clothing)

### France
Paris: Bibliothèque Nationale (manuscripts, ivories, metalwork, coins)
Musée du Louvre (ceramics, metalwork, stucco, ivories, wood-carvings, stone-carvings, manuscript fragments, arms, armour)

### Germany
Berlin: Staatliche Museum Dahlem (ivories, metalwork, ceramics, stucco, armour)

### Iran
Isfahan: Archaeological Museum (archers' thumb-rings)
Tehran: Iran Bastan Museum (ceramics, wall-painting, metalwork, arms, horse harness)

### Iraq
Baghdad: National Museum
Mosul: Church of Mar Hudeni (carvings)

### Israel and Palestine
Jerusalem: Syrian Orthodox Convent of St Mark Library (manuscripts)
Franciscan Museum (grenades)
Rockefeller Museum (ceramics, manuscript fragments)

### Italy
Florence: Museo Nazionale di Bargello (ivories, metalwork)
Palermo: Cappella Palatina (painted ceiling panels)
Rome: Istituto di Studi Medievale Orientale (ceramics)

### Russia
Moscow: State Historical Museum (arms, armour)
St Petersburg: State Hermitage Museum (ivories, metalwork, ceramics,
    stone carvings, arms, armour, horse harness, textiles, clothing)
Oriental Institute, Russian Academy of Sciences (manuscripts)

### Syria
Damascus: National Museum (ceramics, armour)

### Turkey
Bodrum: Castle Museum (arms)
Istanbul: Army Museum (arms, armour)
Museum of Turkish and Islamic Art (metalwork, war drum, stucco, stone carvings)
Suleymaniye Library (manuscripts)
Topkapi Museum (arms, metalwork, ceramics, coins)
Topkapi Library (manuscripts)
Van area: Aght'amar island, Church of Gagik (relief carvings)

### United Kingdom
London: British Library (manuscripts)
British Museum (metalwork, ceramics, ivories, arms, manuscript fragments)
Tower of London (swords)
Victoria and Albert Museum (metalwork, ceramics, ivories, glassware,
    textiles, arms)
Oxford: Bodleian Library (manuscripts)

### United States of America
Boston: Museum of Fine Art (manuscripts, ceramics, metalwork, textiles, stucco)
Los Angeles: County Museum of Art (arms)
New York: Brooklyn Museum (manuscripts, ceramics)
Metropolitan Museum of Art (glass, ceramics, metalwork, ivories, stucco,
    manuscripts, stone carving, wall paintings, arms, horse harness)
Pierpoint Morgan Library (manuscripts)
Washington: Freer Gallery of Art (ceramics, metalwork, manuscripts)
Textile Museum (textiles)

### Vatican City
Vatican Library (manuscripts)

# APPENDIX THREE

## TEMPLAR SITES TODAY

After the dissolution of the Order of the Temple, the pope ordered that its property should be given to the Order of the Hospital, except in the Iberian Peninsula where new military orders were established. But many former Templar properties passed into private hands and never reached the Hospitallers. For example, in England Temple Denney in Cambridgeshire, which had been where the old and sick English brothers lived, passed into the hands of Mary of Valence, countess of Pembroke, who converted it into a nunnery.

The Hospitallers repaired and extended many of the Templars' properties. After the dissolution of the monasteries in Britain and Ireland in the 16th century, these properties were sold. Some fell into disrepair and others were converted for

A modern monument to the Templars outside the Church of the New Temple, London, showing the familiar image of two knights mounted on one horse. (Nigel Nicholson)

secular use. In France, religious buildings were damaged or destroyed in the French Revolution, while in Germany property suffered in the religious wars of the 16th and 17th centuries. In Hungary, the Balkans, Cyprus and Greece Christian property was destroyed or neglected under Ottoman government. As a result, much has disappeared, and where buildings survive they may be very different from those that belonged to the Templars.

Much of the former Templar property in the Middle East has been destroyed or seriously damaged by the ravages of time, enemy action or natural disasters. Some castles, such as 'Atlit, are still important military sites. The site of Safed castle is now a park. The castle of Baghras has been seriously damaged by earthquakes. The Templars' castle at Vadum Iacob, north of Galilee, is in the course of excavation. Most of the Templars' former headquarters at Acre is now under the sea, because the sea level has risen since the 13th century.

Many former Templar sites survive in Europe. Some are being sympathetically restored. The former Templar and Hospitaller sites in the Larzac area of central southern France are being restored and developed as tourist centres as part of a development scheme for this area. The 'Conservatoire Larzac Templier et Hospitalier', based at Millau, organizes a programme of regular events and is producing a series of publications. In England, the massive Templar barns at Cressing in Essex have been restored and there is a small visitor centre. The 'New Temple' Church off Fleet Street, London, is now the chapel of the Temple Inns of Court. The priest in charge of the Temple Church is still called 'the master of the Temple', as he has been since the Middle Ages. The church is open for visitors on certain days during the terms of the Inns of Court.

Many Templar churches survive in Britain, France, Germany, Poland and Italy, with castles and churches in the Iberian Peninsula, the Czech Republic and Croatia. Many of these churches are still in use for Christian worship and readers who visit them should remember this and treat these buildings with respect.

**OPPOSITE**
The fortified village of La Cavalerie in Aveyron, France has recently been restored as part of a government project to revitalise the Aveyron area and to attract tourism. A reconstruction of the Order's banner has been hung from the fortified gate tower, which was built by the Hospitallers in the 15th century. (Author's photograph)

# GLOSSARY

NB – all references to 'the Order' are references to 'the Order of the Temple'

'**Abbasid:** Caliphal dynasty of Sunni Islamic persuasion with its capital normally at Baghdad (750–1262), then in Cairo (1262–1517).

**ahdath:** urban militia in Islamic cities of the Middle East and Egypt.

**arrière ban:** medieval French term for a general levy of men for military service in both Europe and the Crusader States.

'**asabiyah:** tribal solidarity.

'**askar:** a ruler's personal regiments.

**aventail (ventaille):** chinflap of the coif, protecting the neck and chin.

**Ayyubid:** dynasty of rulers in Egypt and the Fertile Crescent, descended from Saladin (1169–1252 in Egypt; after 1462 in part of south-eastern Turkey).

**camera:** literally a chamber: a small house belonging to the Order, administered by a single brother or leased out to a third party, and subject to the authority of a commandery.

**cantle:** rear part of a saddle, raised in a war saddle to support the hips and lower back in combat.

**cappa:** a long, all-covering monastic robe.

**caravan:** raid into enemy territory launched from the Crusader States, usually by lightly equipped troops.

**Catholic:** *see* **Latin Christians.**

**chapter:** an administrative meeting within the Order. The general chapter of the Templars was a general assembly of officials of the Order from the West and East, which took place at intervals of a few years. The meeting appointed officials, passed statutes and dealt with problems of discipline within the Order.

**chausses:** leggings that were normally made of woollen cloth. By the late 12th century, chausses made of mail formed a part of a knight's armour.

**coif:** close-fitting hood, made of mail in the context of armour.

**commander:** general title for an official in the Order.

**commandery (Latin: preceptoria):** a local centre of administration in the military religious orders, typically consisting of a manor house at the centre of an estate. The commandery buildings would include agricultural buildings, accommodation for the brothers and for travellers, and a chapel. Administered by a commander (Latin: preceptor).

**composite bow:** bow made of wood, horn and sinew.

**connétable:** medieval French term for a senior official in a royal or noble household responsible for military discipline and organization; same as constable.

**Constantinople:** capital of the Byzantine Empire, now called Istanbul.

**convent:** a religious community. The central convent of the Templars was their administrative headquarters; the term also referred to the military personnel at that headquarters.

**couched:** method of grasping a cavalry lance tightly beneath the right shoulder.

dir': Arabic term for a mail hauberk.

Druze: follower of a Middle Eastern religious belief springing from Islam but now considered outside the Islamic community or umma.

Fertile Crescent: cultivated and cultivatable zone running from southern Palestine and Jordan through Syria and Lebanon, south-eastern Turkey and Iraq to the Persian Gulf.

faris: cavalryman.

fief: piece of land allocated to a person as a source of income, usually to a knight to enable him to equip himself and a certain number of followers as soldiers.

Franks: see Palestinian Franks.

furusiya: cavalry skills.

ghulam: professional Islamic soldier of slave-recruited origin, also called a mamluk.

gonfanier: the Order's standard-bearer, carrying the Order's banner in battle.

gonfanon bauçant: the 'piebald banner', the Order's black-and-white standard.

Greek fire: see naft.

halqa: elite professional household regiment or regiments during the Ayyubid period, subsequently downgraded to non-elite units in the Mamluk period.

hauberk: form of Western European mail armour to protect the body, upper legs and part or all of the arms.

Holy Land: Christian term for the region of Palestine where Jesus Christ lived and worked.

Holy War: war for a religious cause, fought in the name of God.

Hospitaller: member of the military Order of the Hospital of St John.

hujra: barracks.

infirmarer: senior official of the Order, in charge of supervising the Order's infirmary where sick and elderly brothers were cared for.

iqta': source of income, often a piece of land, allocated to an individual, often a soldier, to enable him to maintain himself and a specified number of followers, but unlike a Western European fief the iqta' could be taken back by the state at any time.

'istina': obligation between soldier and patron.

jamakiyah: military pay.

januwiyah: Arabic name for a tall infantry shield with a flattened base; probably meaning 'Genoese', as much military equipment was imported from Genoa.

jawshan: form of flexible body armour, usually of lamellar construction.

jaysh: army in general.

jihad: Arab-Islamic term for a struggle against evil, either individual and internal, or external in defence of Islam and Islamic territory, often wrongly translated as 'Holy War'.

jubbah: mail-lined armour.

jund: originally a militia army, later the Ayyubid military elite.

kazaghand: mail-lined armour.

lamellar: form of armour construction in which lamels or scales are laced to each other rather than to a fabric base material.

Latin Christians: Catholic (not Greek Orthodox) Christians, whose main religious writings are in Latin. Their religious leader is the pope, whose traditional seat is at Rome.

mamluk: professional soldier of slave-recruited origin, and subsequently the name given to a ruling dynasty in Egypt and Syria, almost invariably headed by a mamluk soldier (1252–1517).

mangonel: stone-throwing siege-machine operating on the beam-sling principle, early forms powered by a team of individuals pulling on ropes.

mantlet: form of large shield, usually rested on the ground to form a shield-wall or barricade.

maréchal: medieval French term for a senior official in a royal or noble household responsible for military equipment, horses and often the summoning of troops; same as marshal.

marshal: the senior military official of the Order.

martyr: a person who chooses to suffer death rather than give up their faith, for the glory of their faith.

martyrdom: the suffering and death of a martyr.

**master:** the chief administrative official of the Order, elected by a committee of brothers.

**mawali:** honorary member of Arab tribe.

**maydan:** parade ground.

**Mongols:** nomadic mounted warriors from north-eastern Asia. They now live mainly in Mongolia.

**mutatawi'ah:** religiously motivated volunteer in an Arab-Islamic army.

**naft:** Arabic term for Greek fire and other petroleum-based incendiary weapons, also apparently applied to some very early forms of gunpowder.

**Outremer:** literally 'the land overseas'; the name given by Western European Christians to the lands conquered by the Crusaders and later in the eastern Mediterranean area.

**Palestinian Franks:** the Western European Christians who settled in the Middle East after 1099. Most of the people on the First Crusade came from France or from the west of Germany, which were the lands that had historically been populated by the Franks, a Germanic people. The Crusaders and the settlers who followed them called themselves Franks, and the Muslims called them Franks.

**penance:** action taken to compensate for sins. Satisfactory penance would wipe out the punishment due for the sin.

**pilgrimage:** a journey, usually with hardships, undertaken to a holy place for the purpose of penance.

**pommel:** front of a saddle, often raised to provide support and protection to the groin; also the large element at the end of a sword-grip.

**province:** an administrative region in the Order, presided over by a grand commander.

**quillons:** the crosspiece or guard of a sword.

**receptor:** Official who received applicants into the Order in a formal admission ceremony.

**relic:** a physical object associated with a holy person, either part of their body or one of their belongings. Medieval Christians believed that God could perform miracles through the relic.

**responsion:** proportion of the income of a commandery that was paid to the Order's headquarters each year. In theory it was a third of income; in practise it varied.

**senéchal:** medieval French term for a governor or ruler's representative in a town or city.

**sergeant-brother:** a brother of the Order who had made the three religious vows of poverty, chastity and obedience, of lower rank than a knight and not a priest. He could play many roles: as a warrior, an administrator, a craftsman, a squire (assistant to a warrior) or a servant.

**Shi'a:** that section of the Muslim *umma* or community which considers that earthly authority and religious guidance (the Caliphate) rests with the descendants of the Prophet Muhammad through his daughter Fatima and his cousin 'Ali.

**sufi:** follower of one of many mystical 'paths' recognized by most but not all Muslims.

**surcoat:** long, loose, lightweight, sleeveless robe worn over mail armour.

**suq al-'askar:** Arab term for the mobile market which followed an army on campaign.

**Teutonic Knight:** member of the military Order of the Knights of the Hospital of St Mary in Jerusalem.

**tawashi:** elite professional cavalryman.

**Templar:** member of the military Order of the Temple of Solomon.

**turcoman:** Turkish tribal nomad.

**turcopolier:** a senior officer in the Order, responsible for commanding the turcopoles and the military sergeant-brothers on the field of battle.

**turcopoles:** lightly armed cavalry employed by the Order, often operating as horse-archers; from a Greek term meaning 'sons of Turks'.

**tympanum:** stone filling the space between the lintel of a doorway and the arch above it.

**visitor:** an official of the Order sent from headquarters to the Order's houses in the West, to ensure that the brothers of the Order were following proper procedures and practices.

**zardkhanah:** arsenal

# BIBLIOGRAPHY AND FURTHER READING

## HATTIN 1187

Most primary sources have been published, the main Islamic ones having been translated into a European language, and are listed in the bibliographies of all serious studies of the Crusades. General accounts of 1187 are found in all histories of the Crusades, but several more detailed descriptions are listed here:

Baldwin, M., *Raymond III of Tripolis and the Fall of Jerusalem* (Princeton, 1936)

Blyth, E., 'The Battle of Hattin', *Palestine Exploration Fund Quarterly Statement*, LIV (1922)

Dalman, G., 'Schlact von Hattin', *Palästinajahrbuch* (1914)

Ehrenkreutz, E.S., 'The Place of Saladin in the Naval History of the Mediterranean Sea in the Middle Ages', *Journal of the American Oriental Society*, LXXV (1955)

Ehrenkreutz, E.S., *Saladin* (New York, 1972)

Elbeheiry, S., *Les Institutions de l'Egypte au temps des Ayyubides*, Service de Reproduction des Thèses, Université de Lille, III (1972)

Fuller, J.F.C., *The Decisive Battles of the Western World* (London, 1954)

Gibb, H.A.R., 'The Armies of Saladin', *Cahiers d'Histoire Egyptienne*, III (1951)

Hamilton, B., 'The Elephant of Christ: Reynald of Châtillon', in D. Blake (ed.), *Religious Motivation: Biographical and Sociological Problems for the Church Historian: Studies in Church History*, XV (Oxford, 1978)

Kedar, B.Z. (ed.), *The Horns of Hattin: Proceedings of the Second Conference of the Society for the Study of the Crusades and the Latin East* (Jerusalem and London, 1992)

Lane-Poole, S., *Saladin and the Fall of Jerusalem* (London, 1898)

Lyons, M.C. and Jackson, D.E.P., *Saladin, the Politics of the Holy War* (Cambridge, 1982)

Nicholson, R.L., *Joscelyn III and the Fall of the Crusader States, 1134–99* (Leiden, 1973)

Prawer, J., 'The Battle of Hattin', *Crusader Institutions* (Oxford, 1980)

Regan, G., *Saladin and the Fall of Jerusalem* (London, 1987)

Smail, R.C., 'The Predicaments of Guy of Lusignan, 1183–87', in B.Z. Prawer (ed.), *Outremer* (Jerusalem, 1982)

## SARACEN FARIS

The following list does not include contemporary chronicles which can be found in any bibliography of the Crusades. Untranslated Arabic, Persian and Turkish sources have also been omitted.

Beshir, B.J., 'Fatimid Military Organization', *Der Islam* LV (1978)

Bombaci, A., 'The Army of the Saljuqs of Rum', *Istituto orientale di Napoli, Annali*, n.s. XXXVIII (1978)

Derenbourg, H., *Ousama Ibn Mounkidh, un Emir Syrien au Premier Siècle des Croisades (1095–1188)* (Paris, 1889)

Ellisséeff, N., *Nur al Din; un Grand Prince Musulman de Syria au Temps des Croisades,* (Institut Français de Damas, Damascus, 1967)

Gibb, H.A.R., 'The Armies of Saladin', *Cahiers d'Histoire Egyptienne*, III (1951)

Glasse, C. and Smith, H., *The New Encyclopedia of Islam* (revised edition), (California, 2001)

Hamblin, W.J., 'Saladin and Muslim Military Theory', in B.Z. Kedar (ed.), *The Horns of Hattin* (Jerusalem and London, 1992)

Hillenbrand, C., 'The History of the Jazira, 1100–1250: A Short Introduction', in J. Raby (ed.) *Oxford Studies in Islamic Art*, vol. I (Oxford, 1985)

Hillenbrand, C., 'The Islamic World and the Crusades', *The Scottish Journal of Religious Studies*, VII (1986)

Humphreys R.R., *From Saladin to the Mongols: The Ayyubids of Damascus 1193–1260* (Albany NY, 1977)

Humphreys, R.S., 'The Emergence of the Mamluk Army', *Studia Islamica*, XLV (1977)

Jackson, M.C., Jackson, D.E.P. and Lyons, M.C., *Saladin: The Politics of the Holy War* (Cambridge, 1982)

Lewis B., *Islam from the Prophet Muhammad to the Capture of Constantinople, vol. I: Politics and War* (New York, 1974)

Løkkegaard, F., 'The Concept of War and Peace in Islam', in B.P. McGuire (ed.), *War and Peace in the Middle Ages* (Copenhagen, 1987)

Mayer, L.A., 'Saracenic Arms and Armour', *Ars Islamica*, X (1943)

McEwen, E. (tr.), 'Persian Archery texts: Chapter Eleven of Fakhr-i Mudabbir's Adab al Harb', *The Islamic Quarterly,* XVIII (1974)

Nicolle, D.C., 'An Introduction to Arms and Warfare in Classical Islam', in R. Elgood (ed.), *Islamic Arms and Armour* (London, 1979)

Nicolle, D.C., *The Arms and Armour of the Crusading Era 1050–1350* (New York, 1988)

Nizam al Mulk (tr. H. Darke), *The Book of Government or Rules for Kings: The Siyasat Nama* (London, 1960)

Parry, V.J., 'Warfare', in P.M. Holt (ed.), *The Cambridge History of Islam* (Cambridge, 1970)

Paterson D., Paterson W. and Lathan, 'Horse-archers of Islam', in R. Elgood (ed.), *Islamic Arms and Armour* (London, 1979)

Peters, R., *Jihad in Medieval and Modern Islam* (Leiden, 1977)

Rabie, H., 'The Training of the Mamluk Faris', in V.J. Parry. and M.E. Yapp (eds.), *War, Technology and Society in the Middle East* (London, 1975)

Ibn al Husayn al Sulami (tr. Tosum Bayrak al Jerrahi al Halveti), *The Book of Sufi Chivalry, Futuwwah* (London, 1983)

al Tarsusi (tr. A. Boudot-Lamotte), *Contribution de l'Étude de l'Archerie Musulmane* (Institut Français de Damas, Damascus, 1968)

al Tarsusi (ed. and tr. C. Cahen), 'Un Traité d'Armurerie composé pour Saladin', *Bulletin d'Etudes Orientales*, XII (1947–8)

Usama Ibn Munqidh (tr. P.H. Hitti), *Mémoires of an Arab-Syrian Gentleman* (Princeton 1929; reprint Beirut, 1964)

Zaki, A.R., 'Military Literature of the Arabs', *Islamic Culture*, XXX (1956)

## KNIGHT TEMPLAR
Primary sources translated into English

Anonymous Pilgrim V,2 in Anonymous Pilgrims I–VIII (11th and 12th centuries), (tr. A. Stewart), *Palestine Pilgrims' Text Society* 6 (London, 1894)

*The Book of Deeds of James I of Aragon: A Translation of the Medieval Catalan Llibre dels Fets*, tr. D. Smith and H. Buffery (Aldershot, 2003)

*The Catalan Rule of the Templars: Barcelona, Archivo de la Corona de Aragon, 'Cartes Reales', MS 3344: A Critical Edition and English Translation*, tr. J.M. Upton-Ward (Woodbridge, 2002)

*Chronicle of the Third Crusade: A Translation of the Itinerarium peregrinorum et gesta regis Ricardi*, tr. H. Nicholson (Aldershot, 1997)

*The Conquest of Jerusalem and the Third Crusade: Sources in Translation*, tr. P.W. Edbury (Aldershot, 1996)

*Crusader Syria in the Thirteenth Century: The Rothelin Continuation of the History of William of Tyre with part of the Eracles or Acre Text*, tr. J. Shirley (Aldershot, 1999)

Jean de Joinville, in Joinville and Villehardouin, *Chronicles of the Crusades*, tr. M.R.B. Shaw (Harmondsworth, 1963)

*Jerusalem Pilgrimage, 1099–1185*, J. Wilkinson, J. Hill and W. F. Ryan (eds.) Hakluyt Society second series 167 (1988)

Matthew Paris (tr. J.A. Giles), *Matthew Paris's English history, from the year 1235 to 1273*, 3 vols (London, 1889–1893)

Matthew Paris (tr. C.D. Yonge), *The Flowers of History, especially such as relate to the affairs of Britain. From the beginning of the world to the year 1307: collected by Matthew of Westminster*, 2 vols (London, 1853)

Odo of Deuil (ed. and tr. V.G. Berry), *De profectione Ludovici VII in orientem: The Journey of Louis VII to the East* (New York, 1965)

Oliver of Paderborn (tr. J.J. Gavigan), 'The Capture of Damietta', in E. Peters (ed.), *Christian Society and the Crusaders, 1198–1229: Sources in Translation* (Philadelphia, 1971)

Roger of Wendover (tr. J.A. Giles), *Flowers of History: Comprising the History of England … formerly ascribed to Matthew Paris*, 2 vols (London, 1849)

*The Rule of the Templars: the French Text of the Rule of the Order of the Temple*, tr. J.M. Upton-Ward (Woodbridge, 1992)

*The Templar of Tyre: Part Three of the 'Deeds of the Cypriots'*, tr. P. Crawford (Aldershot, 2003)

*The Templars: Selected Sources*, tr. M. Barber and K. Bate (Manchester, 2002)

*The Trial of the Templars in Cyprus: A Complete English Edition*, tr. A. Gilmour-Bryson (Leiden, 1998)

Usamah ibn Munqidh (tr. P.K. Hitti), 'Memoirs', in *An Arab-Syrian Gentleman and Warrior in the Period of the Crusades: Memoirs of Usamah ibn-Munqidh* (New York, 1929; reprinted Princeton, 1987)

Walter Map (ed. and tr. M.R. James, C.N.L. Brooke and R.A.B. Mynors), *De nugis curialium* (Oxford, 1983)

William, Archbishop of Tyre (tr. E.A. Babcock and A.C. Krey), *A History of Deeds Done Beyond the Sea*, 2 vols (New York, 1976)

Untranslated primary sources

'Annales de Terre Sancte', ed. R. Röhricht and G. Raynaud, *Archives de l'Orient Latin*, 2 (1884), 427–61.

'Chronique d'Amadi', in R. de Mas Latrie (ed.), *Chroniques d'Amadi et de Strambaldi* (Paris, 1891), vol. 1.

*Chronique d'Ernoul et de Bernard le trésorier*, ed. L. de Mas Latrie (Paris, 1871)

'Fragmentum de captione Damiatae', in R. Röhricht (ed.), *Quinti belli sacri scriptores minores*, Société de l'orient latin, no. 162 (Geneva, 1879)

Guiot de Provins, 'La Bible', in J. Orr (ed.), *Les oeuvres de Guiot de Provins, poète lyrique et satirique*, (Manchester, 1915)

'Henri d'Arci: the Shorter Works', (ed. Perman, R.C.D.) in E.A. Francis (ed.), *Studies in Medieval French Presented to Alfred Ewert in Honour of his Seventieth Birthday* (Oxford, 1984)

'Imad al-Din al-Katib al-Isfahani, *Conquête de la Syrie et de la Palestine par Saladin: (al-Fath al-qussi fi l-fath al-qudsi)*, tr. H. Massé (Paris, 1972)

James of Vitry, 'Sermones', in J. B. Pitra (ed.), *Analecta novissima spicilegii solesmensis: altera continuatio 2*, Tusculana (Paris, 1888)

Philip of Novara, *Mémoires*, published as *Filippo da Novara, Guerra di Federico II in Oriente (1223–1242)*, ed. S. Melani (Naples, 1994)

*Le Procès des Templiers*, ed J. Michelet, 2 vols (Paris, 1841–51: repr. Paris, 1987)

'Ein zeitgenössisches Gedicht auf die Belagerung Accons', ed. H. Prutz, *Forschungen zur deutschen Geschichte*, 21 (1881), 449–94.

Bodley Manuscript 454, the manuscript recording the trial of the Templars in the British Isles. An abridged version was published by David Wilkins, *Concilia Magnae Britanniae et Hiberniae*, 2nd of 4 vols (London, 1737)


Secondary sources

Barber, M. (ed.), *The Military Orders: Fighting for the Faith and Caring for the Sick* (Aldershot, 1994)

Barber, M., *The New Knighthood: A History of the Order of the Temple* (Cambridge, 1994)

Barber, M., *Crusaders and Heretics, 12th–14th Centuries* (Aldershot, 1995)

Balard, M., Kedar, B.Z. and Riley-Smith, J. (eds.), *Dei gesta per Francos: Études sur les croisades dédiées à Jean Richard – Crusade Studies in Honour of Jean Richard* (Aldershot, 2001)

Bennett, M., 'La règle du Temple as a Military Manual, or How to Deliver a Cavalry Charge', in C. Harper-Bill et al. (eds.), *Studies in Medieval History Presented to R. Allen Brown*, (Woodbridge, 1989)

Bulst-Thiele, Marie Luise, *Sacrae domus militiae Templi Hierosolymitani magistri: Untersuchungen zur Geschichte des Templerordens 1118/9–1314* (Göttingen, 1974)

Demurger, A., *Vie et mort de l'ordre du Temple, 1120–1314* (Paris, 1985)

Demurger, A., *Chevaliers du Christ: les ordres religieux-militaires au Moyen Âge XIe–XVIe siècle* (Paris, 2002)

Forey, A.J., *The Templars in the Corona de Aragón* (London, 1973)

Forey, A.J., *The Military Orders from the Twelfth to the Early Fourteenth Centuries* (Basingstoke, 1992)

Forey, A.J., *Military Orders and Crusades* (Aldershot, 1994)

Forey, A.J., *The Fall of the Templars in the Crown of Aragon* (Aldershot, 2001)

Forey, A.J., 'Ex-Templars in England', *Journal of Ecclesiastical History,* 53 (2002)

Huygens, R.B.C., 'Un nouveau texte du traité "De constructione castri Saphet"', *Studi Medievali*, 3rd series, 6 (1965)

Johns, C.N. (ed. D. Pringle), *Pilgrims' Castle ('Atlit), David's Tower (Jerusalem) and Qal'at ar-Rabal ('Ajlun): Three Eastern Castles from the Time of the Crusades* (Aldershot, 1997)

Kedar, B.Z., 'The Tractatus de locis et statu sancte terrae ierosolimitanae', in J. France and W.G. Zajac (eds.), *The Crusades and Their Sources: Essays Presented to Bernard Hamilton* (Aldershot, 1998)

Kennedy, H., *Crusader Castles* (Cambridge, 1994)

Luttrell, A., 'The Earliest Templars', in M. Balard (ed.), *Autour de la première croisade: actes du colloque de la Society for the Study of the Crusades and the Latin East* (Clermont-Ferrand, 22–25 juin 1995) (Paris, 1996)

Marshall, C., *Warfare in the Latin East, 1192–1291* (Cambridge, 1992)

Miquel, J., *Sites Templiers et Hospitaliers du Larzac et commanderies du Rouergue* (Millau, 1989)

Nicholson, H., *Templars, Hospitallers and Teutonic Knights: Images of the Military Orders, 1128–1291* (Leicester, 1993)

Nicholson, H. (ed.), *The Military Orders. Volume 2: Welfare and Warfare* (Aldershot, 1998)

Nicholson, H., *The Knights Templar: A New History* (Stroud, 2001)

Nicholson, H., *Love, War and the Grail: Templars, Hospitallers and Teutonic Knights in Medieval Epic and Romance, 1150–1500* (Leiden, 2001)

Pringle, D., *The Red Tower (al-Burj al-Ahmar): Settlement in the Plain of Sharon at the Time of the Crusaders and Mamluks A.D. 1099–1516* (London, 1986)

Riley-Smith, J., 'The Templars and the Castle of Tortosa in Syria: an Unknown Document Concerning the Acquisition of the Fortress', *English Historical Review*, 84 (1969)

Riley-Smith, J., 'The Templars and the Teutonic Knights in Cilician Armenia', in T.S.R. Boase (ed.), *The Cilician Kingdom of Armenia* (Edinburgh, 1978)

Roncetti, M., Scarpellini, P. and Tommasi, F., *Templari e Ospitalieri in Italia: La chiesa di San Bevignate a Perugia* (Milan, 1987)

Smail, R.C., *Crusading Warfare, 1097–1193*, 2nd edn (Cambridge, 1995)

Tommasi F. (ed.), *Acri 1291: La fine della presenza degli ordini militari in Terra Sancta e i nuovi orientamenti nel XIV secolo* (Perugia, 1996)

# INDEX

References to illustrations are shown in **bold**.

215